Medical Psychedelics

Edited by Dr. Oliver Rumle Hovmand

Copyright © 2019 Oliver Rumle Hovmand

All rights reserved.

ISBN:
ISBN-13: 9781790134083

DEDICATION

To the psychedelic community.

Please visit **medicalpsychedelics.net** if you would like to learn more about the subject, get involved or want to support the research of Dr. Hovmand. If you would like to get in touch write to oh@medicalpsychedelics.net

ACKNOWLEDGMENTS

This text is not an original work. It is my attempt to consolidate the existing literature into a coherent text, which I hope will allow the reader to gain a deeper understanding of the subject.

All credit goes to the original authors of the papers.

INTRODUCTION

The last decade has seen a newfound interest in the clinical applications of psychedelic substances such as LSD, psilocybin, MDMA, DMT, ayahuasca and ketamine—an interest not seen since pre-prohibition days. Back then, these substances were widely used as adjuncts to psychotherapy in the treatment of severe psychiatric and psychological problems such as posttraumatic stress disorder (PTSD), depression and substance abuse.

The current results are extremely promising, and many believe we are on the verge of a new psychedelic revolution, which will transform the field of psychiatry. There is now a push to make these substances legal again, and a lot of great researchers are working to gather evidence of their safety and efficacy in various patient populations.

This book presents an in-depth analysis of what is currently known about the possible medical applications of psychedelics. It examines the pre- and post-prohibition medical literature as well as the manuals used in clinical research, and it focuses on the practical aspects of psychedelic-mediated therapy.

The aim is to update this analysis annually and thus to develop it—along with the ever-expanding body of evidence—into a textbook that can be used when/if these substances again become legal. It is intended for medical and psychological professionals, science-minded psychonauts and any other members of the public who want to know more about psychedelic substances.

CLASSICAL PSYCHEDELICS

The psychedelics:
Herein, the word "psychedelics" refer to the classical psychedelics, sometimes called "hallucinogens," "psychotomimetics," or "entheogens" (Ruck et al., 1979; Grinspoon and Bakalar, 1979; Ott, 1996; Metzner, 2004). In this text, the term "psychedelic" is used because of the fact, that the administration of these substances results in more than just perceptual changes, and the typical perceptual changes engendered by psychedelics at typical doses rarely include frank hallucinations (Grinspoon and Bakalar, 1979; Nichols, 2004; O'Brien, 2006). This, although the term it is the most widely used in the scientific literature, and although the term "psychedelic" is widely used, it has the disadvantage of carrying considerable cultural connotation (i.e., its use as a descriptor of a style of music or art associated with Western counter-culture of the 1960s). The terms "psychotomimetic" (emphasizing model psychosis) and "entheogen" (emphasizing mystical-type experiences, i.e., phenomenologically indistinguishable from classically described mystical experiences) highlight as "hallucinogen" only a single aspect (which may not occur reliably) of the much broader range of psychedelic effects.

LSD   Psilocybin

Psychedelics can be divided structurally into two classes of alkaloids: the tryptamines, including psilocybin (prodrug constituent of Psilocybe and several other mushroom genera), the semi-synthetic d-lysergic acid diethylamide (LSD), and DMT; and the phenethylamines, including mescaline (principle active constituent of peyote) and certain synthetic compounds (Grinspoon and Bakalar, 1979; Shulgin and Shulgin, 1991, 1997; Metzner, 2004, Nichols, 2004). The effects of these substances are primarily mediated by agonist action at 5-HT2A receptors (Glennon et al., 1984; Nichols, 2004; González-Maeso, 2007) and produce a generally similar profile of subjective effects (Hidalgo, 1960; Hollister, 1962; Wolbach, Isbell and Miner, 1962; Wolbach, Miner and Isbell, 1962; Shulgin and Shulgin, 1991, 1997), with the exception of DMT, which therefore is discussed in a separate chapter.

Other classes of substances have sometimes been identified as psychedelics, including 3,4-methylenedioxymethamphetamine or MDMA (perhaps more appropriately labeled an entactogen (Nichols et al., 1986) or empathogen (Metzner, 1985) (see MDMA chapter for more information); dissociative anesthetics such as ketamine (see Ketamine chapter for more information), phencyclidine, and dextromethorphan; and anticholinergic agents such as scopolamine and atropine (Nichols, 2004). However, this text uses the term "psychedelics" to refer specifically to classical psychedelics.

A brief history of psychedelics:
The use of psychedelics can be divided into three eras: The ancient use and the modern use. The following is the history as summed up by Johnson et al (2008):

Psychedelic use by indigenous cultures:
Psychedelics have been used by indigenous cultures for millennia (Schultes, 1969; Lowy, 1971; Schultes et al., 2001). These cultures have restricted psychedelic use to sacramental and healing contexts, with these two often being inseparably intertwined. Remarkably, apparently without exception, such cultures view psychedelic plants and fungi as being of divine origin (Schultes et al., 2001). Given this orientation, it is not surprising that their ingestion is often tightly restricted, with use controlled by ceremonial guidelines including taboos against improper use (Schultes et al., 2001; Weil, 2004). Indigenous cultures restrict use of psychedelics to highly ritualized, sacred ceremonies such as those designed to serve as rites of passage, or to set the occasion for divination and spiritual or physical healing. Even in cases in which certain use extends beyond the shaman and may be more recreational in nature (e.g., use of the DMT-containing epená by the Waiká cultures of Brazil and Venezuela), the psychedelic is prepared and taken in a highly ritualized context (Grinspoon and Bakalar, 1979; Schultes, 2001;

Weil, 2004). Modern, urban syncretic religions, such as the UDV, which have developed in South America and have been influenced by indigenous use of ayahuasca, also incorporate a high degree of structure and guidance into their ayahuasca use, which may minimize adverse reactions (Gonzales v. O Centro Espirita Beneficiente União do Vegetal, 2006).

However, indigenous cultures should not be regarded as absolute role models in the clinical use of psychedelics for at least two reasons. First, some of these cultures also engaged in practices considered unethical in our culture. For example, the Aztecs, who used psilocybin mushrooms and morning glory seeds (containing LSD-related agents), practiced human sacrifice, and even incorporated psychedelic use into sacrificial rituals (Ott, 1996). As another example, the Jivaro in Ecuador who use ayahuasca practice sacramental headhunting, and ayahuasca may be used by the shaman in that society for malevolent intent (i.e., bewitching) as well as for healing (Harner, 1962, 1968; Grof, 1977). Second, risk/benefit tradeoffs that may be acceptable in various religious contexts may fall short of what is expected in the domain of contemporary scientific research with human participants.

Nonetheless, some important themes have emerged in the use of psychedelics by indigenous cultures that may have bearing on the appropriate use of psychedelics in clinical research. Indeed, some of the safeguards developed for clinical psychedelic research and expressed in the guidelines presented herein are similar to important aspects of psychedelic use by indigenous cultures. These common themes are structured use (expressed as ritual in indigenous use), restrictions on use including the need for guidance, and appreciation of psychedelics' powerful psychological effects (expressed as reverence in indigenous use). We believe that these commonalities are more than coincidence. The unique pharmacology of classical psychedelics may have shaped convergent practices across independent cultures. Likewise, the guidelines expressed herein for human clinical research with psychedelics may also be viewed as having been developed in reaction to these same aspects of psychedelic pharmacology. As an example, some of the unique effects and safety concerns for psychedelics may be related to their ability to set the occasion for deeply meaningful, even spiritual experiences (Richards, 2003, 2005). Novak (1997) hypothesised that Western intellectuals in the mid 1950's such as Aldous Huxley and Gerald Heard merely redefined the subjective effects resulting from psychedelic administration as a spiritual experience, thereby popularising such an association in western culture. However, the observation that indigenous cultures that ingest classical psychedelics almost invariably do so under sacramental contexts (Schultes et al., 2001), along with the findings from double-blind clinical studies demonstrating that under supportive conditions psychedelics occasion mystical-type experiences with high frequency (Pahnke, 1963; Griffiths et al., 2006), suggests that the association of psychedelics with spiritual experience relates to the pharmacology of these agents rather than being based entirely on cultural suggestion.

Modern history:
In the 1950s and 1960s, thousands of research participants were administered psychedelics in the context of basic clinical research or therapeutic clinical research, resulting in hundreds of publications (Grinspoon and Bakalar, 1979; Grob et al., 1998; Strassman, 2001; Nichols, 2004). During this time the United States Army investigated classical psychedelics as incapacitating agents in soldiers, and the United States Central Intelligence Agency conducted clandestine research investigating classical psychedelics as interrogation agents in which civilians were administered psychedelics without knowledge or consent. Eventually, both groups ceased to focus on classical psychedelics in favour of non-classical "psychedelics" such as the synthetic anticholinergic compound quinuclidinyl benzilate (BZ), which showed greater promise as a warfare agent than LSD because its effects were marked by greater immobility, delirium, amnesia, and duration (Lee and Shlain, 1992).

Very early academic research on classical psychedelics was designed without considering the powerful influences of set (psychological state) and setting (environment) (e.g., Malitz et al., 1960; Rinkel et al., 1960; Hollister, 1961; Rümmele and Gnirss, 1961; Leuner, 1962). Subsequent research, which included more preparation and interpersonal support during the period of drug action, found fewer adverse psychological reactions, such as panic reactions and paranoid episodes, and increased reports of positively-valued experiences (Chwelos et al., 1959; Leary, 1964; Leary et al., 1963, 1964; Metzner et al. 1965; Pahnke, 1969).

One major area of early research focused on the comparison of psychedelic effects with the symptoms of psychosis (e.g., Stockings, 1940; Hoch et al., 1953; Hoffer and Callbeck, 1960; Leuner, 1962; Kuramochi and Takahashi, 1964). Although the study of psychedelics as models for the psychosis observed in schizophrenia eventually fell out of favor in psychiatry (Grinspoon and Bakalar, 1979; Snyder, 1988; Strassman, 2001), a renewed interest in this area is emerging, in part due to modern brain imaging techniques and neuropharmacological findings that have supported psychedelics as a model of at least certain aspects of acute psychosis (Gouzoulis-Mayfrank, Heekeren et al., 1998; Vollenweider et al., 1997; Vollenweider and Geyer, 2001; Gouzoulis-Mayfrank et al., 2005, 2006).

Other areas of early human research included investigations of therapeutic applications of psychedelics in treatment of psychological suffering associated with cancer and in the treatment of substance dependence. Anecdotal observations and non-blind studies in cancer patients suffering from anxiety and depression suggested that LSD administration resulted in an ability to openly discuss existential fears and be at peace with approaching death, and that this reorientation often outlasted the acute drug effects (Kast and Collins, 1964; Cohen, 1965; Kast, 1967). Follow up investigations involved the administration of a high dose of a psychedelic to carefully prepared patients under highly supportive interpersonal conditions, with the patient wearing eyeshades and listening to classical music through headphones during the course of pharmacological action, a model known as "psychedelic peak therapy" or "psychedelic therapy" (Kurland et al., 1969; Pahnke et al., 1969; Richards et al, 1972; Grof et al., 1973; Kurland et al., 1973; Grof and Halifax, 1977; Richards et al., 1977; Richards et al., 1979; Grof, 1980; Richards, 1980; Kurland, 1985). Unfortunately, these early studies did not include the stringent control conditions or groups that now have become standard in modern clinical psychopharmacology research. The results suggest, however, that these compounds may have improved psychological well-being in the face of anxiety and depression secondary to cancer. Luckily, contemporary researchers have again begun studying psychedelics for the use of this purpose, which is discussed later in this text.

Another focus of study was psychedelic-facilitated therapy in the treatment of alcoholism and other forms of substance dependence (e.g., Smart et al., 1966; Ludwig et al., 1969; Kurland et al., 1971; Savage and McCabe, 1973). While some studies prepared patients and utilised supportive conditions (e.g. Kurland et al. 1971; Savage and McCabe, 1973), others drastically departed from the "psychedelic therapy" model, and involved the administration of high doses to unprepared, restrained patients (e.g., Smart et al., 1966). Results across studies were ultimately inconclusive due to such variations in methods and a lack of modern controls and experimental rigour (Abuzzahab and Anderson, 1971; McGlothlin and Arnold, 1971; Halpern, 1996; Mangini, 1998). Again, contemporary researchers have again begun conducting new trials researching psychedelics for the use of this purpose, and Krebs and Johansen (2012). have made a meta-analysis of some of the old trials, which is too discussed later in this text.
Similarly, some therapists reported that psychedelics administered under supportive contexts could accelerate psychotherapy for a variety of psychological disorders (e.g., Abramson, 1960, 1963; Crochet et al., 1963; Mogar and Aldrich, 1969; Rhead, 1977). However, these reports were

largely based on anecdotal clinical accounts rather than controlled studies.

Escalation in recreational psychedelic use, primarily LSD, in the 1960s, led to considerable sensationalism concerning these drugs in media coverage. Adding to the controversy was the publicised departure and termination of Timothy Leary and Richard Alpert from Harvard University in 1963 following charges of unorthodox methods in psychedelic research (Grinspoon and Bakalar, 1979; Lee and Shlain, 1992; Novak, 1997; Strassman, 2001). Leary's subsequent irresponsible advocacy of psychedelic use by youth further undermined an objective scientific approach to studying these compounds.

The growing controversy and sensationalism resulted in increasing restrictions on access to psychedelics throughout the 1960s (ultimately resulting in the placement of the most popular psychedelics into Schedule I of the 1970 Controlled Substances Act in the United States), creating substantially greater regulatory barriers for researchers to conduct human trials. The negative publicity also resulted in withdrawal of federal research funds, which had previously supported much of the human research, and in the professional marginalisation of clinical investigators interested in pursuing research with psychedelics. Human research with psychedelics in the United States became virtually dormant when the last trials were published in the early 1970s.

After several decades of dormancy, research involving the administration of classical psychedelics to humans has been recently renewed. Although animal research during the intervening decades has substantially advanced our understanding of underlying neuropharmacological mechanisms of the psychedelics, the fact that human research with this historically important and widely used class of compounds remained inactive is remarkable. Renewed human administration research began with the work of Rick Strassman, who initiated research on the effects of the N,N-dimethyltryptamine (DMT) at the University of New Mexico in the early 1990s (Strassman, 1991). Subsequently, investigators both in the United States and in Europe have developed human research programs with psychedelics. This new research has included basic-science studies that have administered psychedelics as tools for investigating cognitive neuroscience and perception (Gouzoulis-Mayfrank, Heekeren et al., 1998; Gouzoulis-Mayfrank et al., 2002; Umbricht et al., 2003; Carter et al., 2004; Carter, Pettigrew, Burr et al., 2005; Carter, Pettigrew, Hasler, et al., 2005), time perception (Wittmann et al., 2007), psychedelic pharmacokinetics and metabolism (Hasler et al., 1997, 2002), model psychosis (Gouzoulis-Mayfrank, Heekeren et al., 1998; Vollenweider et al., 1997, 1998, 1999, 2007; Vollenweider and Geyer, 2001; Gouzoulis-Mayfrank et al., 2005,

2006), and, recently psychedelics' reported facilitation of experiences having enduring personal meaning and spiritual significance (Griffiths et al., 2006). Recent clinical studies have administered psychedelics to evaluate their safety and efficacy in the treatment of psychiatric disorders: specifically, anxiety related to advanced-stage cancer (Grob, 2005) and obsessive-compulsive disorder (Moreno et al., 2006). In addition, several studies have examined the effects of ayahuasca (also known as hoasca or yagé; an admixture containing DMT) in human volunteers outside of the United States (e.g., Grob et al., 1996; Riba et al., 2001) (see the DMT chapter of this text). This clinical research is discussed in dept in this chapter.

Physiological safety:
Psychedelic administration in humans results in a unique profile of effects and potential adverse reactions that need to be appropriately addressed in order to maximise safety. Different risks are associated with different drug classes. For example, because high doses of certain opioids and sedative/hypnotics can cause respiratory depression (Gutstein and Akil, 2006; Charney et al., 2006), when conducting research with high doses of these drugs, respiration rate and/or blood oxygen are monitored, and mechanical breathing assistance and appropriate rescue medications are readily available.
Similarly, human psychedelic administration entails its own unique risk profile. But unlike opioids, the primary safety concerns with psychedelics are largely psychological rather than physiological in nature.

Psychedelics generally possess relatively low physiological toxicity, and have not been shown to result in organ damage or neuropsychological deficits (Strassman, 1984; Gable, 1993, 2004; Halpern and Pope, 1999; Hasler et al., 2004; Nichols, 2004; Halpern et al., 2005). There is no evidence of potential neurotoxic effects with the prototypical classical psychedelics (i.e., LSD, mescaline, and psilocybin). Some physiological symptoms may occur during psychedelic action, such as dizziness, weakness, tremors, nausea, drowsiness, paresthesia, blurred vision, dilated pupils, and increased tendon reflexes (Isbell, 1959; Hollister, 1961; Nichols, 2004). In addition, psychedelics can moderately increase pulse and both systolic and diastolic blood pressure (Isbell, 1959; Wolbach, Miner and Isbell, 1962; Strassman and Qualls, 1994; Gouzoulis-Mayfrank et al., 1999; Passie et al., 2002; Griffiths et al., 2006). However, these somatic effects vary and are relatively unimpressive even at doses yielding powerful psychological effects (perceptual, cognitive, and affective) (Metzner et al., 1965; Passie et al., 2002; Metzner, 2004).
The early literature examining psychedelics in the treatment of anxiety and depression secondary to cancer indicated that the classical psychedelics

LSD and N,N-dipropyltryptamine (DPT) were physiologically well-tolerated. The physical adverse effects of these agents observed in cancer patients were manageable and similar to effects observed in physically healthy individuals. These researchers noted that any other symptoms experienced during sessions with cancer patients were symptoms already associated with their existing illness (Richards et al., 1972; Kurland et al., 1973; Kurland, 1985). Early clinical research also safely administered LSD to chronic alcoholics and cancer patients with "considerable liver damage," suggesting hepatic concerns are "negligible unless the dysfunction is of a critical degree" (Grof, 1980, p. 164).

In older times, participants and review committees were concerned that LSD or other psychedelics were associated with chromosomal damage. These concerns originated from an anti-LSD media campaign by the United States government in the late 1960s that was based on and followed soon after initial reports (Cohen, Hirschhorn and Frosch, 1967; Cohen, Marinello and Back, 1967; Irwin and Egozcue, 1967) suggesting LSD caused chromosomal damage in human leukocytes (Ott, 1996; Weil, 2004). This campaign included pictures of deformed children (Grinspoon and Bakalar, 1979) at a time when the thalidomide tragedies of a decade earlier were relatively fresh in the public's memory (Ott, 1996). However, many follow up investigations soon squarely refuted the hypothesis that LSD use in humans was a significant risk for chromosomal damage or carcinogenic, mutagenic, or teratogenic effects (e.g., Bender and Siva Sankar, 1968; Tjio et al., 1969; Dishotsky et al., 1971; Long, 1972).

Subjective Effects:
Drug dosage is a primary factor in predicting the types of effects that will occur (Strassman et al., 1994; Riba et al., 2001b; Hasler et al., 2004; Hintzen and Passie, 2010; Studerus et al., 2011, 2012; Liechti et al., 2017). Effects unfold temporally over a drug session; onset effects are distinct from peak effects and some effects have a higher probability of occurring at specific timepoints over the total duration of drug effects (Masters and Houston, 1966; Preller and Vollenweider, 2016).

Furthermore, effects are influenced by two crucial extra-pharmacological factors referred to as *set and setting*. *Set describes* factors such as personality, pre-dose mood, while setting describes factors as drug session environment, and external stimuli (Leary et al., 1963; Studerus et al., 2012; Hartogsohn, 2016; Carhart-Harris and Nutt, 2017).

Perceptual effects:
Swanson (2018) conducted a comprehensive review of the perceptual effects of the classical psychedelics:

The range of subjective experience under psychedelics can be remarkably broad (Blewett and Chwelos, 1959; Richards, 1980; Masters and Houston, 1966; Strassman, 2001; Nichols, 2004; Stolaroff, 2004).
Perceptual effects occur along a dose-dependent range from subtle to drastic. The range of different perceptual effects includes intensifications of color saturation, texture definition, contours, light intensity, sound intensity, timbre variation, and other perceptual characteristics (Kometer and Vollenweider, 2016; Kaelen et al., 2018). The external world is often experienced as if in higher resolution, seemingly more crisp and detailed, often accompanied by a distinct sense of 'clarity' or 'freshness' in the environment (Hofmann, 1980; Huxley, 1991; Díaz, 2010; Kometer and Vollenweider, 2016). Sense of meaning in percepts is altered, e.g., 'Things around me had a new strange meaning for me' or 'Objects around me engaged me emotionally much more than usual' (Studerus et al., 2010).

Perceptual distortions and illusions are extremely common, e.g., 'Things looked strange' or 'My sense of size and space was distorted' or 'Edges appeared warped' or 'I saw movement in things that weren't actually moving' (Dittrich, 1998; Muthukumaraswamy et al., 2013). Textures undulate in rhythmic movements, object boundaries warp and pulsate, and the apparent sizes and shapes of objects can shift rapidly (Kometer and Vollenweider, 2016). Controlled psychophysical studies have measured various alterations in motion perception (Carter et al., 2004), object completion (Kometer et al., 2011), and binocular rivalry (Frecska et al., 2004; Carter et al., 2007).

Perceptual distortions and illusions are dose-dependent and can be divided in subcategories. In e*lementary hallucinations*—e.g., 'I saw geometric patterns'— the visual field can become permeated with intricate tapestries of brightly coloured, flowing latticework and other geometric visuospatial 'form constants' (Klüver, 1928; Siegel and Jarvik, 1975; Kometer and Vollenweider, 2016). In *complex hallucinations* visual scenes can present elaborate structural motifs, landscapes, cities, galaxies, plants, animals, and human (and non-human) beings (Shanon, 2002; Studerus et al., 2011; Carhart-Harris et al., 2015; Kaelen et al., 2016; Preller and Vollenweider, 2016; Roseman et al., 2016; Kraehenmann et al., 2017b). Complex hallucinations typically succeed elementary hallucinations and are more likely at higher doses (Kometer and Vollenweider, 2016; Liechti et al., 2017), and especially appear under DMT (Strassman et al., 1994; Shanon,

2002). Both elementary and complex hallucinations are more commonly reported behind closed eyelids ('closed eye visuals'; CEVs) but can dose-dependently occur in full light with eyes open ('open eye visuals'; OEVs) (Kometer and Vollenweider, 2016). CEVs are often described as vivid mental imagery. Under psychedelic drugs, mental imagery becomes augmented and intensified— e.g., 'My imagination was extremely vivid'— and is intimately linked with emotional and cognitive effects (Carhart-Harris et al., 2015; Preller and Vollenweider, 2016). "Sometimes sensible film- like scenes appear, but very often the visions consist of scenes quite indescribable in ordinary language, and bearing a close resemblance to the paintings and sculptures of the surrealistic school" (Stockings, 1940, p. 31).

Psychedelic mental imagery can be modulated by both verbal (Carhart-Harris et al., 2015) and musical (Kaelen et al., 2016) auditory stimuli - a phenomena known as synaesthesia (Ward, 2013) - e.g.,—'Sounds influenced the things I saw' or 'seeing sounds or hearing colours'—but classification of these effects as 'true' synaesthesia is actively debated (Sinke et al., 2012; Brogaard, 2013; Luke and Terhune, 2013; Terhune et al., 2016).

Somatosensory perception can be drastically altered—e.g., 'I felt unusual bodily sensations'—including body image, size, shape, and location (Savage, 1955; Klee, 1963; Preller and Vollenweider, 2016). Sense of time and causal sequence can lose their usual linear cause-effect structure making it difficult to track the transitions between moments (Heimann, 1963; Wittmann et al., 2007; Wackermann et al., 2008; Studerus et al., 2011; Schmid et al., 2015).

Overall the perceptual effects of psychedelics are extremely varied, multimodal, and easily modulated by external stimuli. Perceptual effects are tightly linked with emotional and cognitive effects.

Emotional Effects:
Swanson (2018) too made a comprehensive review of the emotional effects of the classical psychedelics:

Emotional psychedelic effects are characterised by a general intensification of feelings, increased (conscious) access to emotions, and a broadening in the overall range of emotions felt, both in a positive and negative manner. They are highly dependent on the two extra-pharmacological factors "set" and "setting." The setting is as mentioned the environment the psychedelic is administered in, and emotional effects can thus be modulated by all types of external stimuli, especially music (Bonny and Pahnke, 1972; Shanon, 2002; Kaelen et al., 2015, 2018). Psychedelics can induce unique states of euphoria characterised by involuntary grinning, uncontrollable laughter, silliness, giddiness, playfulness, and exuberance (Preller and Vollenweider,

2016). Negatively experience emotions—e.g., 'I felt afraid' or 'I felt suspicious and paranoid'—are often accompanied by a general sense of losing control, e.g., 'I feared losing control of my mind' (Strassman, 1984; Johnson et al., 2008; Barrett et al., 2017a). However, the majority of emotional psychedelic effects in supportive contexts are experienced as positive (Studerus et al., 2011; Schmid et al., 2015; Carhart-Harris et al., 2016b; Belser et al., 2017; Watts et al., 2017). Both LSD and psilocybin can bias emotion toward positive responses to social and environmental stimuli (Kometer et al., 2012; Carhart-Harris et al., 2016b; Dolder et al., 2016; Pokorny et al., 2017). Spontaneous feelings of awe, wonder, bliss, joy, fun, excitement are too consistent themes across experimental and anecdotal reports (Huxley, 1991; Kaelen et al., 2015; Preller and Vollenweider, 2016; Belser et al., 2017). In supportive environments, classic psychedelic drugs can promote feelings of trust, empathy, bonding, closeness, tenderness, forgiveness, acceptance, and connectedness (Dolder et al., 2016; Belser et al., 2017; Carhart-Harris et al., 2017b; Pokorny et al., 2017; Watts et al., 2017).

Cognitive Effects:
Swanson (2018) characterised the cognitive effects of psychedelics as follows:

Acute changes in the normal flow of linear thinking—e.g., 'My thinking was muddled' or 'My thoughts wandered freely'—are extremely common (Hasler et al., 2004; Studerus et al., 2011). This is reflected in reduced performance on standardised measures of working memory and directed attention (Carter et al., 2005; Vollenweider et al., 2007); however, reductions in performance have been shown to occur less often in individuals with extensive past experience with the drug's effects (Bouso et al., 2013). Cognitive impairments related to acute psychedelic effects are dose-dependent (Wittmann et al., 2007). Extremely low doses, known as microdoses, have been anecdotally associated with improvements in cognitive performance (Waldman, 2017; Wong, 2017) Theoretical attempts to account for the reported effects of microdosing have yet to emerge in the literature.

Certain cognitive traits associated with creativity can increase under psychedelics (Sessa, 2008; Baggott, 2015) such as divergent thinking (Kuypers et al., 2016), use of unlikely language patterns or word associations (Natale et al., 1978b), expansion of semantic activation (Spitzer et al., 1996; Family et al., 2016), and attribution of meaning to perceptual stimuli (Liechti et al., 2017; Preller et al., 2017) especially musical stimuli (Kaelen et al., 2015, 2018; Atasoy et al., 2017b; Barrett et al., 2017b).

Primary-process thinking (Rapaport, 1950)—a widely validated psychological construct (Arminjon, 2011) associated with creativity (Suler, 1980)—is characterized phenomenologically by "image fusion; unlikely combinations or events; sudden shifts or transformations of images; and contradictory or illogical actions, feelings, or thoughts" (Kraehenmann et al., 2017a, p. 2). et al., 2016) have been measured after just one psychedelic experience.

Ego Effects and Ego Dissolution Experiences

Klüver (1926, p. 513) observed that under peyote "the line of demarcation drawn between 'object' and 'subject' in normal state seemed to be changed. The body, the ego, became 'objective' in a certain way, and the objects became 'subjective.'" Similar observations continued throughout first-wave and second-wave psychedelic science (Beringer, 1927b; Klüver, 1928; Savage, 1955; Eisner and Cohen, 1958; Klee, 1963; Leary et al., 1964; Grof, 1976).

Effects on sense of self and ego occur along a dose-dependent range spanning from subtle to drastic (Letheby and Gerrans, 2017; Millière, 2017). Subtle effects are described as a 'softening' of ego with increased insight into one's own habitual patterns of thought, behaviour, personal problems, and past experiences; effects which were utilized in 'psycholytic' psychotherapy (Grof, 1980). Drastic ego-effects, known as "ego dissolution", are described as "the dissolution of the sense of self and the loss of boundaries between self and world" (Millière, 2017) —e.g., 'I felt like I was merging with my surroundings' or 'All notion of self and identity dissolved away' or 'I lost all sense of ego' or 'I experienced a loss of separation from my environment' or 'I felt at one with the universe' (Dittrich et al., 2010; Nour et al., 2016; Millière, 2017). These descriptions resemble non-drug 'mystical-type' experiences (James, 1902; Huxley, 1945; Stace, 1960; Forman, 1998; Baumeister and Exline, 2002); however, the extent of overlap here remains an open question (Hood, 2001; Maclean et al., 2012; Barrett and Griffiths, 2017; Millière, 2017; Winkelman, 2017).

Ego dissolution is more likely to occur at higher doses (Griffiths et al., 2011; Studerus et al., 2011, 2012; Liechti et al., 2017). Furthermore, certain psychedelic drugs cause ego dissolution experience more reliably than others; psilocybin, for example, was found to produce full ego dissolution more reliably compared with LSD (Liechti et al., 2017). Ego dissolution experiences can be driven and modulated by external stimuli, most notably music (Carhart-Harris et al., 2016c; Atasoy et al., 2017b; Kaelen et al., 2018). Interestingly, subjects who experienced 'complete' ego dissolution in psychedelic-assisted therapy were more likely to evidence positive clinical outcomes (Griffiths et al., 2008, 2016; Majić et al., 2015; Ross et al., 2016; Roseman et al., 2017) as well as long- term changes in life outlook and the personality trait openness (MacLean et al., 2011; Carhart-Harris et al., 2016b; Lebedev et al., 2016).

Psychological safety:
Although psychedelics have relatively low physiological toxicity and are not associated with compulsive drug seeking, there is still concern that they may pose other psychological risks. The most likely risk associated with psychedelic administration is commonly known as a "bad trip" and is characterised by anxiety, fear/panic, dysphoria, and/or paranoia. Distressing effects may be experienced in a variety of modalities: sensory (e.g., frightening illusions), somatic (e.g., disturbing hyperawareness of physiological processes), personal psychological (e.g., troubling thoughts or feelings concerning one's life) and metaphysical (e.g., troubling thoughts or feelings about ultimate evil forces) (McCabe, 1977; Grinspoon and Bakalar, 1979; Strassman, 1984). Because emotional experience is often intensified when under the influence of a psychedelic, in unprepared individuals or uncontrolled situations any of these effects may potentially escalate to dangerous behaviour. For example, fear and paranoid delusions may lead to erratic and potentially dangerous behaviour, including aggression against self or others (Strassman, 1984). Although very rare, in hazardous and unsupervised conditions, individuals under the influence of psychedelics have ended their lives by such acts as jumping from buildings (Keeler and Reifler, 1967; Reynolds and Jindrich, 1985; Reitman and Vasilakis, 2004; O'Brien, 2006). We recognise that even under unsupervised and unprepared conditions, reactions to psychedelics involving violence and self-destructive behaviour are rare, and our intention is not to create an unrealistic account of the dangers of psychedelics. Nonetheless, even infrequent reports of such dangers require that investigators take seriously such risks and take steps to avoid their occurrence.

Prolonged psychosis:
Another potential risk of psychedelic administration is provoking the onset of prolonged psychosis, lasting days or even months (Strassman, 1984). Although determining causation is difficult, it appears that individuals who experience such reactions have premorbid mental illness before taking psychedelics. However, it is unknown whether the precipitation of psychosis in such susceptible individuals represents a psychotic reaction that would have never occurred in the absence of psychedelic use, or whether it represents an earlier onset of a psychotic break that would have inevitably occurred (Grinspoon and Bakalar, 1979; Strassman, 1984). Unlike acute psychological distress, these cases will be extremely rare in well-

selected and well-prepared participants. In a survey of investigators who had administered LSD or mescaline, Cohen (1960) reported that only a single case of a psychotic reaction lasting more than 48 hours occurred in 1200 experimental (non-patient) research participants (a rate of 0.8 per 1000). Notably, the individual was an identical twin of a schizophrenic patient and thus would have been excluded in modern research. Prolonged reactions over 48 hours were slightly more frequent in patients undergoing psychotherapy than in experimental non-patient participants, but still relatively rare, occurring at a rate of 1.8 prolonged reactions per 1000 patients. Cohen (1960) also reported that suicide attempts and completed suicides occurred at a rate of 1.2 and 0.4, respectively, per 1000 patients. The causal link between psychedelic exposure and suicide or suicide attempt was only clear for a portion of these cases in patients, and no suicides or suicide attempts were noted for the 1200 non-patient, experimental participants. However, it is important when evaluating these data to consider that only 44 of the 62 researchers queried by Cohen returned survey results (Cohen, 1960; Novak, 1997). Although Cohen and Ditman (1962) subsequently expressed misgivings over the increased incidence of adverse effects due to the increasing recreational use of LSD and some questionable clinical practices, they maintained that when used under the proper guidelines, LSD was an important tool for use in human research (Novak, 1997). McGlothin and Arnold (1971) reported 1 case out of 247 individuals who received LSD in either experimental or psychotherapeutic studies in which an LSD-related psychotic reaction lasting more than 48 hours occurred. That single case was a patient who received repeated LSD administrations in a psychotherapeutic context. Although very rare, care must be taken to minimise the risks of such an episode. Proper selection guidelines, will be the key factor in minimising the risk of prolonged psychosis in human psychedelic use.

Some clinical observations suggest the possibility that unconscious psychological material may be activated during psychedelic sessions, and that such material, if not properly worked through and psychologically integrated, may lead to psychological difficulties of a non-psychotic nature, such as negative emotions and psychosomatic symptoms, lasting beyond the session (e.g., McCabe, 1977; Grof, 1980). Although these observations have not been examined experimentally, they deserve consideration. Johnson et al (2008) believe that the strong interpersonal support from session monitors before, during, and following sessions will minimise any enduring untoward psychological effects.

Lasting perceptual abnormalities:

Another potential risk of psychedelic administration is psychedelic persisting perception disorder (HPPD). In order to meet DSM-IV-TR criteria for this disorder, a psychedelic user must re-experience perceptual effects similar to those experienced under acute psychedelic action after cessation of psychedelic use, these effects must be clinically distressing or impair functioning, and the effects must not be caused by a medical condition or be better explained by another psychiatric disorder or hypnopompic hallucinations (American Psychiatric Association, 2000). WHO ICD-10 doesn't have a similar diagnosis.

The incidence of HPPD is unknown, although it is thought to be very uncommon given the relatively few cases reported out of the millions of psychedelic doses consumed since the 1960s (Halpern and Pope, 2003). Although the term "flashback" is sometimes used interchangeably with HPPD, the former term is often used to describe any brief perceptual effects reminiscent of acute psychedelic effects but occurring beyond acute psychedelic use, usually in the absence of clinical distress or impairment (Lerner et al., 2002). Indeed, many illicit psychedelic users report some brief visual abnormalities occurring after acute psychedelic effects, but only for a small minority of users are these effects troubling or impairing enough to be considered clinically significant or warrant the diagnosis of HPPD (Lerner et al., 2002; Baggott et al., 2006). Many illicit users regard such sub-clinical effects as benign and pleasurable (Strassman, 1984; Lerner et al., 2002; Frecska and Luna, 2006). Importantly, the incidence of HPPD or other perceptual abnormalities appears to be much lower in therapeutic or research contexts with careful screening and preparation than in the context of illicit recreational use which may include the confounds of polydrug use and unscreened psychiatric disorders (Cohen, 1960; McGlothlin and Arnold, 1971; Strassman, 1984; Halpern and Pope, 2003). Because such perceptual abnormalities are poorly understood, researchers administering psychedelics to humans should probe for perceptual disturbances in follow up contact (Johnson et al, 2008).

Abuse and dependence:

Like many classes of psychoactive drugs, psychedelics are sometimes used in a manner that jeopardises the safety or well-being of the individual or others (e.g., driving while impaired; a pattern of use that interferes with work, school, or relationships). Under such circumstances psychedelics are said to be abused.

However, psychedelics are not typically considered drugs of dependence in that they do not engender compulsive drug seeking (National Institute on Drug Abuse, 2001, 2006; O'Brien, 2006), consistent with the observation that they are not reliably self-administered in nonhuman animals (Poling and Bryceland, 1979; Griffiths et al., 1980; Fantegrossi et al., 2004). Further, they are not associated with a known withdrawal syndrome (O'Brien, 2006). Therefore, there is little risk that exposing human volunteers to psychedelics will leave participants physically or psychologically dependent on these compounds.

Psychedelic Therapy
According to Johnson et al (2008) these are the main domains of consideration for selection of individuals fit for psychedelic ingestion in a clinical setting:

Somatic conditions:
Participants must be in good general health as assessed by detailed medical history, physical exam, 12-lead ECG, blood chemistry profile, haematology, and urinalysis. Pregnant women or those not practicing effective means of birth control are excluded, and a negative urine pregnancy test must be present at ingestion of the substance. Relevant to general medical screening, classical psychedelics do as previously described, increase pulse and both systolic and diastolic blood pressure. Therefore contemporary research have excluded volunteers if their resting blood pressure exceeded 140 systolic and 90 diastolic (mmHg), averaged across four assessments on at least two separate days. None of the recent clinical research of classical psychedelics has resulted in blood pressure increases considered medically dangerous, and it has never been needed to administer an anti-hypertensive medication in response to psilocybin effects.

Certain medications may alter the effects of a psychedelic and therefore individuals taking these medications should be excluded from participation. Specifically, chronic administration of tricyclic antidepressants and lithium (Bonson and Murphy, 1996), and acute administration of serotonin reuptake inhibitors (Fiorella et al., 1996) and the antipsychotic medication haloperidol (Vollenweider et al., 1998) have been shown to potentiate psychedelic effects, and therefore participants' use of these represents a safety concern. Chronic administration of SSRI (Stolz et al., 1983; Strassman, 1992; Bonson et al., 1996) and MAO (Bonson and Murphy, 1996) have been shown to decrease sensitivity to psychedelics, and therefore participants' use of these represents a scientific concern. Johnson et al (2008) further advice to include questions concerning over-the-counter dietary supplements in addition to prescription medications when probing medication history, and to exclude those taking potentially problematic substances (e.g., 5-hydroxytryptophan and St. John's Wort may affect serotonergic function, and, therefore, it is appropriate to exclude individuals currently or recently taking these products). It should also be noted that administration of ayahuasca (which contains monoamine oxidase inhibitors in addition to DMT) to individuals taking serotonin reuptake inhibitors may lead to a severe serotonin syndrome reaction (Callaway and Grob, 1998).

Psychiatric conditions:
Psychiatric screening criteria are important for minimising the already low chances of precipitating a longer-term psychotic reaction by psychedelic administration. Thorough psychiatric interviews (e.g., SCID; First et al., 2001) should be conducted in order to identify contraindicated psychological functioning or history. In modern research, individuals are excluded who have a current or past history of meeting ICD-10 and DSM-IV criteria for schizophrenia or other psychotic disorders (unless substance-induced or due to a medical condition), or bipolar I or II disorder, which are the most important conditions to exclude for ensuring safety. In addition, those with a first or second-degree relative with these disorders are excluded, since there is considerable evidence from family, twin, and adoptive studies that genetic factors make a robust contribution to the aetiology of schizophrenia, with genetic factors established as relevant to some, perhaps all cases (Buchanan and Carpenter, 2005). In fact, data indicate there is approximately a six-fold greater chance of developing schizophrenia in second-degree relatives of individuals with schizophrenia (Patel et al., 2003). Other investigators have also excluded individuals scoring high on the personality traits of rigidity and emotional lability on the grounds that these have been significantly associated with negative experiences during psychedelic action and during non-pharmacologically induced altered states of consciousness (Dittrich, 1993; Hasler et al., 2004). It may be appropriate to exclude those with other psychiatric disorders as well (Johnson et al, 2008).

Clinical Personnel:
The clinical staff plays a big part in creating a beneficial psychedelic experience, and the interpersonal atmosphere created by clinical staff in influencing a participants response to a psychedelic. Most critically, this applies to the interpersonal environment created by the session monitors (Leary et al., 1964; Masters and Houston, 1966). The "monitor" is the staff members who will be with the participant in the session room during the course of psychedelic action. Johnson et al (2008) advice, that the monitors should be knowledgeable about the medical and psychological markers of potential adverse reactions to the psychedelic drug. Furthermore, monitors should have significant human relation skills and be familiar with descriptions of altered states of consciousness induced by psychedelics. They have experienced that experience with techniques such as meditation, yoga, or breathing exercises may also prove to be helpful in facilitating

empathy for the participant that experience altered states of consciousness during psychedelic action. They further believe that clinical sensitivity (e.g., empathy, respect) is likely more important than formal degrees when considering monitor qualifications.

They recommend the presence of at least two monitors during psychedelic administration sessions so that the participant will never be alone should one monitor need to briefly leave the session room (e.g., to the restroom). During their clinical studies, they had specified a primary monitor (who takes the lead in participant interactions) and an assistant monitor, with differing required levels of involvement for the two monitors during participant preparation. In early research into potential treatment applications of psychedelic, the presence of both genders in the monitoring team has been recommended (Grof and Halifax, 1977; Grof, 1980; Kurland, 1985). Having both genders present may foster feelings of security. Johnson et al (2018) counsel against both members of the monitoring team being the opposite gender of a participant unless there is a staff member of participant's gender who has established some rapport with the participant in advance, and who can quickly be summoned to assist should support be needed in the restroom.

Although the participant's interactions with the monitors are of paramount importance, all individuals at the study site having contact with the participant on or before the session day may influence a participant's reaction to a psychedelic. Pre-session negative mood consisting of anxiety or depression has been shown to significantly predict anxious or other negative experiences during the session (Metzner et al., 1965). Strassman (2001) reported that a visiting medical student's unexpected interaction with a volunteer before the session may have contributed to an adverse event resulting in the participant leaving the study site under the influence of psilocybin. To the degree possible, the people in charge of the session, should work with all personnel that the participant may encounter (e.g., receptionist, building security, nurses) to ensure that participants are treated with courtesy and respect. Other staff members should be friendly, welcoming, and compassionate, as he or she interact with the participant, and should maintain a positive social rapport with the volunteer to reduce the likelihood of adverse psychological reactions during the session and to gain accurate information on the volunteer's condition so that other study staff may be notified if there is any potential reason to postpone or cancel the session (e.g., if the participant is experiencing a particularly stressful life event or is feeling ill). If any staff member treats the participant disrespectfully or coldly (i.e., "like a guinea pig"), this may negatively influence the participant's psychological state and subsequent psychedelic experience. This, given the powerful influence of set and setting on psychedelic effects.

Physical environment:
The physical environment during psychedelic sessions is extremely important for ensuring safety for participants. The physical environment is the setting of the session, and an aesthetically pleasing environment may decrease the probability of acute psychological distress. Most of the recent clinical studies of psychedelics utilise a living room-like setting. The furniture should be comfortable, and should preferably not resemble a typical medical-setting. According to Johnson et al (2008), an overly "clinical" environment with an "antiseptic" look (e.g., white walls, extraneous medical equipment, personnel in white lab coats) may increase anxious reactions. Strassman (2001) noted that the medically oriented environment in which his DMT studies were conducted may have contributed to volunteers having unpleasant subjective experiences. For example, some volunteers reported vivid and realistic experiences of being medically examined by extraterrestrials. It has also been noted that many of the potentially unpleasant physical reactions to psychedelics (e.g., subjective changes in temperature, difficulty in breathing, various bodily sensations) might be in part psychosomatic in nature (Blewett and Chwelos, 1959), and therefore possibly more likely in settings evocative of medical conditions (Masters and Houston, 1966).

Beyond the psychological importance of a comfortable, relaxing environment, attention must be paid to the physical safety of the environment. The environment should be designed keeping in mind the perceptual changes and disorientation that can occur under the influence of psychedelics. Thus, any potentially dangerous objects (e.g., furniture with sharp corners; glass lamps) should be avoided. If there is a window in the room, the study staff need to be confident that the participant could not exit the window if in a delusional state. Additionally, the session room should not have a telephone, and the participant should surrender her or his cellular telephone before the session. Not only may an incoming telephone call be distracting or alarming while under the influence of a psychedelic, but it may also represent a safety risk, as Strassman (2001) has reported a case in which a participant used a session room telephone to call a companion, which culminated in the two fleeing the study site. Having a private restroom located near the session room would be ideal for volunteer use during the session, ensuring that the participant doesn't meet other individuals than the monitors.

Preparation of participants:
Participant preparation must according to Johnson et al (2008), at the earliest include an explanation in plain language, of the range of experiences that may result from psychedelic administration, including changes in perception, sense of time and space, time course of drug-action and emotion (possibly including anxiety, fear, panic, and paranoia). The subjective effects of psychedelic are likely more difficult to describe to a naïve participant; why additional time may be necessary to fully discuss these potential effects with participants. The relatively small risk of adverse effects that last for hours to days after the psychedelic session should be communicated to the participant, including mood disorders (such as depression), psychotic disorders, and anxiety disorders, including rare reports in which psychedelic exposure appears to cause, accelerate, or precipitate the onset of significant or lasting psychiatric illnesses such as psychoses and flashbacks/HPPD.

The next step in participant preparation is to conduct a series of meetings between the monitors and volunteer in order to build rapport and trust. The relationship between the monitors and the participant should be well established by the time of the first session (Masters and Houston, 1966). One of these preparatory meetings should be conducted in the room in which the psychedelic is to be administered, in order to familiarise the participant with the physical environment. The primary monitor meets with the volunteer during all of these meetings, while the assistant monitor is required to be present on at least one occasion. It is important that the assistant monitor, in addition to the primary monitor, has developed a trusting relationship with the participant because this assistant monitor will be the only person in the session room with the participant if the primary monitor needs to leave briefly.

During these preparatory meetings, the monitors discuss meaningful aspects of the participant's life. The main purpose of the participant-monitor meetings is to develop rapport and trust, which Johnson et al (2008) believe helps minimise the risk of fear or anxiety reactions during the psychedelic session. This typically includes discussions of the participant's childhood, romantic life, current relationships with family and friends, and the participant's philosophical and/or spiritual beliefs.
Reviewing personal history and feelings may be important for two reasons. First, this discussion helps establish a significant level of trust. The interaction should convey that all aspects of the person are welcome, from the petty to the noble, from embarrassments to achievements, and from sorrow to joy. By the time of the psychedelic session day, the volunteer will ideally feel completely comfortable with the monitor, reducing the

likelihood of paranoia (e.g., feeling that the monitors are trying to control her or his mind, or have deceived the participant about the nature of the study). Second, related personal material may "emerge" under the effects of the psychedelic. That is, the volunteer may experience intense thoughts, feelings, and visions related to his or her personal history or world-view. Knowing about the volunteer's life will allow the monitor to better understand her or his session experience and help the monitor in providing interpersonal support should strong emotions arise. If it is felt that sufficient rapport and trust have not developed during these monitor meetings, then either additional contact hours should be provided, or the psychedelic session should be cancelled. A high dose of a psychedelic should not be administered to a volunteer if sufficient trust has not been established.

At some point during preparatory meetings, time must be devoted to explaining the session logistics. These should include the timing of the session (e.g., what time to arrive at the facility, what time the session is likely to end), any restrictions on diet or contraindicated medicines, drugs, or nutritional supplements (e.g., if fasting or a low-fat diet is required the morning before session), and any requirements of other people (e.g., if a family member or friend is to pick up the participant at the end of the session).

The preparation of the volunteer should involve a detailed discussion of the possible range of experiences that may be encountered after psychedelic administration. This includes the typical onset and duration of the drug(s) under investigation. Preparation involves discussion of the various potential physical sensations, such as nausea, or heightened awareness of physiological processes such as breathing and heartbeat. Volunteers are encouraged to trust that their bodies will continue to function properly regardless of such sensations, and that these bodily processes will continue without the volunteers' volitional control.

The major categories of potential psychological experiences during psychedelic action should too be discussed with the participant. The volunteers should be given guidance on how to handle difficult psychedelic experiences. Whether the disturbance consists of frightening illusions or internal imagery, difficult thoughts and feelings about some past or present personal issue, or anxiety related to a radical change in sense of self (e.g., temporary loss of self-identity), the volunteer is encouraged to mentally surrender to the experience, trusting that her or his usual state of consciousness will return when the drug effects resolve (Blewett and Chwelos, 1959; Masters and Houston, 1966; McCabe, 1977). For example, if the participant experiences disturbing internal imagery of a demon or monster, he or she is encouraged to mentally approach the figure and interact with it (e.g., imagine asking the figure why it has appeared), rather than attempt to flee from the disturbing imagery. The participant should be alerted that sometimes people experience extremely convincing sensations of dissolving, melting, exploding, and so forth, and that the best way to deal with all such situations is to surrender to the experience, subjectively allowing oneself to dissolve, melt, or explode. Similar advice applies to physical symptoms such as nausea; for example, participants may be encouraged to "dive in" to their stomachs, which may alleviate the nausea, as it has been suggested anecdotally that nausea and other somatic discomforts may in part be of a psychosomatic nature (Blewett and Chwelos, 1959; Masters and Houston, 1966).

Conduct of the psychedelic session:
Johnson et al (2008) recommend that a physician should be available during psychedelic sessions should any untoward medical complications arise. Furthermore, medication for the treatment of acute hypertension (e.g., intravenous labetalol) should be immediately available in the event that blood pressure exceeds pre-determined safety parameters.

Adverse psychological reactions to psychedelics will be minimised when studies are conducted under conditions that provide strong interpersonal support to the participants (Blewett and Chwelos, 1959; Chwelos et al., 1959; Pahnke, 1969; Masters and Houston, 1966). The monitors should carefully observe the participant and be vigilant for signs of psychological distress. If the volunteer needs to walk in order to go to the restroom, the monitors should stand close by in order to assist by gently holding an arm or shoulder. Even with high doses of psychedelics, individuals do not typically show substantial motor impairment, and will likely be able to ambulate without considerable difficulty (with the exception of psychedelics such as parenteral DMT with abrupt effects and short duration of action). However, perceptual and proprioceptive effects may make walking disorienting, which is why gentle guidance may be helpful. One of the monitors should always be present in the session room with the participant. Because the session monitors will have developed rapport and trust with the participant, they should be the only people to interact with the volunteer during the course of psychedelic action, barring any non-routine event (e.g., fire alarm, medical intervention by a specialist). Individuals who are anticipated to have contact with the volunteer during the course of psychedelic action (e.g., nurse, physician) should have at least met with the volunteer once prior to session to develop some degree of rapport and trust.

For all but the shortest acting psychedelics (e.g., parenteral DMT), the participant is likely to need to use the restroom at some point while experiencing psychedelic effects. If a private restroom is not available, then staff should escort the volunteer to assure that no one is in the restroom, and that the participant doesn't leave the facility. Any attempt by a disoriented volunteer to leave the session area would be met with compassionate but firm direction to return to the session room.

The restroom door needs to have no lock, or staff should have a key readily available if needed. Cohen (1960) reported a case in which a depressed patient who had been administered LSD barricaded himself into a room in order to attempt suicide.

Strategies for handling non-routine scenarios should be considered. For example, how are study monitors and the volunteer expected to respond in the event of a fire alarm or fire? If any non-routine events occur, the monitors should maintain contact with the volunteer throughout.

If participants become anxious during the course of psychedelic action, O'Brien (2006) recommend that the appropriate first response is to provide strong personal support and reassurance. This primarily includes interacting with the volunteer in a comforting and reassuring manner. If the volunteer is behaving anxiously and a negative psychological reaction seems to be escalating, the monitors should convey a solid sense of security and calm, while empathising with what may be an incredibly intense and unpleasant experience. Attempts to "talk down" the participant (i.e., the use of reality-defining techniques in order to distract the participant from or attenuate the altered state of consciousness) may be counterproductive and aggravate a difficult reaction (McCabe, 1977). Instead, participants should be reminded to surrender to the experience. Appropriate forms of reassurance may include a supportive touch to the arm or shoulder with verbal reminders that the participant is in a psychedelic session, has taken the psychedelic, and that he or she will return to normal consciousness in "a few minutes" or "a few hours" (or whatever the appropriate estimate may be, depending on the specific drug under study and when it was administered). During an intense psychedelic-occasioned experience when verbal interactions may be of limited help, a powerful form of reassurance (sometimes called "interpersonal grounding") is simply holding the hand of the participant (McCabe, 1977). Many volunteers report that during such experiences, a reassuring hand provides an incredible sense of stability and connection. Monitors should demonstrate this practice during preparation to normalise hand holding during sessions.

If volunteers have been appropriately screened and the guidelines herein followed, reassurance should be sufficient to diffuse acute psychological distress in the vast majority of cases (Johnson et al, 2008). Although pharmacological intervention is a last resort and should rarely, if ever, be needed, medications should be readily available for use if the need arise. For cases in which acute psychological distress is insufficiently managed with reassurance alone, treatment with a benzodiazepine anxiolytic is the pharmacological intervention of choice (Abraham and Aldridge, 1993; Frecska and Luna, 2006; O'Brien, 2006). In these cases Johnson et al (2008) recommend a 10 mg oral dose of diazepam, although oral doses of 15–30 mg per hour or every few hours as needed have been recommended for pharmacological treatment of "bad trips" that do not respond to reassurance in emergency department settings (Ungerleider and Frank, 1976). Because of its high lipid solubility, diazepam has a more rapid onset, a shorter time until peak plasma concentration, and a shorter duration of therapeutic action than many other benzodiazepines including lorazepam, despite the fact that lorazepam has a shorter elimination half-life (Greenblatt and Shader, 1985; Funderburk et al., 1988). Although the intravenous route may be considered, the oral route is preferable because intravenous injection procedures may further exacerbate the participant's anxiety. Also, antipsychotic medications (e.g., risperidone, olanzapine) should be available in the event that an adverse reaction escalates to unmanageable psychosis. However, experienced clinicians have suggested that although antipsychotic medications may reduce psychotic behaviour through sedation, their use may be problematic because the effects may be abrupt, unpleasant, and intense and their use may result in subsequent psychological problems (McCabe, 1977; Grinspoon and Bakalar, 1979; Grof, 1980). Furthermore, pretreatment with the antipsychotic haloperidol has been shown to exacerbate the psychosis-like effects of psilocybin (Vollenweider, et al., 1998), suggesting that haloperidol should not be used as a rescue medication.

Ketanserin (a 5-HT2A antagonist) pretreatment has been shown to attenuate psilocybin effects (Vollenweider, et al., 1998), suggesting possible use as a rescue medication for psychedelic administration. Ultimately the decision to medicate will depend on whether the monitors and responsible physician judge that they are capable of maintaining the safety of the volunteer and others without medical intervention. Bringing the participant to the emergency department represents an ultimate "last resort" in the treatment of a very difficult (i.e., psychotic) reaction. However, medical evaluation by well-meaning emergency department personnel who are inexperienced with psychedelic effects can readily escalate and prolong an adverse reaction. Therefore, all possible efforts should be made to treat a difficult experience in the session context.

The employment of eyeshades and headphones (through which supportive music is played) may contribute to safety by reducing the distractions of environmental stimuli and social pressures to verbally interact with monitors. This may be especially important for volunteers who are experiencing the effects of a psychedelic for the first time. Johnson et al (2008) kept eyeshades and headphones in place for most of the session. In the latter hours of the session some time were spent with the volunteer sitting on the couch, interacting without eyeshades and headphones, although music still might be played through speakers to provide nonverbal structure and continuity. As a whole, they encourage their participants to "collect experiences" to discuss after the drug effects have abated, and discourage attempts to analyse material or communicate excessively while the atypical states of consciousness were still occurring.

After the effects of the psychedelic have resolved, the participant should either be released into the care of a friend or family member or required to stay overnight at the facility for monitoring. If participants are released from the study site after the session, they should be instructed not to drive an automobile or engage in any other potentially dangerous activity for the remainder of the day. If released, the participant should be given the primary monitor's phone number to call if he or she feels the need for support that evening.

Post-session procedures:
After the session, safety monitoring should continue in the form of one or more post-session meetings (typically the next day) between the primary monitor and participant to ensure psychological stability and provide an opportunity for the volunteer to discuss thoughts or feelings from the session. As with any acute, intense positive or negative emotional experience, participants often feel the need for, and seem to benefit from, additional time for reflecting on the novel thoughts and feelings that may have arisen in the session. Given the potentially intense and unusual psychological nature of psychedelic effects, the volunteer may have difficulty discussing the experience with others in her or his life. Because the monitors were present during the session when the psychedelic effects were experienced and have knowledge of a broad range of reported phenomena during drug action, the volunteer may feel more comfortable discussing her or his experiences with the monitors than with others. This follow up contact also allows the assessment of any potentially persisting adverse effects, including perceptual abnormalities. More than one post-session meeting may be necessary if the volunteer is experiencing psychological difficulty concerning thoughts and feelings encountered

during the session. If the primary session monitor is not a clinically trained psychiatrist, it is prudent to have available for consultation a clinically trained psychologist or psychiatrist familiar with altered states of consciousness, who can work with patients who appear to have developed psychological difficulties stemming from psychedelic administration (Johnson et al, 2008).

Clinical Research

The following part of the text deal with the ongoing research concerning clinical applications of the classical psychedelics.

Psychedelics for the treatment of alcohol dependence

Possible biological mechanisms in the treatment of alcohol dependence:

Although classic psychedelics bind to many serotonin receptor subtypes and other receptors (Ray, 2010), the psychoactive effects of all classic psychedelics appear to depend primarily on their actions at 5HT2A receptors (Nichols, 2004; Vollenweider and Kometer 2010; Vollenweider et al., 1998). Administration of classic psychedelics in rat models has been shown to induce down-regulation of 5HT2A receptors, particularly those in the anterior cingulate and frontomedial cortex, likely accounting for the rapid development and reversal of behavioural tolerance to most classic psychedelics (Buckholtz et al., 1990; Gresch et al., 2005).

The behavioural correlates and effects of 5HT2A receptor activity are complex. Increased 5HT2A receptor binding has been found in relation to pathological conditions in humans including depression (Shelton et al., 2009), impulsive aggression (Rosell et al., 2010), neuroticism (Frokjaer et al., 2008), borderline personality disorder (Soloff et al., 2007), and suicide (Anisman et al., 2008). The relationship of 5HT2A receptor binding/activity and alcoholism or alcohol exposure is less clear. Family history of alcoholism may be associated with lower 5HT2A binding (Underwood et al., 2008), and alcoholism is not consistently associated with change in 5HT2A receptor levels (Thompson et al., 2012; Underwood et al., 2008). Among alcoholics, one small post-mortem study reported that higher impulsivity was associated with increased 5HT2A receptor binding (Thompson et al., 2012). In animal models, alcohol exposure has been associated with region-specific increases (Akash et al., 2008) and decreases (George et al., 2010) in 5HT2A receptors binding.
Studies indicate that increased activity in 5HT2A-mediated pathways relative to 5HT2C activity increases cue response and impulsivity in rat models of cocaine addiction (Cunningham and Anastasio, 2014). 5HT2A antagonists suppress alcohol consumption in animal models (Johnson, 2008). However, two large trials of the 5HT2A antagonist ritanserin failed to demonstrate beneficial effects in people with alcohol dependence (Johnson et al., 1996; Wiesbeck et al., 1999). Animal studies suggest mechanisms by which acute activation of 5HT2A receptors could activate

intracellular signalling pathways resulting in persisting changes in cellular structure and synapses. The classic psychedelic DOI increases expression of glial cell line-derived neurotrophic factor (GDNF) mRNA in glioiblastoma cells by a 5HT2A-dependent mechanism (Tsuchioka et al., 2008). Through its action on 5HT2A receptors, DOI has also been shown to increase levels of mRNA for brain derived neurotrophic factor (BDNF) in rat parietal cortex and other neocortical regions, with decreases in the hippocampus and no change in piriform cortex (Vaidya et al., 1997). These findings are relevant because levels of BDNF and GDNF
are inversely related to alcohol consumption and conditioned place preference in animal models (Ghitza et al., 2010). DOI activates intracellular signalling cascades associated with dendritic
spine remodelling on rat pyramidal cells, and transiently increases the size of dendritic spines on cortical neurons (Jones et al., 2009).

Possible psychological models of psychedelic treatment of alcohol dependence:

Clinical work with classic psychedelics has emphasised the central role of the altered state of consciousness experienced during the drug's acute effects (Grof, 2008; Hoffer, 1967; Masters and Houston, 2000; Pahnke et al., 1970; Sherwood et al., 1962). The "psycholytic" model of treatment emphasised the use of classic psychedelics to enhance the process of psychodynamic psychotherapy by making unconscious material more accessible (Leuner, 1967).

The "psychedelic" treatment model on the other hand emphasised the use of relatively high doses of classic psychedelics (usually LSD) to occasion a "peak-psychedelic" or mystical experience of ego loss, often likened to psychological death and rebirth (Kurland et al., 1967). The latter model was used in most of the clinical studies conducted in North America using LSD in the treatment of addiction or existential anxiety in the dying. The concept of a singular transformative experience
leading to lasting behaviour change is consistent with classic descriptions of religious conversion (James, 1902), "spiritual awakening" in the context of Alcoholics Anonymous (Forcehimes,
2004), and spontaneous Quantum Change experiences (Miller and C'de Baca, 2001). Recent studies have demonstrated that the self-reported "mystical" dimension of the psilocybin experience (feelings of unity, sacredness, ultimate reality, transcendence of time and space, deeply felt positive mood, and ineffability (Pahnke, 1963)) significantly predicts the lasting personal significance of the experience (Griffiths et al., 2008) and personality change (Maclean et al., 2011) in normal volunteers receiving psilocybin.

Previous research:

In the 1950s through early 1970s there was extensive research on the use of LSD, psilocybin and other classic psychedelics in the treatment of addiction (Abuzzahab and Anderson, 1971; Dyck, 2006; Grinspoon and Balakar, 1997; Halpern, 1996; Mangini, 1998). One particular field of interest were the treatment of alcohol dependence.

Many reports of clinical experience, non-randomised controlled and open-label studies of LSD for alcoholism were published in the 1970's and 1980's, and about 30 of these are reviewed in Mangini (1998). Unfortunately, early investigators did not employ rigorous clinical methods such as randomized controlled trials, outcome measures, and treatment settings, and thus those studies did not provide definitive results. Abuzzahab and Anderson (1971) reviewed studies of 1100 alcoholic patients treated with LSD in the period from 1953 to 1969 and came to a similar conclusion; however, they did find reports of improvement at 10 months for 75% of patients who received a single dose of LSD compared with only 44% of controls. For patients who received multiple doses of LSD, 58% were "improved" compared with 54% of the controls.

Some studies of good quality were published in the pre-prohibition era. These randomised controlled trials were examined in a meta-analysis from 2012 of LSD for alcoholism (Krebs and Johansen, 2012).
This study, as well as the evidence summarised above provides a convincing rationale to continue investigating whether a classic psychedelic can improve treatment response among patients with alcohol and substance dependence.

Contemporary research:

To begin the exploration of the contemporary research, we first examine the meta-analysis of the pre-prohibition randomised controlled studies:

Krebs and Johansen (2012). Lysergic acid diethylamide (LSD) for alcoholism: meta-analysis of randomized controlled trials.

Methods:

Krebs and Johansen (2012) searched the PubMed and PsycINFO databases (1943–2010) for randomized controlled trials of LSD for alcoholism, in which control condition involved any type of treatment, including doses of up to 50 mcg LSD as an active control. If a trial included multiple randomized treatment arms, all participants in the eligible LSD arms and all participants in the eligible
control arms were pooled for analysis. We excluded participants with

schizophrenia or psychosis from analysis, as psychosis is recognized as a contraindication for treatment with LSD.

They identified identified six eligible randomised controlled trials (Bowen et al., 1970; Hollister et al., 1969; Ludwig et al., 1969; Pahnke et al., 1970; Smart et al., 1966; Tomsovic and Edwards, 1970), including additional reports on three of the trials (Kurland et al., 1971; Ludwig et al., 1970; Smart et al., 1967).
Among the excluded studies were five non-randomised controlled trials (Ables and Eng, 1967; Ables et al., 1970; Jensen, 1962; Jensen, 1963; Van Dusen et al., 1967), one quasi-randomised controlled trial (allocation by alternating assignment) (Osmond et al., 1967), two randomised controlled trials without any outcome data related to alcohol use (both measured only general psychological variables) (Denson and Sydiaha, 1970; Ditman et al., 1970), and one randomised controlled trial without extractable outcome data on alcohol misuse (this trial reported only 'no statistically significant difference' between LSD and control groups on alcohol misuse at 12 months follow-up) (Johnson, 1969).

The six eligible trials included a total of 536 adults; of these 325 (61%) had been randomly assigned to receive full-dose LSD and 211 (39%) to a control condition. Participants were male inpatients, except for two females and a small number of day-care patients in one of the trials (Smart et al., 1966). All participants were seeking treatment for 'alcoholism' as their primary problem and had been admitted to alcohol-focused treatment programs before clinical trial recruitment. Alcoholism were defined according to DSM-I as a 'well established addiction to alcohol without recognisable underlying disorder'.
Among the reported exclusion criteria, trials excluded potential volunteers with 'psychiatric complications' (Bowen et al., 1970), with a 'past history of schizophrenic reaction or severe affective disorder' (Hollister et al., 1969), or overt psychosis (Ludwig et al., 1969; Smart et al., 1966; Tomsovic and Edwards, 1970). One trial included a subgroup of patients with schizophrenia (Tomsovic and Edwards, 1970), which were excluded from the meta-analysis. Two trials included additional non-randomized control groups or non-randomised sub-studies, which too were excluded from the meta-analysis (Bowen et al., 1970; Tomsovic and Edwards, 1970).
Single oral doses of LSD ranged from approximately 210 mcg (3 mcg/kg) to 800 mcg, with a median dose of 500 mcg. No studies used multiple doses of LSD. The control conditions
included low-dose LSD (25 mcg or 50 mcg), d-amphetamine (60 mg), ephedrine sulphate (60 mg), or non-drug control conditions,

Before the experimental drug session, all participants had equivalent treatment within each trial; however, between the trials the preparation for the experimental drug session varied from
minimal to extensive, with most studies providing brief orientation, often with little or no description of the possible effects of LSD. During the experimental drug session, the most common treatment was simple observation with brief reassurance by clinic staff, only three studies included treatment groups who received clinical interviews, psychotherapy, or active guidance. In four studies, the experimental drug session took place in comfortable surroundings with music available. After the experimental drug session, only one study included multiple review sessions focused on discussing the experiences during the drug session, while the other studies provided only one brief review session or no review session at all. Each trial used clearly defined, standardised methods to assess outcomes on alcohol misuse, although methods varied between trials. Extracted dichotomous or categorical outcomes included maintained abstinence from alcohol, alcohol use rating scales, or composite alcohol use and social adjustment rating scales; the one continuous outcome was percentage change in time abstinent from alcohol.

Results:
Adverse effects:
Five trials reported a total of eight acute adverse reactions to LSD, without any lasting harmful effects. Trial investigators did not specifically mention whether there were adverse events among
participants in the control conditions. During the LSD experience, two people 'acted bizarrely' (Tomsovic and Edwards, 1970), one person became agitated (Hollister et al., 1969), another person had a grand mal seizure during a period of agitation (this patient had a
history of alcohol withdrawal seizures and had been abstinent from alcohol for only a few days) (Hollister et al., 1969) and two people had unspecified 'adverse reactions' (Ludwig et al., 1969).

In the days after LSD, one person experienced transient 'moderate confusion' (Hollister et al., 1969) and one person had a transient 'adverse reaction' (Pahnke et al., 1970). Additionally, investigators in one trial reported mild adverse reactions to LSD in a small number of participants, including nausea, vomiting and 'moderate agitation' that was relieved by social support, relaxation, or changing the lights and music (Hollister et al., 1969).
Furthermore, in one trial, about a third of the participants who received LSD reported briefly experiencing 'any perceptual thought or feeling experience which impressed the patient with its vividness and which was

clearly related to the [LSD] experience' on one or a few occasions within a year after LSD, typically after using alcohol (Tomsovic and Edwards, 1970), while participants in another trial specifically did not mention such experiences at follow-up (Hollister et al., 1969).

Effects:
- The pooled odds ratio on improvement in alcohol misuse between the LSD and control groups was 1.96 (95% CI, 1.36–2.84; p = 0.0003) at the first reported follow-up. Among the five trials with dichotomised data, 185 of 315 (59%) LSD patients and 73 of 191 (38%) control patients were improved at the first reported follow-up, and the pooled benefit difference was 16% (95% CI, 8%–25%; p = 0.0003), or, equivalently, the number needed to treat were six. Including an estimated dichotomised outcome for the one trial that reported only continuous outcome.
- Among the three trials that reported maintained abstinence from alcohol use, there was a beneficial effect of LSD at the first reported follow-up (1–3 months post-treatment) (OR, 2.07; 95% CI, 1.26– 3.42; p = 0.004) and short-term follow-up (2–3 months post-treatment) (OR, 1.80; 95% CI, 1.07–3.04; p = 0.03), which was not statistically significant at medium-term follow-up (6 months post-treatment) (OR, 1.42; 95% CI, 0.65–3.10; p = 0.38).
- Heterogeneity of the between-trial treatment outcome was negligible in the pooled comparisons for abstinence at first reported follow-up and short-term follow-up (I2 = 0%, for both p ≥ 0.38 for the χ2 test), while heterogeneity was moderate at medium-term follow-up (I2 = 44%, p = 0.41 for the χ2 test).

Discussion:
- In a pooled analysis of six randomised controlled clinical trials, a single dose of LSD had a significant beneficial effect on alcohol misuse at the first reported follow-up assessment, which ranged from 1 to 12 months after discharge from each treatment program. This treatment effect from LSD on alcohol misuse was also seen at 2 to 3 months and at 6 months, but was not statistically significant at 12 months post-treatment. Among the three trials that reported total abstinence from alcohol use, there was also a significant beneficial effect of LSD at the first reported follow-up, which ranged from 1 to 3 months after discharge from each treatment program.
- The findings from randomised controlled trials of a sustained treatment effect of a single dose of LSD on alcohol misuse, which may fade within 12 months, are consistent with many reports of clinical experience and with data from most non-randomised controlled and open-label studies

of LSD for alcoholism.
- In addition, the effectiveness of a single dose of LSD in the trials included in this meta-analysis, compares well with the effectiveness of daily naltrexone, acamprosate, or disulfiram (Krampe and Ehrenreich, 2010; Rösner et al., 2010a, 2010b).
- Given the emerging evidence for a beneficial effect of LSD on alcoholism, the authors of the meta-analysis felt it is puzzling why this treatment approach has been largely overlooked. Based on reviewing the literature, they had four suggestions for why this happened. First, the randomised controlled trials were underpowered and most did not reach statistical significance when considered individually. Second, trial authors expected unrealistic results and tended to discount moderate or short-term effects. Third, early non-randomised clinical trials were poorly described and had methodological problems, creating the mistaken impression that well-designed studies did not exist. Finally, the complicated social and political history of LSD led to increasing difficulties in obtaining regulatory approval for clinical trials.
- Estimates of the rate of adverse events of LSD in alcoholics and others should include data from non-randomised as well as randomised trials. Based on extensive animal research and human experience, there is now widespread recognition that LSD and similar psychedelic substances are physically safe, but acute psychiatric adverse events such as anxiety and confusion should be anticipated, and LSD administration should occur in a comfortable environment with informed participants.
- Several matters in this meta-analysis deserve discussion. First, trials typically lacked detailed descriptions of the populations studied, including diagnosis methods. However, all participants were recruited into the trials after admission to alcohol treatment programs with a primary diagnosis of alcoholism, making it likely that the patients are representative of typical clinical practice. Second, there were not enough trials to examine the effect of LSD dose or other treatment variables; all of the trials used a high or very high dose of LSD and employed different treatment frameworks. Third, it is possible that additional randomised controlled trials were never published or were missed by our literature search. Fourth, three trials either concealed for the participant that LSD might be used (Hollister et al., 1969; Smart et al., 1966) or gave very little information about its likely effects (Ludwig et al., 1969), and in two of these trials participants were left alone in a room during much of the LSD effects (Ludwig et al., 1969; Smart et al., 1966); including people who might be reluctant to participate in a trial of LSD or who were unprepared for the LSD effects may have attenuated the treatment effect and increased the risk of adverse events. Fifth, blinding is a common problem to clinical trials of active interventions, including most

pharmacological and behavioural treatments; most trials included in this meta-analysis attempted to minimise risks of bias related to blinding by using active placebos and/or using explicitly treatment-independent, allocation blind interviewers for outcome assessment. However, the use of low-dose LSD as an active placebo in two of the trials may have attenuated the between-group treatment effect. Finally, primary outcome measures on improvement in alcohol misuse varied between trials; however, all of the clinical trials used standardised questionnaires. Additionally, three trials also reported data on the same clearly-defined outcome: maintained abstinence from alcohol use.

Conclusion:
The meta-analysis showed there was evidence for a beneficial effect of LSD on alcohol misuse (OR, 1.96; 95% CI, 1.36–2.84; $p = 0.0003$), and that a single dose of LSD, in the context of various alcoholism treatment programs, is associated with a decrease in alcohol misuse.

In addition to this meta-analysis, two smaller post-prohibition studies on psilocybin for alcohol dependence have been conducted:

Bogenschutz et al (2015). Psilocybin-assisted treatment for alcohol dependence: a proof-of-concept study.

Methods:
Bogenschutz et al (2015) recruited 10 participants (six men) age 25-65 (mean age 40.1) years, with a diagnosis of active alcohol dependence (mean duration of alcohol dependence was 15.1 years) and at least two heavy drinking days in the past 30 days, who were concerned about their drinking and not currently in treatment. Participants were required to be abstinent and not in alcohol withdrawal at the time of the psilocybin sessions. Somatic and psychiatric screening as well as the practical aspects of the study were carried out according to the principles in Johnson et al (2008).

Participants received a 12-week, 14-session manualised intervention including two open-label psilocybin sessions in which psilocybin was administered: the first after 4 weeks of psychosocial
treatment, the second after 8 weeks. Outcome data were collected for a total of 36 weeks.
The psychosocial intervention comprised a total of 12 sessions: seven sessions of Motivational Enhancement Therapy (MET: a structured approach using the principles of motivational interviewing), three preparation sessions, and two debriefing sessions. Four sessions occurred before the first psilocybin session, four sessions between the first and

second psilocybin sessions, and four sessions after the second psilocybin session. The psychosocial intervention was conducted by a team of two therapists. One performed the seven MET sessions focused on changing drinking behaviour, while the other was responsible for preparation before, support during, and debriefing after the psilocybin sessions. Both therapists were present for the preparation and debriefing sessions, as well as the psilocybin sessions. The first and third MET sessions were coded using the Motivational Interviewing Treatment Integrity (MITI 3.1).

On the morning of the psilocybin sessions, participants were required to be afebrile, non-hypertensive, non-tachycardic, and without evidence of alcohol withdrawal symptoms, in addition Individualised doses of psilocybin (based on participant weight) were ingested by the participants. For the first psilocybin session, participants received a dose of 0.3 mg/kg. For the second session, the dose was increased to 0.4 mg/kg unless the participant (i) was unwilling to increase the dose; (ii) experienced adverse effects during the first session which suggested that a higher dose would pose significant risk; or (iii) reported a "complete" mystical experience during the first session indicating very strong effects from 0.3 mg/kg.

Ten participants completed the first psilocybin session. Of the seven participants completing the second psilocybin session, six received psilocybin 0.4 mg/kg and were included in analysis of second session effects. One received psilocybin 0.3 mg/kg due to meeting criteria for "complete mystical experience" in the first session. Nine participants completed all follow-up assessments and were included in outcome analyses. One participant discontinued participation shortly after the first psilocybin session and did not provide usable outcome data.

Participants remained under observation for at least 8 h following psilocybin administration. Both therapists were present throughout the session. Interactions with the participants were supportive and non-directive. Medications were available for administration if needed to treat hypertension (sublingual nitroglycerin), anxiety (lorazepam), or acute psychosis (ziprasidone).
Beginning 7 h after drug administration, participants completed questionnaires and assessments, and a brief clinical interview was performed, including mental status exam.

Self-report scales (administered 7 h after drug administration) and monitor ratings (0–6 hours after drug administration) were used to quantify acute subjective effects. The Intensity subscale of the Hallucinogen Rating Scale (HRS) was used as a global measure of the intensity of the drug experience.

The 5-Dimensional Altered States of Consciousness Scale (5D-ASC) and The States of Consciousness Scale was used to measure states of consciousness in the psychedelic experience. The Addiction Research Center Inventory (ARCI) was also administered following each drug administration session. In addition, a Monitor Session Rating Form was completed by both monitors at intervals during the psilocybin sessions to provide ratings of participants' behaviour and affect during the session. The Time-Line FollowBack (TLFB) procedure was used to assess drinking behaviour at baseline (covering the 12 weeks preceding enrolment) and follow-up visits. Heavy drinking days were defined as days during which participants consumed five or more standard drinks if the participant was male, or four or more standard drinks if the participant was female, a standard drink being defined as 14 g of alcohol. Drinking days were defined as days during which participants consumed any amount (even a sip) of an alcoholic beverage. The Short Inventory of Problems (SIP), past 3 month version, was used to measure consequences of alcohol use. Breath Alcohol Concentration (BAC) was measured at each visit, but was used to ensure safety of treatment and validity of assessments rather than as an outcome measure.

The Stages of Change Readiness and Treatment Eagerness Scale (SOCRATES 8A) was used as a measure of motivation. The Alcohol Abstinence Self-Efficacy Scale (AASE) was used as a measure of self-efficacy to abstain from drinking. The Penn Alcohol Craving Scale (PACS) was used to assess craving. The Profile of Mood States (POMS) was used as a measure of mood. Vital signs were obtained at each visit and measured frequently during psilocybin sessions: every half hour for the first 2 hours, then hourly for the next 4 hours, with more frequent readings as needed.

Results:
Adverse Effects:
- BP was significantly increased, but HR did not change significantly.
- Five participants reported mild headaches which resolved within 24 hours following psilocybin administration.
- One participant had nausea with one episode of emesis during one psilocybin session.
- One participant with irritable bowel syndrome experienced diarrhoea during one psilocybin session. One participant reported insomnia on the night following a psilocybin session.
- No participant required medication or other intervention for blood pressure, anxiety, or other psychiatric symptoms.
- There was no report of illicit psychedelic use by any participant during study participation.

Effects:
- Self-report intensity measures of subjective experience obtained 7 hours following administration of psilocybin 0.3 mg/kg in the first session and for the six participants who received psilocybin 0.4 mg/kg in the second session varied markedly from patient to patient. For the six participants who received psilocybin 0.4 mg/kg in the second session, subjective ratings were not significantly different between the two sessions, but were strongly correlated between the sessions for most of the scales intended to measure psychedelic effects.
- Percent heavy drinking days decreased during weeks 5–12 relative to baseline (mean difference (SD) = 26.0 (22.4), 95% CI 8.7–43.2, p = 0.008), and also decreased relative to weeks 1–4 (during psychosocial treatment but prior to psilocybin) (mean difference (SD) = 18.2 (20.0), 95% CI 2.8 33.5, p = 0.026). Percent drinking days also decreased during weeks 5–12 relative to baseline (mean difference (SD) = 27.2 (23.7), 95% CI 9.0–45.4, p = 0.009) and relative to weeks 1–4 (mean difference (SD) = 21.9 (21.8), 95% CI 5.1– 38.6, p = 0.017).
- Improvement were not statistically significant during the first 4 weeks of participation, when participants received weekly counselling but had not yet received psilocybin.
- Following the first psilocybin session, percent heavy drinking days and percent drinking days were significantly lower than baseline at all follow-up points. Further, these measures were significantly decreased relative to weeks 1–4 with the exception of heavy drinking days during weeks 9–12 (p = 0.059). Fifteen out of 16 contrasts were significant at the nominal 0.05 level, and all of these remained significant at a false discovery rate of 0.05. E
- Changes in POMS scores were not significant with one exception (increased vigour at week 24 relative to baseline).
- Because the acute effects of psilocybin were quite variable, it was possible to explore the relationships between the intensity of acute effects and changes in drinking behaviour. Large correlations were observed between measures of acute effect intensity and change in drinking behaviour, as well as changes in craving and self-efficacy in some cases.

Discussion:
- Psilocybin-related adverse effects were transient and mild.
- The subjective response was highly variable among participants in the study, and numerically weaker on average for some of the measures than that reported in normal volunteers at comparable doses. This is

consistent with observations beginning in the 1950s that alcoholics tended to require larger doses of LSD to have a strong effect. The study thus suggested that some alcohol-dependent patients were relatively insensitive to the effects of psilocybin, although larger samples are necessary to confirm this. The lack of significant differences between the 0.3 mg/kg and 0.4 mg/kg doses were most likely accounted for by the small sample size (n = 6) and/or idiosyncratic responses in a small number of participants.

- Participants exhibited significant improvement in drinking, with large pre–post effect sizes, as well as significant changes in psychological measures relevant to drinking. Importantly, much of the improvement occurred following the administration of psilocybin, at which time participants had already received 4 weeks of psychosocial treatment and 4–6 hours of assessment.
- Also, strong correlations were observed between measures of intensity of the acute drug effects and clinical outcomes. Although change in drinking was correlated with the mystical quality of the experience, it was similarly associated with ratings of other acute effects. More work should determine whether there are particular characteristics of the acute psilocybin experience that were predictive of therapeutic benefit in alcohol use disorder.
- A major, self-evident limitations of the present study is the small sample size, lack of a control group or blinding, and lack of biological verification of alcohol use. Due to these limitations, it is not possible to separate unequivocally the effects of attention, psychosocial treatment, and time; expectancy effects related to knowledge of receiving psilocybin; and the specific effects of psilocybin. However, the time course of the observed changes and the striking relationship between intensity of response and clinical improvement provide support for the concept that psilocybin may produce lasting benefits in alcohol use disorder when administered under controlled conditions to carefully screened patients, in the context of appropriate psychosocial interventions.
- Adequately powered randomised trials should help determine this. In addition to this, neuroimaging studies in alcohol use disorder trial participants could help characterise the persisting effects of psilocybin on brain activity.
- Studying the genetics of response to psilocybin may shed light on the variability of response, ultimately aiding in dose selection or identifying patients particularly likely to benefit.

Conclusion:
The study showed that psilocybin can be safely administered to a carefully screened population of patients with alcohol dependence. Abstinence did not increase significantly in the first 4 weeks of treatment (when participants had not yet received psilocybin), but increased significantly following psilocybin administration. Gains were largely maintained at follow-up to 36 weeks. These preliminary findings provide a strong rationale for controlled trials with larger samples to investigate efficacy and mechanisms.

Psilocybin for the treatment of Nicotine Dependence:

Previous research:
The psychedelics were newer explored as a mean to help people quit smoking in the pre-prohibition era - possibly because smoking weren't viewed as something problematic and unhealthy.
Thus, no pre-prohibition literature exist on the subject.

Contemporary research:
Johnson et al (2014) carried out an open-label pilot study using psilocybin as an adjunct to psychotherapy in a structured 15-week smoking cessation program, which is explored in the following paragraph:

Johnson et al (2014). Pilot study of the 5-HT2AR agonist psilocybin in the treatment of tobacco addiction.

Methods:
Johnson et al (2014) recruited 15 participants (10 males) who smoked a minimum of 10 cigarettes per day for a 15-week course of smoking cessation treatment, with psilocybin administration occurring in weeks 5, 7, and 13.
Somatic and psychiatric screening as well as the practical aspects of the study were were carried out according to the principles in Johnson et al (2008).

Participants were assigned to a team of two or three study staff who conducted treatment and oversaw psilocybin sessions. At least one member of each team was a doctoral level psychologist trained in delivering the study intervention and conducting psilocybin sessions. Participants attended four weekly meetings in which a manualised intervention consisting of cognitive-behavioral therapy (CBT) for smoking cessation and preparation for psilocybin administration were delivered. Participants were administered a moderate dose of psilocybin (20mg/70kg). Participants then continued meeting weekly with study staff, and received another dose of psilocybin at week 7, and optionally again at week 13. Although the default dose for sessions 2 and 3 was a high dose (30mg/70kg), participants were permitted to repeat the moderate dose on these sessions.

The second and third sessions were intended as additional quit opportunities for those who failed to achieve abstinence after the first session. For those who did quit on the first session, the additional psilocybin sessions were meant to support motivation for long-term abstinence. This approach was informed by studies of psychedelic-facilitated substance dependence treatment in which investigators described an extended, time-limited, post-session period (sometimes referred to as an "afterglow") associated with decreased substance use, elevated mood and energy, decreased anxiety, and increased capacity for close interpersonal relationships.

The doses and dosing sequence used in this study were based on previous psilocybin dose-response research showing greater prevalence of mystical experience at 20mg/70kg and 30mg/70kg over other lower doses, and that ascending dose sequences produced significantly increased well-being, life satisfaction, and persisting positive mood at 1-month post-session as compared to descending dose sequences (Griffiths et al., 2011). Study staff met with participants the day after each psilocybin session to discuss session experiences and provide support for smoking cessation, for a total of 19 in-person meetings. A staff member made brief (<5 min.) daily phone calls to participants for two weeks after the sessions to provide encouragement for smoking abstinence. Participants were instructed to abstain from using any additional smoking cessation treatments (e.g., nicotine replacement) during the study.

Participants made a brief motivational statement for smoking cessation, which they stated before each psilocybin administration, and participated in a guided imagery exercise at the resolution of psilocybin effects on the first psilocybin sessions. Participant blood pressure and heart rate were monitored at ≤60 min. intervals, and at least one staff member was present throughout sessions. For each session a physician was on call, and rescue medications were available in case of adverse cardiovascular or psychological events. During sessions, participants were encouraged to lie down on a couch and focus on their internal experience. Participants wore an eye mask and listened to a music program through headphones. During sessions, staff provided non-directive interpersonal support for managing psilocybin effects, but did not deliver smoking cessation specific content. After drug effects subsided, participants were asked to write an open-ended narrative describing their session for discussion with staff the following day.

In addition to the psilocybin-sessions, participants participated in four weekly preparation meetings, where participants received smoking cessation Cognitive-behavioral therapy, largely based on the Quit For Life program. Sessions started with a brief (<10 min) "body-scan" meditation. In preparatory sessions participants developed their most important reasons to quit smoking into a brief motivational statement (e.g., "I want to be free, clean, and clear"). Study treatment also included two components of an effective group based smoking cessation therapy (Zernig et al., 2008). First, participants smelled a scented oil during preparatory and support meetings before each exercise. This oil was provided to the participant at the target quit date (TQD) and the participant was encouraged to smell it when experiencing cravings. Second, brief (<10 min) guided imagery exercises were conducted during preparatory and support meetings, and at the end of the first psilocybin session.

Two measures of recent smoking, exhaled carbon monoxide (CO) and urinary cotinine level were assessed at intake, weekly throughout the intervention, and at 6-month follow-up. Breath CO was measured using a Bedfont Micro III Smokerlyzer to detect smoking over approximately the past 24 hours. Urine cotinine levels of <200ng/mL, and breath CO of ≤6ppm were considered as biological verification of non-smoking status. These two were assessed at intake, weekly throughout the intervention, and at 6-month follow-up.

The participants were assessed with the Fagerström Test for Cigarette Dependence (FTCD) at intake. Three supplemental measures related to smoking cessation were administered at intake, weekly post-Target Quit Date until end of treatment (excluding psilocybin session weeks), and at 6-month follow-up. These were the Questionnaire on Smoking Urges (QSU), a multidimensional assessment of smoking craving with demonstrated sensitivity to smoking cessation, The Smoking Abstinence Self-Efficacy scale (SASE) which provides a measure of smokers' confidence to abstain from smoking in 20 hypothetical situations, and temptation to smoke in those situations, and The Wisconsin Smoking Withdrawal Scale (WSWS), which measures severity of smoking withdrawal and exhibits good validity and reliability in smoking cessation studies.

As well as these ratings, the participants completed the 32 item Mysticism Scale to assess primary mystical experience across the lifetime. Participants completed the Mysticism scale at intake, 1-week post psilocybin session 2, and 1-week post session 3 (when applicable).

They also completed the States of Consciousness Questionnaire (SOCQ) in order to assess the occurrence of fearful or otherwise challenging experiences. Participants completed the SOCQ at the conclusion of each psilocybin session, approximately seven hours after psilocybin administration.
Finally they completed the Persisting Effects Questionnaire. This 145-item questionnaire was designed to measure changes in attitudes, moods, behaviour, and spiritual experience. This questionnaire was administered 1-week after each psilocybin session.

Twelve participants completed three psilocybin sessions. Three participants did not undergo a third session, but completed the study. One participant chose a moderate dose on the second psilocybin session; all other participants chose the default recommended dosing sequence (moderate in first session and high in subsequent sessions).

Results:
Adverse Effects:
- No clinically significant adverse events requiring physician or pharmacologic intervention occurred.
- BP and HR were significantly increased, but were self-limiting and did not require medical intervention.
- States of Consciousness Questionnaire data showed that one participant (7%) reported extreme ratings, and five others (33%) reported strong ratings of fear, fear of insanity, or feeling trapped at some time during a session. These episodes occurred in six participants (40%), and occurred during five moderate and five high dose sessions. They were readily managed by interpersonal support, and had resolved by the end of the sessions.
- None experienced flashbacks at follow-up.
- Eight participants reported at least one post-psilocybin headache which resolved during the following day.

Effects:
- Based on the Timeline Follow-back and verified by CO and cotinine measures, 12 of 15 (80%) participants showed seven-day point prevalence abstinence at 6-month follow-up.
- Eleven of these 12 self-reported quitting smoking on their target quit date and demonstrated biologically verified smoking abstinence throughout the following 10 weeks of active treatment. One participant of these 12 reported quitting on the TQD and was biologically verified as abstinent at all attended meetings, but was unexpectedly required to leave the country for business, and was therefore unable to undergo a third

psilocybin session, or provide CO and urine samples for weeks 6–10 post-TQD.
- Three of these 12 participants reported self-corrected lapses (consisting of 1, 4, and 48 cigarettes) during the 16-week period between end of treatment and 6-month follow-up. Another participant reported a relapse after 13 weeks of continuous abstinence, smoking an average of 5 cigarettes/day for 14 weeks (compared to a mean of 19 cigarettes/day at intake), but resumed smoking abstinence prior to 6-month follow-up, as biologically confirmed. This participant also reported use of nicotine replacement (lozenges and gum) during the relapse. No other participant reported use of smoking cessation medications throughout the study.
- Two-tailed paired T-tests demonstrated significant reductions in self-reported daily smoking from intake to 6-month follow-up (TLFB; $t14=11.1$, $P<.001$) among the entire study sample. Smoking biomarker data among the entire sample also demonstrated statistically significant reductions from intake to 6-month follow-up for breath CO levels ($t14=3.8$, $P<.01$), and urine cotinine ($t14=2.3$, $P=.04$).
- Three participants tested positive for smoking at 6-month follow-up, and reported periods of 4, 11, and 22 days of smoking abstinence post-TQD, with two showing >6 days biologically verified continuous abstinence. These individuals ultimately resumed daily smoking. However, a 2-tailed paired T-test analysis of Timeline Follow-back data for these three participants revealed significantly reduced smoking post-TQD, with a reported average of 20 cigarettes/day before TQD, and an average of 14 cigarettes/day afterwards ($t2=5.3$, $P=.03$). Two-tailed paired T-tests found no significant differences in these three participants' smoking biomarker data from intake to 6-month follow-up for breath CO or urine cotinine levels.
- Lifetime Mysticism scale scores indicated a significant increase in mystical experience from intake to 1-week post final psilocybin session (difference $M=+54$; $t14=3.5$, $P=0.004$). Participants reported greater positive than negative effects across all Persisting Effects Questionnaire subscales, with a mean (SD) score of 5.3% (3.6) across negative subscales, and a mean (SD) score of 55.8% (12.1) across positive subscales (scores expressed as percentage of maximum possible score).
- Participants attributed substantial personal meaning to their psilocybin experiences, with 13 (87%) rating at least one psilocybin session among the 10 most meaningful experiences of their lives. Eleven (73%) rated at least one psilocybin session among the 5 most spiritually significant experiences of their lives, and 13 (87%) reported that their personal well-being or life satisfaction had increased very much as a result of at least one psilocybin session.
- Participants were asked to rate several mechanisms by which psilocybin

may have helped in quitting smoking at 3-weeks post-TQD. The most commonly endorsed items (paraphrased) included: changing orientation toward the future, so that long-term benefits outweighed immediate desires (73%); strengthening participants' belief in their ability to quit (73%); and changing life priorities/values, such that smoking was no longer more important than quitting (68%). One participant (7%), who exhibited the shortest duration of abstinence (4 days) among the study sample, responded that psilocybin had not helped in smoking cessation.

Discussion:
- No serious adverse effects were experienced during the study. Adverse effects included increases in BP and HR, headaches (<24 hours) along with psychological discomfort, but all were self limiting.
- Such time-limited effects stand in contrast to adverse effects (e.g., nausea, insomnia, abnormal dreams) associated with approved smoking cessation medications requiring daily administration (e.g., bupropion, varenicline).
- 80% of participants were abstinent at 6-month follow-up. Results should be interpreted with caution given the small study population and open-label design. Therefore, no definitive conclusions can be drawn about the causal role of psilocybin per se.
- However, abstinence rates were substantially higher than typical. For example, when paired with 12 brief weekly counseling meetings, pharmacotherapies have shown seven-day point prevalence abstinence rates of 24.9% to 26.3% (bupropion) and 33.5% to 35.2% (varenicline) at approximately 6 months post-TQD. Furthermore, a randomised controlled trial of the Quit for Life CBT program that provided the primary foundation for the manualised intervention used in this study found a 17.2% abstinence rate at 6-month follow-up.
- The present study provided higher levels of psychosocial support than typical in smoking cessation treatment. However, efficacy rates were higher than observed in studies utilising similarly extensive CBT-based support. For example, in two trials of extended smoking cessation treatments using a combination of bupropion, nicotine replacement, and CBT ranging from 5 to 12 months in duration, participants showed 45% to 59% seven-day point prevalence abstinence at approximately 6 months.
- The study design was unable to discern differential benefits of moderate psilocybin dose (20mg/70 kg) and high dose (30mg/70kg) sessions. All participants who quit smoking (n=12) did so after their initial moderate dose session, and those who did not quit (n=3) were unable to do so even after their subsequent high dose sessions.

Conclusion:
This study were the first to examine psilocybin in the treatment of tobacco addiction, and illustrates a viable framework for psilocybin-based addiction treatment interventions, which in this small study shows promising effects. The novel approach presented here warrants further investigation with a randomised controlled trial.

In a follow-up to the report by Johnson et al. (2014), Garcia-Romeu et al. (2014) reported that abstainers scored significantly higher on a measure of psilocybin-occasioned mystical experience. There were no significant differences found between groups in general intensity of drug effect, suggesting that mystical-type subjective effects, rather than overall intensity of drug effect, were responsible for smoking cessation. Smoking cessation outcomes were significantly correlated with measures of mystical experience on drug session days. The authors proposed a mediating role for mystical experience in psychedelic-facilitated addiction treatment.

Psilocybin for the treatment of OCD:

Previous research:
The earliest indication of efficacy for a psychedelic in treatment of OCD was reported by Jackson (1962), in which a patient suffering from depression and violent obsessive sexual thoughts experienced dramatic and permanent improvement after only two doses of LSD. Brandrup and Vanggaard (1977) report on the outcome of LSD treatment of a 30-year-old man suffering from a completely disabling OCD. The treatment took place over 15 months, and surprisingly, without any other therapy provided. While under the influence of LSD, the patient was simply left alone except for brief visits by the doctor or the nurse. At 3 years, the patient was completely symptom free and remained so at 12-year follow-up, the point at which the therapists published the case report.

In addition to these reports of LSD treatment, anecdotal accounts of OCD symptom reduction by consumption of Psilocybe mushrooms have also been published (Leonard and Rapoport, 1987; Moreno and Delgado, 1997). Hanes (1996) reported on a 27-year-old male patient with body dysmorphic disorder who spent up to 4 hours every day checking his appearance in the mirror. The intensity of his somatic distress markedly improved on occasions when he had ingested psilocybin mushrooms, noting that at those times, when he looked in the mirror, he no longer appeared deformed.

These promising results provide support for more extensive controlled clinical trials of a psychedelic, either LSD or psilocybin, in OCD. The relative lack of efficacy for current therapies argues for more effort to be put into studies of the efficacy of psychedelics for this very-difficult- to-treat condition.

Moreno et al (2006). Safety, tolerability, and efficacy of psilocybin in 9 patients with obsessive-compulsive disorder.

Methods:
Moreno et al (2006) recruited nine participants (7 male) with OCD for a proof-of concept, modified double-blind study investigated the safety, tolerability, and clinical effects of psilocybin. Three were employed, one were a housewife and five were unable to work because of their illness. All had as a minimum previously received standard treatment with SSRI. They had a baseline Yale-Brown Obsessive Compulsive Scale (YBOCS) score ranging from 18 to 36 (mean 24.1).
None had abuse or other major psychiatric diagnosis or a family history of psychosis. They were screened and educated according to the principles outlines by Johnson et al (2008), and the practical aspects of the study were also carried out according to these principles.

Participants received up to four different doses in a modified escalating blinded protocol, but only one dose per session: Doses were 25 (VLD), 100 (LD), 200 (MD) and 300 (HD) / μgkg of body weight. LD, MD and HD were assigned in that order, and VLD were inserted randomly and in double-blind fashion at any time after the first (LD) dose. Testing days were separated by at least one week. All participants received LD, 7 also received VLD and MD and 6 received all doses. Data assessment were carried out before ingestion of psilocybin (baseline), and at 1, 4, 8 and 24 hours past baseline.

Results:
Adverse effects:
- No prolonged adverse effects were observed.
- Transient hypertension which didn't require medical intervention were observed.
- Two participant declined further participation due to psychological discomfort.

Effects:
- Marked decreases in OCD-symptoms were observed in all subjects at one or more sessions (23 100% reduction in YBOCS scores). Repeated measures analysis of variance for all YBOCS values revealed a significant main effect of time for LD and MD, but not VLD and HD. Changes in

obsessions and compulsions were comparable.
- Improvement generally lasted past the 24-hour timepoint, and some of the participants described improvement in the days following the session.

Discussion:
- When administered in a clinical setting to a screened group of OCD-patients, psilocybin were generally well-tolerated and safe.
- Administration of psilocybin were associated with a transient reduction in OCD-symptoms in treatment resistant patients, which often lasted for several days. This indicate that the effects of psilocybin lasted beyond the time that psilocybin were in the body of the participants.

Conclusion:
In a controlled clinical environment, psilocybin was safely used in subjects with OCD and was associated with acute reductions in core OCD symptoms in several subjects.

Psychedelics for the management of cluster headaches and other types of pain:

Possible biological mechanism:
According to Whelan et al (2018) do the contemporary perspectives on pain suggest, that pain is a perceptual experience inferred from bodily sate (i.e., embodied) and socioenvironmental context (i.e., embedded in the environment in which pain is experienced). An individual's experience of pain is influenced by a wide variety of sensory, affective, cognitive, social and bodily cues interpreted within current and evolutionary contexts (Tabor et al, 2017; Anchisi et al , 2015; Nicholas et al, 2017 and Di Lernia et al, 2016). Pain is defensive, promoting actions that attempt to reduce the impact of threat on the integrity of the body. Pain involves inferences associated with rationalising complex, uncertain environments and is defined by the boundaries of actions available to the person. The ability to detect physiological state through interoceptive awareness diminishes when pain becomes chronic (Duschek et al, 2017 and Di Lernia et al, 2016).

Psychedelic drugs produce acute psychedelic experiences by influencing activity in brain regions involved in processes that regulate emotion, cognition, memory and self-awareness. These brain regions are also associated with processes leading to perceptual experience of 'embodied' and 'embedded' pain (Dos Santos et al, 2016). Brain imaging studies have found that the thalamus, anterior cingulate cortex, posterior insula and medial and lateral frontal cortices become active in response to transient noxious stimuli (Jensen et al, 2016), although these regions also become active to non-noxious auditory, visual, mechanical and thermal stimuli (Mouraux et al, 2011). The right anterior insula cortex is as an integration hub for autonomic, immune, hormonal and cardiovascular systems creating a 'metacognitive map' of active processes such as pain, touch and temperature, and subjective and emotional feelings (Adolfi et al, 2017 and Craig et al, 2011). The left anterior insular region and the frontoparietal region contribute to a sense of 'body ownership' and the temporoparietal regions to a sense of peripersonal space (Grivaz et al, 2017). These regions are interconnected with the anterior cingulate cortex forming an emotional motivational appraisal system associated with pain (Craig et al, 2009). There is a shift of activity from the posterior to anterior insula with the development of persistent pain reflecting the transition from nociception to emotional responses associated with pain (Hashmi et al, 2013). Evidence also suggests that chronic pain impairs resting state activity in the brain by disrupting processing in the default mode network contributing to intrusive cognition and a breakdown of the normal self (Baliki et al, 2011; Baliki et al, 2008; Baliki et al, 2014). Mindfulness training alleviates chronic pain and improves quality of life by developing interoceptive attention to bodily sensations (Zeidan et al, 2016). Psychedelic agents act at regions modulated during mindfulness including the medial prefrontal cortex, posterior cingulate cortex and posterior insula of the default mode network (Allen et al, 2012; Brewer et al, 2014 and Farb et al, 2013). Evidence that 5-HT2A agonists inhibit activity in the default mode network and connector hubs, such as the thalamus and anterior cingulate cortex (Buckner et al, 2008), may provide opportunities to influence activity in brain regions implicated in chronic pain.

Previous research:
Since the dawn of psychedelic research, have psychedelics been explored as a mean to treat pain. One of the first documented human clinical trials assessing the analgesic effects of LSD was in 1964 when Kast et al (1964) administered a single-dose of dihydromorphine HCl (2 mg) and pethidine (meperidine HCl 100 mg in a randomized sequence with a 6-h interval to 50 patients with pain related to cancer or gangrene of hands or feet. Patients who were still experiencing pain 6 h after the administration of the second analgesic drug were administered a single dose of LSD (100 μg p.o.). Data presented in the report were difficult to interpret, although it appeared that 48.9% of the patients receiving LSD experienced no pain for at least 19-h post-dose. Kast et al (1964) concluded that LSD provided a longer and more effective analgesic action than pethidine and dihydromorphone. In 1967, Kast et al (1967) reported that LSD (100 μg p.o.) had analgesic actions in a series of 128 terminally ill patients, commencing at 2–3 h after

administration and lasting for 12 h. In 1969, Pahnke et al. (1969) reported the findings of a case series of 22 patients that had terminal metastatic cancer with depression and received LSD psychotherapy. Pahnke et al. claimed that LSD psychotherapy improved pain, mood, anxiety and fear of death, with no adverse effects for some but not all patients, although there was no quantitative nor qualitative data provided in the report. In 1973, Grof et al. (1973) administered LSD-assisted psychotherapy for 31 patients with pain, anxiety and depression associated with terminal metastatic malignancies and found significant improvements in pain severity, preoccupation with pain and physical suffering, anxiety, depression and fear of death.

Fanciullacci et al. (1977) reported that five out of seven patients with phantom limb pain who were administered sub-psychedelic doses of LSD (25 μg p.o. per day for 1 week followed by 50 μg p.o. per day for a further 2 weeks) reported improvement in pain and reductions in analgesic consumption.

Contemporary research:
Psychedelics has in the post-prohibition age been explored as a possible mean to treat cluster headages. At present, there is an absence of controlled clinical trial evidence to judge clinical efficacy, although internet surveys have found that patients report benefits from using LSD and psilocybin for treatment resistant cluster headaches. This evidence is discussed in the following paragraph:

Sewell et al (2006). Response of cluster headache to psilocybin and LSD.

Methods:
Sewell et al (2006) located through cluster headache support groups and an Internet-based survey several hundred people with cluster headache who reported use of psilocybin containing mushrooms or LSD, specifically to treat cluster headaches. They recruited 53 individuals who agreed to be contacted for evaluation by telephone or e-mail, met International Classification of Headache Disorders-2 criteria for cluster headache and allowed the authors to obtain copies of medical records documenting a diagnosis of cluster headache by an MD or DO.

Results:
- Of the 32 subjects with episodic cluster headache, 19 had used sublingual psilocybin during cluster attacks; 17 found psilocybin to be effective in aborting attacks (defined as ending the attack within 20 minutes). Only one subject had used sublingual LSD for an acute attack, reporting it to be effective.
- Twenty-nine subjects had used psilocybin prophylactically during a cluster period; 15 (52%) reported that it was effective (defined as causing total cessation of attacks), and a further 12 (41%) reported partial efficacy (defined as attacks decreasing in intensity or frequency but not ceasing).
- Five of six LSD users reported cluster period termination. Twenty subjects ingested psilocybin during a remission period; 19 reported an extension of their remission period, in that their next expected cluster period was delayed or prevented entirely. Four of five subjects reported similar remission extension with LSD.
- Of the 21 subjects with chronic cluster headache, 5 of 7 reported that psilocybin aborted a cluster attack; 10 of 20 reported that psilocybin induced a complete termination of cluster attacks; and a further 8 reported partial efficacy.
- Of two chronic cluster headache patients who ingested LSD, both at sub-psychedelic ("microdosing") doses, one reported no attacks for 10 days, and the other reported none for 2 months. Interestingly, 22 (42%) of the 53 subjects reported partial or complete efficacy (as defined above) from sub-psychedelic ("microdosing") doses of psilocybin or LSD.

Discussion:
- The authors found the results interesting for three reasons. First, no other medication, to their knowledge, has been reported to terminate a cluster period. Second, unlike other ergot-based medications, which must be taken daily, a single dose of LSD was described as sufficient to induce remission of a cluster period, and psilocybin rarely required more than three doses. Third, given the apparent efficacy of sub-psychedelic doses, these drugs might benefit cluster headache by a mechanism unrelated to their psychoactive effects.
- They identified several limitations of their study: First, it were subject to recall bias, because it relies primarily on participants' retrospective reports, even through 6 participants (11%) provided detailed headache diaries. Secondly, it could be subject to selection bias, since individuals with a good outcome may have been more likely to participate. Third, participants were not blind to their treatment, raising the possibility of a placebo response (Vlan Vlilet et al (2003).

Conclusions:
Sewell et al (2006) concluded, their "(...) observations must be regarded as preliminary, but given the high reported efficacy for this notoriously refractory condition, it is difficult to dismiss this series of cases as entirely artifactual. Further research is warranted."

Psilocybin for alleviation of anxiety and depression

Possible biological mechanisms in the treatment of depression:
As a prodrug of psilocybin (4-hydroxy-dimethyltryptamine), a serotonin receptor agonist and classic psychedelic drug whose principal psychoactive effects are mediated by serotonin 2A (5-HT2A) receptor agonism (Halberstadt et al, 2011), psilocybin has a novel pharmacology in the context of currently available antidepressant medications, because selective serotonin- reuptake inhibitors are not direct 5-HT2A receptor agonists.

Enhanced cognitive flexibility (Boulougouris et al, 2008), associative learning (Harvey et al, 2003), cortical neural plasticity (Vaidya et al, 1997), and antidepressant responses have been reported with 5-HT2A receptor agonism in animals (Buchborn et al, 2014), and increased and sustained improvements in wellbeing (Griffiths et al, 2008) and optimism (Carhart-Harris et al, 2016) have been observed after psychedelic experiences in human beings. Findings from human imaging studies with psilocybin have supplemented these discoveries, showing changes in brain activity suggestive of antidepressant potential; for example, a range of effective antidepressant treatments have been found to normalise hyperactivity in the medial prefrontal cortex and we found reduced blood flow in this region with intravenous psilocybin (Carhart-Harris et al, 2012). Moreover, data obtained from large-scale population studies have recently challenged the view that psychedelics negatively affect mental health (Hendricks et al, 2015; Krebs et al, 2013 and Bouso et al 2012), with one study's findings showing lower rates of psychological distress and suicidality among people who had used psychedelics within their lifetime than among those who used no psychedelics but an equivalent amount of other drugs (Hendricks et al, 2015).In modern trials, psychedelics have been found to reduce anxious (Gasser et al, 2014 and Grob et al, 2011), and depressive symptoms (Grob et al, 2011 and Osorio et al, 2015), often for several months after just one or two exposures.
Antidepressant medications and cognitive behavioural therapy can be effective for some patients, but around 20% do not respond to any intervention, and many of those who do respond, eventually relapse (Gaynes et al, 2009).

Possible psychological mechanism in the treatment of depression:
The American psychologist and LSD researcher, Betty Eisner, summarised the psychotherapeutic mechanism by which LSD, and by implication other psychedelics, may work as follows (Eisner and Cohen, 1958):

(1) LSD lessens defensiveness;
(2) there is a heightened capacity to relive early experiences with accompanying release of feelings;
(3) therapist–patient relationships are enhanced;
(4) there is an increased appearance of unconscious material.

If the aetiology of UMD in some patients can be understood, at least in part, as the present day emotional and behavioural sequelae of unresolved traumas and emotional conflicts from the past, with anxieties about the future, it is reasonable to hypothesise that psychedelic psychotherapy will catalyse the resolution of such conflicts in a proportion of patients where other treatment modalities have failed.

Previous Research:
Rucker et al (2016) made a systematic review, of the pre-prohibition literature on the therapeutic use of psychedelics on unipolar mood disorder, within which they include contemporary depressive disorder with co-morbid anxiety, as well as disorders grouped under the old-fashioned terms 'neurotic' and 'psychoneurotic' disorders. This, with the aim of evidencing the debate on whether these substances should be reinvestigated with the benefit of modern, more systematic trial methodology. They identified 21 papers which they included in their review, from the first report of therapeutic use of LSD in 1949 (Condrau, 1949) to Savage et al. (1973) which investigated LSD-assisted psychotherapy in the treatment of inpatients with 'severe chronic neuroses. LSD was, by far, the most commonly used psychedelic. Mescaline was occasionally used. Psilocybin weren't used, properly because psilocybin (and its active metabolite, psilocybin) were not isolated until 1959, and the drug marketed after this (Hofmann et al 1959). By this time, LSD research was well underway and it is likely that most clinicians would have wanted to stick to what was an established pharmaceutical entity, rather than risk the potential complications of trying a new one (Rucker et al, 2016). The sample size ranged from 5 to 77, with a total aggregated sample size of 423 across all the studies where this was clearly defined. The number of psychedelic sessions ranged from 1 to 58 and the therapeutic paradigms applied were

variable. The dose of LSD used ranged from 20 to 1500 µg. Mescaline was used at doses of 200–400 mg, in combination with LSD. Many studies used titrated dosing schedules that took account of individual patient responses to the drug. They concluded that (…) psychedelic therapy may represent a form of catalysed psychotherapy whereby the drug acts to hasten the breakdown of habitual maladaptive templates of thinking and behaviour in supportive therapeutic environments. The evidence from the pre-prohibition literature, whilst unsystematic and methodologically suboptimal, suggests that this is worth re-investigating (Rucker et al, 2016)."

Carhart-Harris et al (2016). Psilocybin with psychological support for treatment-resistant depression: an open-label feasibility study:

Method:
Carhart-Harris et al (2016) recruited 12 participants (six men) with moderate-to-severe, unipolar, treatment-resistant major depression of a moderate to severe degree (17+ on the 21-item Hamilton Depression Rating scale [HAM-D]), and no improvement despite two adequate courses of antidepressant treatment of different pharmacological classes lasting at least 6 weeks within the current depressive episode.
Nine of the 12 patients met criteria for severe or very severe depression at baseline
(BDI score ≥30), with the remaining three participants meeting criteria for moderate depression (BDI score 19 to <30). 11 participants had received some form of psychotherapy before participation in the study.

None had abuse or other major psychiatric diagnosis or a family history of psychosis. They were screened and educated according to the principles outlines by Johnson et al (2008), and the practical aspects of the study were also carried out according to these principles.

The enrolled participants were given an opportunity to meet with the two clinical psychiatrists who would support them through the remainder of the trial. The participants then attended a subsequent visit involving a baseline functional MRI (fMRI) scan [for the use of a separate study], followed by an extensive preparatory session with the psychiatrist. Here, they had the chance to talk openly about their personal history and any thoughts on the origins of their depression.

The participants then attended two subsequent dosing sessions that were separated by 7 days.
At the first session the participant received a low oral dose of psilocybin 10 mg and a high oral dose of psilocybin 25 mg on the second dosing day,

separated by 1 week. The low-dose session was conceived a priori as a safety session rather than a treatment session.
Blood pressure, heart rate, and observer ratings of the intensity of psilocybin's acute
psychoactive effects (0–4, with 0 signifying no effects and 4 signifying extreme effects) were measured at baseline and 30, 60, 120, 180, 240, 300, and 360 min after dosing. Subjective ratings of the acute altered state of consciousness using the revised 11D ASC were completed 6-7 hours after dosing.

After the session the patient were accompanied by a relative or close friend to their home, and had the option of staying overnight in accommodation adjacent to the hospital. Participants were contacted via telephone 1 day after their low-dose session to check on their wellbeing and monitor for any adverse events. One day after the high-dose session participants returned to the research facility for a post treatment fMRI scan. After the scan, participants completed interim questionnaires (QIDS, STAI-T, and HAM-D), and were seen by their psychiatrists in order to discuss their experience the previous day. Participants then attended one further study visit to the research
facility 1 week after their high-dose session, during which all baseline questionnaires and assessments were repeated.
Subsequent assessments of clinical progress were done via email 2, 3, and 5 weeks after the high-dose session. Final follow-up was done remotely at 3 months after the high-dose session, and
included QIDS, BDI, STAI-T, and SHAPS. Participants were lastly made aware that they could contact the study psychiatrists at any time if their depression deteriorated.

Results:
Adverse Effects:
- The acute effects of psilocybin were well tolerated by all of the patients, none required tranquillising medications, and no serious or unexpected adverse events occurred.
- The most common adverse events were transient anxiety (mostly mild) during drug onset (n=12), transient confusion or thought disorder (n=9), mild and transient nausea (n=4), and transient headache (n=4;).
- Subacute headache typically presented 1 day after the psilocybin session, and subsided after 1–2 days. Paranoia presented in only one patient, but this was mild and transient. No prolonged psychotic symptoms were observed in any of the patients. One patient contacted the study psychiatrists during the 3 months of follow-up due to deterioration of their depression, and was referred to their general practitioner.

Effects:
- Mean self-rated intensity of the psilocybin experience was 0·51 (SD 0·36) for the low-dose session and 0·75 (0·27) for the high-dose session (difference 0·24 [95% CI 0·06–0·41], Z –2·4, p=0·019).
- Results from interim patient questionnaires (QIDS, BDI, and STAI-T), done immediately before the low-dose session to monitor for substantial changes since enrolment, did not differ from baseline. Interim questionnaires done the day after the high-dose session showed some reduction in depressive symptoms.
- QIDS depression scores were significantly reduced from baseline to 1 week and 3 months post-treatment, with the maximum effect at 2 weeks. BDI and clinician-administered ratings confirmed these results. All patients showed some reduction in depression severity at 1 week that was sustained in the majority for 3 months. According to standard criteria for determining remission (eg, a score of ≤9 on the BDI), eight (67%) of the 12 patients achieved complete remission at 1 week and seven patients (58%) continued to meet criteria for response (50% reduction in BDI score relative to baseline) at 3 months, with five of these (42%) still in complete remission. STAI-T anxiety scores were also significantly reduced at 1 week and 3 months post-treatment, as were SHAPS anhedonia scores for 1 week and 3 months post-treatment.

Discussion:
- With the pilot-study the researchers sought to examine the feasibility of administering psilocybin to patients with treatment-resistant depression as a prelude to a larger randomised controlled trial. The results support the view that, done with appropriate safeguards such as careful screening and adequate therapeutic support), psilocybin can be safely administered to this patient group.
- The response rate to psilocybin was 67% (n=8) at 1 week after treatment (HAM-D and BDI), and seven of these eight patients also met criteria for remission. Moreover, 58% (n=7) of the patients maintained their response for 3 months, and 42% (n=5) remained in remission.
- These were great results in the light of the fact, that spontaneous recovery in refractory depression is rare, and many of the patients in the present study reported having depression for much of their adult lives (mean estimated illness duration 17·8 years [SD 8]).
- Because of the small sample-side and the open label design, strong inferences could be made about the treatment's therapeutic efficacy. But the data is promising and do suggest that further research is warranted.
- The researchers stated that key questions for future research should

address why the therapeutic effect observed in the present study is so large, and if it can be replicated when tighter experimental controls are introduced, such as a placebo-controlled double-blinded design. And since the treatment in the study consisted of not just psilocybin but also psychological support before, during, and after these sessions, as well as a positive therapeutic environment for the sessions, the relative effects of these factors need to be determined in further trials. For example in a placebo controlled randomised trial in which the level of therapist contact is consistent between conditions. This would enable any between-group differences in clinical outcomes to be attributed to psilocybin rather than the psychological support provided.

Conclusion:
This study provides preliminary support for the safety and efficacy of psilocybin for treatment-resistant depression and motivates further trials, with more rigorous designs, to better examine the therapeutic potential of this approach.

Carhart-Harris et al (2018). Psilocybin with psychological support for treatment-resistant depression: six-month follow-up:

Methods:
Carhart-Harris et al (2018) reported on the follow-up completed on the participants from Carhart-Harris et al (2016). The original 12 participants were following the beginning of the first study supplemented by an additional 6 subjects, in order to increase the sample-size. Thus, 20 participants with psilocybin (10 and 25 mg), 7 days apart. The primary outcome was mean change in the severity of self-reported (SR) depressive symptoms (measured primarily with the Quick Inventory of Depressive Symptoms, QIDS-SR16) from baseline to 1–3 and 5 weeks and 3 and 6 months post-treatment, with 5 weeks post-treatment regarded as the primary endpoint. In addition, BDI (depression) and STAI (anxiety) ratings were collected at 1 week and 3 and 6 months. SHAPS (anhedonia) was collected at 1 week and 3 months and HAM-D (depression, clinician-administered) and GAF (global functioning, clinician administered) ratings were collected at 1 week only. These secondary measures were collected to enable comparisons to be made with other studies that use the same measures.

Twenty participants were recruited for the trial and 19 completed all measures. Data on 12 of the 20 have been previously reported in Carhart-Harris et al. (2016), and these 12 were included in the analysis conducted for this paper. Eighteen of the 20 patients met the criteria for severe or very severe depression at baseline (QIDS-SR16 score of ≥ 16); the remaining two meeting the criteria for moderate depression (QIDSSR16 score ≥ 11, < 16). The median number of (lifetime) failed previous medications was 4, the mean was 4.6 ± 2.6 and the maximum was 11. The mean duration of illness of the sample was 17.7 ± 8.4 years (range = 7–30 years).

Results:
Adverse Effects:
- Treatment was generally well tolerated and there were no serious adverse events.
- One patient became uncommunicative during the peak of his 25-mg psilocybin experience but this normalised after the acute drug effects had abated. Follow-up discussions revealed that his experience had been blissful and beneficial but also overwhelming. This patient chose not to complete further follow-up measures, with the exception of the QIDS-SR16 and BDI scores at 6 months post-treatment.
- Consistent with Carhart-Harris et al. 2016, transient anxiety lasting for minutes (n = 15) and headaches lasting no more than 1–2 days (n = 8) were the most common AE. Five reported transient nausea but there were no cases of vomiting.
- Three reported transient paranoia within the duration of the acute drug experience but this was short-lived in every case.
- There were no reported cases of flashbacks or persisting perceptual changes.
- Fourteen patients reported visions of an autobiographical nature. In most cases, such visions were regarded as insightful and informative. But one patient reported a vision of his father attempting to physically harm him when he was child, something he claimed not to have been previously conscious of. This participant subsequently felt confused about the authenticity of this putative memory and this was associated with a transient worsening of symptoms. Appealing to clinical equipoise, the study team felt it best practice not to make a judgement on the veridicality of this alleged memory but open and compassionate listening was maintained and the patient subsequently improved.

Effects:
- Relative to baseline, QIDS-SR16 scores were significantly reduced at all six post-treatment time points, with the maximum effect size at 5 weeks ($- 9.2$, 95% CI = $- 11.8$ to $- 6.6$, $t = - 7.2$, $p < 0.001$, Cohen's $d = 2.3$). Of the 19 patients who completed all assessments, all showed some reduction in depression severity at 1 week and these were sustained in the majority for 3–5 weeks.
- Changes in HAM-D ratings from baseline to 1-week post treatment

showed a reasonable correspondence with changes in QIDS-SR16 data across the same period (r = 0.61, p < 0.001) and the relationship between the QIDS-SR16 and BDI at 1 week was very strong (r = 0.81, p < 0.001).

- BDI scores, STAI-T anxiety and SHAPS anhedonia scores were significantly reduced at 1 week, 3 months and 6 months post-treatment.
- HAM-D scores were significantly reduced at 1 week post-treatment; and GAF scores were significantly increased 1 week post treatment.
- Suicidality scores on the QIDS-SR16 were significantly reduced 1 and 2 weeks post-treatment, with trend decreases at 3 and 5 weeks. Scores on the suicide item of the HAM-D were significantly decreased 1-week post-treatment, with 16 of 19 patients scoring 0 at this time point and none showing an increase from baseline nor scoring the maximum on this measure. Scores on the genital/sexual dysfunction item of the HAM-D were also significantly reduced 1-week post-treatment and no one scored the maximum nor showed an increase in sexual dysfunction from baseline.
- Previous work on the use of psilocybin has indicated a strong relationship between the following 11D-ASC factors: experience of unity, spiritual experience and blissful state, and positive effects. A multiple correlation analysis confirmed their interrelatedness here (r > 0.92 for all permutations). Therefore, the team decided to treat them as one factor (assigned the acronym 'USB'), taking mean values for each patient.
- Testing the hypothesis that this USB factor and insight would predict better clinical outcomes, they found significant relationships between mean scores of USB and insight during the 25-mg psilocybin experience and changes in QIDS-SR16 scores at 5 weeks (r = − 0.49, p = 0.03 and r = − 0.57, p = 0.01, respectively). This is further discussed in Roseman et al (2018).
- After the 6-month endpoint, information was collected on other treatments received by the patients (Watts et al. 2017). With the exception of one participant (who remained on venlafaxine throughout the trial and also received CBT shortly afterwards), no patients received additional treatments within 5 weeks of the 25-mg psilocybin dose. Six began new courses of antidepressant medication after the 3-month time point. Five received psychotherapy (CBT, psychodynamic, counselling and group therapy × 2) shortly before or after the 3-month period and five sought and successfully obtained psilocybin (without sanction from the study team) between 3 and 6 months. Removing the five that obtained psilocybin from the 3- and 6-month analyses did not substantially alter the main results: at 3 months, the effect size increased to 1.6 and the p value remained < 0.001; and at 6 months, the effect size

increased to 1.7 and the p value became 0.018.
- Assessing relapse at 6 months in responders (at 5 weeks) revealed only three of nine cases—with the remaining six maintaining response—even when using conservative criteria for relapse of QIDS score of 6+ or above at 6 months. These data tentatively imply that psilocybin may protect against relapse.

Discussion:
- The findings corroborated Carhart-Harris et al. (2016) and others' previous results (Griffiths et al. 2016; Ross et al. 2016; Grob et al. 2011), supporting the safety and efficacy of psilocybin for depressive and anxiety symptoms. A fast and sustained response exceeding what might be expected from a placebo response was observed in many of the patients. All 19 completers showed some reductions in the QIDS-SR16 scores at 1-week post-treatment and maximal effects were seen at 5 weeks.
- As in Carhart-Harris et al. 2016, conclusions on efficacy are limited by the absence of a control condition in the trial and the small sample size. A comprehensive RCT designed to properly assess psilocybin's efficacy for major depressive disorder, with some form of placebo control, is therefore warranted. Relatedly, psychotherapeutic models used to support and mediate the psilocybin experience need to be better defined, tested and potentially manualised.
- An obvious limitation of the present study is its open-label design and absence of a control condition. The researchers wrote that their initial plan was to conduct a placebo-controlled RCT but regulatory and drug procurement challenges meant that their available resources could only support a smaller trial.
- Thus, the present results may be viewed as a successful demonstration of proof-of-principle, however, supporting the view that psilocybin can be given safely, even in severe cases of depression, with the caveat that appropriate control of context.

Psychedelics for autism spectrum disorders:

Previous research:
Between 1959 and 1974, a number of studies were reported on the use of LSD to treat children with autism. Sigafoos et al. (2007) reviewed these reports. Unfortunately, the vast majority of those studies had serious methodological flaws. Typically, after the drug was administered, the children were simply observed and their reactions were recorded in a narrative format. Thus, the resulting data were for the most part qualitative and were presented in a form that was highly subjective, potentially biased

by observer expectations, and of unknown reliability and validity. Furthermore, when enthusiastic investigators obtained neutral or negative findings, they often were cast in a more positive light than was warranted.

Thus, despite a good number of independent studies, it remains impossible to determine whether LSD had any therapeutic value for children with autism. When judged by today's standards of RCT, or a properly controlled and systematically replicated single-case study, most of the early autism/LSD studies were so flawed as to be little better than anecdotal.

Current research:
No post-prohibition papers on the use of psychedelics for treatment of autism spectrum disorders have been published.

Psychedelics for the alleviation of anxiety and depression in life-threatening illness:

Possible psychological mechanisms in the treatment of Anxiety and Depression in Life-Threatening Illness:
According to Gasser et al (2015) does it appears that psychedelic-assisted psychotherapy involves a combination of mechanisms operating in conventional psychotherapy, such as a facilitated access to emotions, relieving of traumatic memories, abreaction and catharsis, facilitation of emotional and intellectual insights (Grof, 1980; Leuner, 1981). The most significant effects of LSD in psychotherapeutic contexts can be described as follows:

1.The cognitive experience, with astonishingly lucid thoughts and altered associations, with problems seen from novel perspectives, and relationships of many levels seen at once;
2. The psychodynamic experience, characterised by an emergence of material into consciousness that was previously excluded. A symbolic portrayal of important conflicts as well as abreaction and catharsis are elements of a (sometimes hypermnestic) reliving of incidents from the past;
3. The psychedelic peak experience, with (i) loss of usual sense of self with positive ego transcendence, (ii) transcendence of time and space, (iii) sense of awe and reverence, and (iv) meaningful new insights

All of these dimensions of the LSD experience may contribute to treatment effects, especially within the psychedelic approach. Studies in the past have demonstrated more treatment effects for individuals who had psychedelic peak experiences, but those without them have also found significantly bettered (Pahnke et al., 1970; Richards et al., 1977). Several authors in addition focus on the fact that psychedelics can facilitate 'peak experiences' or 'mystical experiences'. Even just one of these experiences was proven to have an inherent potential to change the psychological make-up of the person (Griffiths et al., 2006; McGlothlin et al., 1967; Savage et al., 1966).

Possible biological mechanisms in the treatment of anxiety and depression in life-threatening illness:
Gasser et al (2015) proposed the following biological model of action in their paper:
Neuroimaging studies suggest that the LSD-like psychedelic psilocybin makes a greater repertoire of functional connectivity in the brain's networks available than in normal waking consciousness. Brain regions implicated as the base for the normal state of consciousness are represented in the default-mode network (DMN), which also hosts important 'connector hubs' (Hagmann et al., 2008) that allow communication and integration between different brain regions (Bullmore et al., 2009). The highly organised activity within the DMN is a requirement for mood regulation and high-level constructs, such as the self (Gusnard et al., 2001) or 'ego' (Carhart-Harris and Friston, 2010) as well as the ability for self-reference (Raichle, 1998).
Psilocybin-induced reduction of blood flow in DMN regions alters the integrity of the DNM and thereby leads to 'unconstrained cognition' and changes in the experience of the self (Carhart-Harris et al., 2012a). Changes in functional connectivity may contribute to changes in perspective and re-evaluations of situations and persons (Carhart-Harris et al., 2014; Vollenweider and Geyer, 2001), sometimes supported by intensified memory (Carhart-Harris et al., 2012b). However, some of these reductions in brain activity are not congruent with earlier findings (e.g. Vollenweider et al., 1997).

The long-term results of the findings of Gasser et al (2014) and (2015) as well as the impact of peak experiences in changing psychological traits, behaviour and basic emotional tone (Griffiths et al., 2006, 2011; MacLean et al., 2011) suggest sustained neurobiological alterations.
Hypothetically, psychedelics in psychotherapy may improve the patients by 'breaking up' a more fixated and less dynamic neurobiological matrix of functioning, accompanied by emotional bias, altered responsiveness and reduced flexibility in the emotional and cognitive sphere (Carhart-Harris et al., 2014; Vollenweider and Geyer, 2001). Patients may regain mental flexibility as a result of treatment with LSD, which has been found to be reduced in depressive and anxiety disorders (Stuhrmann et al., 2011). Through intensification of affectivity and weakening of ego boundaries, LSD may also function as an 'opener' to another emotional basic

experience, enabling subjects to have 'deeper' insights and perspective-altering outlooks.

Previous research: LSD has since the 1960's been used to alleviate anxiety and depression in acutely ill patients. The research began with the observations by Kast and Collins (1964), who found found that LSD had an analgesic effect at least comparable to opiates, but that the LSD analgesia outlasted its acute psychologic effects. Subsequent study revealed that patients treated with LSD had improved psychologic adjustment, were more responsive to their families and environments, and had enhanced ability to enjoy everyday life (Kast, 1966, 1970). Beginning in 1963, a group at the Spring Grove State Hospital in Maryland developed an extensive research program to study the value of psychedelic-assisted psychotherapy of patients with alcoholism or neuroses, patients who were addicted to narcotics, and patients who were dying of cancer (Pahnke et al., 1970a). With respect to treatment of dying cancer patients, this group found that about two-thirds of cancer patients who received LSD treatment had improved mood and reduced anxiety and fear of death (Pahnke et al., 1969, 1970b; Grof et al., 1973).

Contemporary research:
Psychedelics for the treatment of Anxiety and Depression in Life-Threatening Illness, is one of the most researched applications of psychedelics in the post-prohibition era. The following paragraph explore the contemporary research in-depth:

Grob et al (2011). Pilot study of psilocybin treatment for anxiety in patients with advanced-stage cancer.

Grob et al (2011) recruited twelve (11 women) subjects with advanced-stage cancer and a DSM-IV diagnosis of acute stress disorder, generalised anxiety disorder, anxiety disorder due to cancer, or adjustment disorder with anxiety, to a within-subject, double-blind, placebo controlled study to examine the safety and efficacy of psilocybin in the treatment of psychological distress associated with the existential crisis of terminal disease.

Primary cancers included breast cancer in 4 subjects, colon cancer in 3, ovarian cancer in 2, peritoneal cancer in 1, salivary gland cancer in 1, and multiple myeloma in 1. All subjects were in advanced stages of their illness. The duration of their primary cancers ranged from 2 months to 18 years. Eight subjects completed the 6-month follow-up assessment, 11 completed at least the first 4 months of assessment, and all 12 completed at least the first 3 months of follow-up. Two subjects died of their cancer during the follow-up period, and 2 others became too ill to continue participating.

Exclusion criteria included central nervous system involvement of the cancer, severe cardiovascular illness, untreated hypertension, abnormal hepatic or renal function, diabetes, lifetime history of schizophrenia, bipolar disease, other psychotic illness, and anxiety or affective disorders within 1 year prior to the onset of cancer. Medication contraindications included active cancer chemotherapy, anti-seizure medications, insulin and oral hypoglycemics, and psychotropic medications in the previous 2 weeks. Participants also were asked to refrain from taking any medications the day of and the day after the experimental treatment sessions, except for prescription or over-the-counter nonnarcotic pain medications at any time and narcotic pain medications up to 8 hours before and 6 hours after administration of psilocybin.
Screening and education of patients, and practical aspects of the study were carried out according to the principles described in the beginning of this chapter (Johnson et al, 2008).

Each participant acted as his or her own control and was provided 2 experimental treatment sessions spaced several weeks apart. They were informed that they would receive active psilocybin (0.2 mg/kg) on one occasion and the placebo, niacin (250 mg), on the other occasion. The order in which subjects received the 2 different treatments was randomised and known only by the research pharmacist. Treatment team personnel remained at the bedside with the subject for the entire 6-hour session.

Psilocybin or placebo was administered at 10:00 hours. Various self-report inventories and questionnaires were administered from 2 weeks prior to the first treatment session to up to 6 months after the second.
A number of psychological measures were administered the day before each of the experimental sessions, at the conclusion of the experimental sessions, the day after the session, at at 2 weeks after each session and at monthly intervals for 6 months after the final session.

Results:
Adverse Effects:
- All participants tolerated the treatment sessions well, with no indication of severe anxiety or a "bad trip."
- The administration of psilocybin induced a mild but statistically significant elevation of HR and BP. The elevation were self-limiting and didn't require medical intervention.

Effects:
- The 5D-ASC (which measures alterations in mood, perception, experience of self in relation to environment, and thought disorder) demonstrated marked subjective differences between the psilocybin and placebo experiences.
- Psilocybin particularly affected the oceanic boundlessness and visionary restructuralisation dimensions. Psilocybin had smaller but significant effects on anxious ego dissolution and auditory alterations. Psilocybin also produced increased positive derealisation, positive depersonalization, altered sense of time, positive mood, manialike experiences, elementary hallucinations, visual pseudohallucinations, synesthesia, changed meaning of percepts, facilitated recollection, and facilitated imagination, compared to placebo.
- Subscales with no appreciable differences between the 2 treatments included anxious derealisation, thought disorder, delusion, fear of loss of thought control, and fear of loss of body control.
- For the Beck Depression Inventory (BDI), which measures depressive symptoms, there was an overall interaction of psilocybin, but it did not attain statistical significance. There was no appreciable change from 1 day prior to placebo administration to 2 weeks after experimental treatment, whereas a trend was observed after psilocybin administration, from a mean (SEM) score of 16.1 (3.6) one day before treatment to 10.0 (2.7) two weeks after treatment. BDI scores dropped by almost 30% from the first session to 1 month after the second treatment session, a difference that was sustained and became significant at the 6-month follow-up point.
- The Profile of Mood States (POMS) which describes the subjects mood during the past week, similarly revealed a trend for reduced adverse mood tone from 1 day before treatment with psilocybin to 2 weeks later, a difference that was not seen after placebo. Improvement of mood, indicated by reduced POMS scores, was observed in 11 subjects after administration of psilocybin. The elevation of POMS scores 1 day before psilocybin treatment occurred regardless of whether the subjects were treated with placebo or psilocybin first (ie, there was no interaction between treatment order and drug). POMS scores were not altered during the 6 months of follow-up compared with the day before the first treatment session.
- The State-Trait Anxiety Inventory (STAI), a measurement of anxiety, revealed no significant changes from 1 day before to 2 weeks after treatment, although a substantial but nonsignificant decrease was evident for the state anxiety subscale 6 hours after psilocybin administration,

which was not observed after placebo. Although minimal change was observed in the STAI state anxiety score for follow-up data, a sustained decrease in STAI trait anxiety was observed for the entire 6-month follow-up, reaching significance at the 1-month and 3-month points after the second treatment session.
- The Brief Psychiatric Rating Scale (which provides clinician assessment of the level of symptoms such as hostility, suspiciousness, hallucination, and grandiosity) at the end of the experimental session revealed no appreciable difference between psilocybin and placebo administration.
- Common themes reported by subjects included examining how their illness had impacted their lives, relationships with family and close friends, and sense of ontological security. In addition, subjects reported powerful empathic cathexis to close friends and family members and examined how they wished to address their limited life expectancy. In monthly follow-up discussions, subjects reflected on insights and new perspectives gained during their psilocybin treatment.

Discussion:
- According to Grob et al (2011), were the initial goals to establish feasibility and safety for psychedelic treatment in patients with advanced-stage cancer and anxiety. Following discussion with authorities, they choose a modest 0.2-mg/kg psilocybin dose, not comparable to higher doses of psychedelics administered in previous research on the subject. This in order to determine safe parameters with this novel treatment paradigm, and establishing a strong foundation for future investigations.
- When psychedelics were administered to patients with terminal cancer in the 1960s and early 1970s, the occurrence of a profound psychospiritual experience was correlated with therapeutic outcome (Pahnke et al, 1969 and Grof et al, 1973). Such transcendent states of consciousness are usually associated with higher doses of psychedelics, so Grob et al's (2011) expectation of demonstrating efficacy was limited (Griffiths et al, 2006). But even the lower dose of psilocybin used in the current study gave some indication of therapeutic benefit in quantitative psychological evaluations.
- In particular, the STAI trait anxiety subscale demonstrated a sustained reduction in anxiety, which might reflect a reduced level of stress and anxiety over time. Mood also improved for 2 weeks after treatment with psilocybin, with sustained improvement on the BDI reaching significance at the 6-month follow-up point. The POMS scores also reflected improved mood 2 weeks after receiving psilocybin. Although not statistically significant, there was a trend toward positive outcome.
- Grob et al (2011) noted that with a larger cohort of subjects and use of a higher dose of psilocybin, it seems possible that significant results

could be obtained on these measures.
- POMS scores declined after administration of psilocybin in 11 of 12 subjects, suggesting that psilocybin produces mood-elevating effects that persist after the acute effects of the drug.
- Most of the subjects knew if they were treated with psilocybin or placebo, which certainly affect blinding. Future studies also will need to address the issue of controlling for a placebo effect that might otherwise be attributed to the active treatment.

Conclusion:
Despite the limitations, Grob et al (2011) concluded the study demonstrates that the careful and controlled use of psilocybin may provide an alternative model for the treatment of the profound existential anxiety and despair that often accompany advanced-stage cancers, and that the results provided by the study indicate the safety and promise of continued investigations into the range of medical effects of psychedelic compounds such as psilocybin.

Gasser et al (2014). Safety and efficacy of lysergic acid diethylamide-assisted psychotherapy for anxiety associated with life-threatening diseases.

Methods:
Gasser et al (2014) recruited 12 participants with anxiety associated with life-threatening diseases, for a RCT exploring LSD and drug-free psychotherapy sessions.
The screening and education of the participants, as well as the practical aspects of the study, was carried out according to the principles described in the beginning of this chapter (Johnson et al, 2008).

The primary intervention consisted of two full-day experimental sessions scheduled 2 to 3 weeks apart with a male/female co-therapist team, embedded within an ongoing process of drug-free psychotherapy sessions for preparatory and integrative purposes. The participants were randomly assigned to the experimental dose groups, receiving either an oral dose of 200 μg of LSD (n = 8) or an active placebo of 20 μg of LSD (n = 4). The experimental dose was a moderate amount expected to produce the full spectrum of a typical LSD experience, without fully dissolving normal ego structures. The 20-μg dose of LSD was chosen as an active placebo to produce short-lived, mild, and detectable LSD effects that would not substantially facilitate a therapeutic process, but could help blind the participants and therapists.

After each experimental session, three drug-free psychotherapy sessions

lasting 60 to 90 minutes took place, during which the participant's experiences were reviewed for integration and deepening the therapeutic process. Two months after the second experimental session, a follow-up evaluation was completed, and the treatment period was finished by breaking the blind for each individual.
The participants who received the active placebo could cross over to an identical but open-label treatment with 200 μg of LSD. A long-term follow-up evaluation was conducted 12 months after the last experimental session with LSD in either the blinded portion of the study or the open-label crossover.

Outcome measures were completed at baseline, 1 week after experimental sessions, 2-month follow-up, and 12-month follow-up. The participants completed a daily dairy on changes in medication, adverse effects of LSD or medications, and pain using the Visual Analog Pain Scale. After each experimental session, the State of Consciousness Questionnaire was completed.

Results:
Adverse effects:
- The administration of LSD induced a mild and statistically insignificant elevation of HR and BP. The elevation were self-limiting and didn't require medical intervention.
- In addition to this, LSD only produced mild and self-limiting psychological adverse effects.

Effects:
- For STAI trait anxiety, no significant difference was found between group mean scores at baseline. Comparing trait anxiety at baseline with 2-month follow-up yielded an effect size of 1.1. However, only three of eight experimental dose subjects dropped lower than the threshold value of 40 after the intervention. In contrast, all active placebo subjects experienced increases in trait anxiety. Comparison of 2-month and 12-month follow-up results in the subjects who received 200 μg of LSD in either the blinded sessions or the open-label crossover indicate that the benefits were sustained over time.
- For STAI state anxiety, no significant difference was found between the groups at baseline. Comparing state anxiety at baseline with 2-month follow-up yielded an effect size of 1.2. However, only three of eight experimental dose subjects dropped lower than the diagnostic cutoff of 40 after the intervention. In contrast, two active placebo subjects experienced increases in state anxiety. Comparison of 2-month and 12-month follow-up results in the subjects who received 200 μg of LSD in

either the blinded sessions or the open-label crossover indicates that the benefits were sustained over time.
- Changes in secondary outcome measures were, overall, quite supportive of the STAI results. Global health scores from the EORTC-QLQ increased from a mean (SD) of 37.4 (10.0) at baseline to 50.0 (14.9) after treatment with two sessions of 200 μg of LSD, whereas mean scores decreased from 44.3 (12.7) to 36.0 (12.8) in the active placebo group. Scores increased on average in the subjects who received 200 μg of LSD treatments and continued to 12-month follow-up, indicating that most of the subjects receiving the experimental dose were able to attain and maintain comparable quality of life with the general European population by participating in this study (Scott et al., 2008).
- The SCL-90-R is a widely used measure of overall psychological problems and psychopathology. Global Severity Index (GSI) scores from the SCL-90-R decreased from a mean (SD) T-score of 69.6 (6.7) at baseline to 60.2 (7.2) in the experimental dose group whereas increasing from 66.0 (15.1) to 67.7 (10.2) in the active placebo group. The active placebo group experienced an improvement comparable with the full-dose group after receiving the experimental dose in the open-label crossover, with mean (SD) T-scores dropping to 57.3 (15.0). Both Positive Symptom Distress Index (PSDI) and Positive Symptom Total (PST) scores from the SCL-90-R mirrored these improvements, indicating that overall psychopathology improved in this subject sample 2 months after treatment.
- The Hospital Anxiety and Depression Scale (HADS) results were also generally supportive of overall improvements in this subject sample. The experimental dose group mean (SD) anxiety scores decreased from 11.7 (3.4) to 8.1 (3.2) after two sessions, whereas the active placebo group anxiety scores decreased only from 11.3 (2.1) to 10.7 (3.0). The active placebo subjects who continued to the crossover experienced an even greater decline lower than the diagnostic cutoff for anxiety to 7.0 (2.6). All subjects who received the experimental dose were lower than the diagnostic cutoff at the 12-month follow-up, with a mean (SD) of 7.6 (4.5). The depression results also mirrored the anxiety results.
- Overall, the secondary outcome measures of the study were useful in supporting the results of the primary outcome measure.

Discussion:
- The study by Gasser et al (2014) were the first in more than 40 years to evaluate safety and efficacy of LSD as an adjunct to psychotherapy, in participants with anxiety after being diagnosed with a life-threatening illness. It utilises modern research methods, and no adverse effects of significance were observed.

- The primary outcome variable in this study was of the STAI anxiety measure. Patients with life-threatening illnesses confront an existential threat from shortened life expectancy that often causes periods of suffering, pain, and anxiety. Congruent with earlier studies (Pahnke et al., 1970), the results in the experimental dose group show a significant reduction in state anxiety, as experienced on a daily basis.
- Furthermore, the more stable personality-inherent feature of anxiety proneness (trait anxiety) showed a strong trend toward reduction. Trait anxiety is not expected to be altered by short-term psychotherapy (Spielberger et al., 1970), but a comparable finding was reported by Grob et al. (2011).
- Therefore, this trait change may be supported by neurobiological effects of adjunctive use of LSD, which was originally introduced for deepening and accelerating psychotherapeutic processing (Abramson, 1967) and, in some studies, was shown to alter personality traits (MacLean et al., 2011; McGlothlin et al., 1967; Savage et al., 1966).
- In this study, the experimental dose reduced anxiety when administered in either the blinded treatment or the open-label crossover for the active placebo subjects. These results were stable over time as shown by the 12-month follow-up.
- A moderate dose (200 μg) provided a psychologically manageable first LSD experience. Most of the participants stated a preference for more than two LSD sessions and a longer treatment period. The results demonstrated a decrease in STAI scores most prominently after the second LSD session, suggesting that at least two LSD sessions are needed to demonstrate these effects.
- The study had limited sample size, which reduced precision in effect size estimates and significance testing. Moat participants also correctly guessed whether they were treated with LSD or active placebo. The imperfect blinding also limits the validity of the results. Using a slightly higher LSD dose in the comparator group can increase blinding, it can also increase efficacy of the comparator, compromising the estimates of effect size.
- Given the safety of the moderate experimental dose, results might have been improved with a larger dose of 250 μg.

Conclusion:

This pilot study in participants with anxiety associated with the diagnosis of a life-threatening illness has demonstrated safety in 22 psychotherapy sessions assisted by 200 μg of LSD with no drug-related severe adverse events. Group comparison results support positive trends in reduction of anxiety after two sessions of LSD-assisted psychotherapy, with effect size estimates in the range of 1.1 to 1.2. In view of promising historical studies with adjunctive LSD treatment in this population and a recent promising study using psilocybin, as well as the urgent need for more effective treatments of anxiety in these participants, further study is warranted into the potential of LSD-assisted psychotherapy.

Gasser et al (2014). LSD-assisted psychotherapy for anxiety associated with a life-threatening disease: A qualitative study of acute and sustained subjective effects.

Methods:
The participants from Gasser et al (2014) were as described earlier randomly assigned to a full-dose group (N=8) with two guided LSD sessions (LSD 200 µg) or to an active placebo group (N=4) with two guided active placebo sessions (LSD 20 µg). A dose of 200 µg was chosen so as not to overwhelm the patients, but being high enough to allow psychedelic peak experiences.
When un-blinding the assignments at the 2 month follow-up therapy session, those who learned that they had been in the placebo group could choose to crossover to two guided sessions with 200 µg of LSD. Participant #2 chose not to crossover (= no full dose) and did not qualify for LTFU. Participant #4 died 6 months after end of the initial study. The remaining 10 participants qualified for LTFU. Participant #3 did not send back the STAI questionnaire and was excluded from the quantitative analysis. Participant #9 did not allow audio recording of the LTFU interview thus was not included in the qualitative analysis.

The remaining participants were included in the follow-up programme (Gasser et al, 2015). To explore subjective experiences and elements of the therapeutic process of the participants in more detail, qualitative semi-structured interviews were conducted to gain a more holistic understanding from a client-centred perspective (Maxwell, 2009; Weiss, 1995).
Interviews focused on subjective experiences, changes in daily life, quality of life, anxiety, attitudes and values as related to the LSD-assisted psychotherapy.
In total, nine participants who received two doses of LSD (200 µg) were evaluated.

Results:
- LTFU results demonstrated that STAI state anxiety and STAI trait anxiety scores did not rise after end of the study. For STAI state, a significant main effect of time and significant reductions between baseline and end of study and follow-up. For STAI trait scores, the main effect of time was too significant at the end of study and of follow-up.

- The interviews conducted with the nine participating subjects found that all of them reported benefits from the LSD-assisted psychotherapy. Data from the interviews confirmed the data obtained with the STAI. Of the nine participants, 77.8% reported sustained reductions in anxiety. Seven participants (77.9%) reported less fear of death and an improved quality of life (66.7%). Most reported (subjectively perceived) positive personality changes such as increased openness and deepened awareness. Generally, the research participants stated that they felt more relaxed and patient with themselves and others. These findings were congruent with the stable improvement in STAI scores between the end of the study and the LTFU. These results were even more impressive in light of the awareness that all participants were experiencing an ongoing severe somatic disease.
- Three participants died a few months after the LTFU. None of the participants reported lasting negative effects from the LSD sessions. Beyond the temporary difficulty reported by some in dealing with the initial effects of LSD (e.g. intense emotions, alteration in self-control), no adverse events were mentioned.

The following quotes were chosen to illustrate the core elements of the subjective experiences and some of the sustained changes reported:

"It encouraged me to let the feelings flow … to free myself from my fears. To look at my grief. It was necessary. It was relieving. Afterward I was able to laugh about it. It is a fluctuating world of emotions you have to pass during these eight hours (…) Except the feeling of grief and fear … there were other sequences and nuances. … A lot is happening there (#1)."

"The LSD session sets things free in my mind, which under normal conditions may not have appeared, because they might have been suppressed. I mean I did sense certain freeing moments for myself. That I could let go of the weight of the fear … Well I was surprised to find real stirring of emotions, which I usually would not have felt with all my self-control and restraint (#5)."

"I was very very sad, I cried, never desperate, but a lot of sad things came up. And that resolved later on and became lightness. But at the beginning, at first I did not go 'in' for long, but then I dove away. … I was very sad. … What was very, very important to me was that I got access to my emotions, I went relatively deep inside. I went through heaviness and sadness. But I felt all emotions very intensely (#7)."

It is known from the extensive experience with LSD-assisted psychotherapy during the 1960s that (if dosing and setting are appropriate) only those emotions/thoughts/memories come up into consciousness which can be coped with by the psychological capacities of the individual patient (Grof, 1980; Leuner 1981). The quotes appear to confirm this observation. Virtually all patients valued the intensified emotional experiences as positive, in spite of sometimes coping with difficult emotional experiences. None of the patients interviewed reported any serious psychological problems resulting from their LSD treatments.

LSD is known for its capacity to alter the usual frame of reference, especially in respect to cognitive concepts and habits and by altering contextualizations and validations of persons and events (Grof, 1975). One important aspect of this 'de-schematizing' is a change in perspective, i.e. the frame in which an individual perceives him/herself and others. An appropriate metaphor for these changes in perspective could be a set of photographic lenses, that can focus, either bringing things nearer than usual or enabling the observation of them from a much more distant perspective, i.e. a mountain-top.
Also, there appears to be the experience of a wide-angle lens giving a much broader picture, providing the opportunity to see many different aspects and/or dimensions of situations, persons, etc., at once (Leuner, 1981). The following examples convey an idea about such changes in concepts and perspectives:

"I had the opportunity to relax. I rather connected to my inner world. Closed eyes. It was less about my illness. I was able to put it into perspective. (…) Not to see oneself with one's sickness as centre. There are more important things in life. (…) The evolution of humankind for example. (…) Your Inner Ego gets diminished, I believe, and you are looking at the whole (…) you are indeed starting to build relations with plants or with the entire living world around. You think less about yourself, you are thinking – across borders (#1)."

"Dying is as usual or unusual as life itself. You cannot separate it. I simply have to familiarize myself with the idea and the process. And for that an LSD session is of priceless worth (#10)."

Some of the participants reported impressive changes in their emotional state during the LSD experiences. Some experienced these changes during the experience itself; or even
manipulate the emotional state in the second LSD session after getting accustomed to the state during their first LSD experience:

"Emotionally it was a roller coaster ride. (…) The first time it was very brutal, painful, at least emotionally very painful. I could not even say in which direction – it just hurt, like heartache, like being disappointed, like everything you once had experienced as a negative feeling. (…) It was pure pain. Pain of memories, well, or memory of pain. (…) it was quite hard. During the second time it was sublime. Really. Love, expansion, holding, I knew that this sometimes happens, that participants talk about spiritual experiences. I thought they just meant this dissolution of oneself – everything is okay, everything is great. That was a very important experience for me. Very, very important (#6)"

"During the session the thoughts were … 'Do I travel the right path'? That was my question. Not dealing with death during the session but if I am on the right path. LSD gave me the feeling intensively that I am on the right path. That was nice. I was just floating for six hours, but felt a total assurance inside. That everything I do is actually good. … It gave me assurance. I was content. I had to giggle a lot and smile and I knew it is the right path. … everything will be fine (#8)."

It appears from the quotes that the patients initially were confronted with aspects of their situation related to 'negative' emotions such as anxiety, depression, hopelessness and feeling
tortured by the gravity of their situation, etc. Later during the course of their experience (or during their second LSD experience), the basic experience transformed to a much more positive basic emotional tone. The patients described this as an intensity that never was experienced before and that gave them 'a new baseline' for how to feel in their life situation.

Another frequently mentioned benefit was the long-term increase in quality of life:
"Quality of life changed extremely insofar as I became calmer, that I take things easier. It makes a difference if I look upon death with stress or with equanimity. I believe that is an enormous difference in quality of life. That I don't have to cry every night like in the first months. Instead I laugh and the illness, well the pain, when I get up and walk like an old grandmother I have to giggle and think 'What is this?'. Well I think quality of life has changed (#8)."

All patients interviewed reported that there were no negative effects that lasted beyond the duration of the sessions. A few mentioned that during the initial phase of the LSD experience they experienced difficulty in 'letting go' or giving up some of the usual self-control. For some others it was a difficult experience to feel their emotions with more intensity and to be confronted with anxiety, hopelessness and fear of death. But all patients were able to handle these unusually intense emotions and reported that a lot of tension was dissolved afterwards.

Discussion:
The present study has shown that psychological improvement as achieved during 3 months of LSD-assisted psychotherapy is stable over a 12-month period. The results from the QCA suggest that the improvement (as demonstrated by the significantly lower STAI trait scores) were also perceived as valid in personal statements.

Conclusion:
LSD-assisted psychotherapy in patients with life-threatening diseases demonstrated safety and positive stable treatment outcomes at LTFU. Systematic evaluations of semi-structured qualitative interviews with the participants point to cognitive, psychodynamic, and emotional experiences induced by LSD which contribute to sustained treatment effects. In particular, the emotional 'peak experiences' were deeply moving and established another inner frame for addressing and/or coping with the stressful situation.

Griffiths et al (2016). Psilocybin produces substantial and sustained decreases in depression and anxiety in patients with life-threatening cancer: A randomized double-blind trial.

Methods:
Griffiths et al (2016) recruited 56 participants with a potentially life-threatening cancer diagnosis and a disorder in the anxiety and/or depression spectrum. These were randomised to two groups: The Low-Dose-1st Group received the active placebo, low dose (1 or 3 mg/70 kg) of psilocybin on the first session and the high dose (22 or 30 mg/70 kg) on the second session, whereas the High-Dose-1st Group received the high dose on the first session and the low dose on the second session. The doses were decreased from 30 to 22 mg/70 kg after two of the first three participants who received a high dose of 30 mg/70 kg were discontinued from the study (one from vomiting shortly after capsule administration and one for personal reasons). The low dose of psilocybin was decreased from 3 to 1 mg/70 kg after 12 participants because data from Griffiths et al. (2011) showed significant psilocybin effects at 5 mg/70 kg, which raised concern that 3 mg/70 kg might not serve as an inactive placebo.

The practical aspects of the study and the education of the participants was carried out according to the principles described in the beginning of this chapter (Johnson et al, 2008). The sessions took place in a environment similar to the one described by Johnson et al (2008), and the psychiatric and somatic screening were according to the recommendations by Johnson et al (2008).

The participants were followed up for six months. Various self-report inventories and questionnaires were administered: (1) immediately after study enrollment (Baseline assessment); (2) on both session days (during and at the end of the session); (3) approximately 5 weeks (mean 37 days) after each session (Post-session 1 and Post-session 2 assessments); (4) approximately 6 months (mean 211 days) after Session 2 (6-month follow-up). Data assessments included cardiovascular measures and monitor ratings assessed throughout the session.

In addition to this, structured telephone interviews with community observers (e.g. family members, friends, or work colleagues) provided ratings of participant attitudes and behaviour reflecting healthy psychosocial functioning. The structured interview (Community Observer Questionnaire) consisted of asking the rater to rate the participant's behaviour and attitudes using a 10-point scale (from 1 = not at all, to 10 = extremely) on 13 items reflecting healthy psychosocial functioning: inner peace; patience; good-natured humour/playfulness; mental flexibility; optimism; anxiety (scored negatively); interpersonal perceptiveness and caring; negative expression of anger (scored negatively); compassion/social concern; expression of positive emotions (e.g. joy, love, appreciation); self-confidence; forgiveness of others; and forgiveness of self. Changes in each participant's behaviour and attitudes after drug sessions were expressed as a mean change score (i.e. difference score) from the baseline rating across the raters. Of 438 scheduled ratings by community observers, 25 (<6%) were missed.

Results:
Adverse Effects:
- The administration of psilocybin induced a mild but statistically significant elevation of HR and BP. The elevation were self-limiting and didn't require medical intervention.
- Nausea or vomiting occurred in 15% of participants in the high-dose session, and an episode of physical discomfort (any type) occurred in

21% of participants in the high-dose session and 8% in the low-dose session.
- Psychological discomfort (any type) occurred in 32% of participants in the high-dose session and 12% in the low-dose session. An episode of anxiety occurred in 26% of participants in the high-dose session and 15% in the low-dose session. One participant had a transient episode of paranoid ideation (2% of high-dose sessions).
- There were no cases of flashbacks or prolonged psychosis.
- One participant reported mild headache starting toward the end of the high-dose session and lasting until 9 p.m. that evening. Of the 11 participants for whom headache was assessed on the day after sessions, two reported a delayed moderate headache after the high-dose session.

Effects:
- Psilocybin produced dose- and time-related increases on all 16 monitor-rated (anxiety, joy, peacefulness) dimensions of the participant's behaviour or mood assessed throughout sessions, with a generally similar time-course in both dose conditions. Significant differences between the dose conditions generally first occurred at 30- or 60-min, with the high dose usually showing peak effects from 90–180 min and decreasing toward pre-drug levels over the remainder of the session.
- End-of-session measures that assessed subjective experiences during the session were significantly greater after the high than the low dose. Psilocybin produced large and sustained effects on the two primary clinician-rated therapeutically relevant outcome measures as well as most of the secondary measures assessed at Baseline, 5 weeks after each session, and at 6-month follow-up.
- Of the 17 measures (focusing on mood states, attitudes, disposition, and behaviours thought to be therapeutically relevant in psychologically distressed cancer patients) assessed, 16 showed significant effects (i.e. a between-group difference at the Post-session 1 assessment and/or a difference between Post-session 1 and Post-session 2 assessments in the Low-Dose-1st Group). Conservative criteria for concluding that psilocybin dose affected these outcomes is to consider only those measures that showed both a between-group difference at Post-session 1 and a difference between Postsession 1 and Post-session 2 assessments in the Low-Dose-1st Group.
- Rates of clinically significant response and symptom remission for the two primary outcome measures of clinician-rated symptoms of depression (GRID-HAMD-17) and anxiety (HAMA) showed large effects of psilocybin that were sustained at 6 months. For instance, 5 weeks after Session 1, 92% of participants in the High-Dose-1st Group showed a clinically significant response (i.e. $\geq$50% decrease relative to

Baseline) on the GRID-HAMD-17 compared with a 32% response rate in the Low-Dose-1st Group. At 6 months 79% of those in the High-Dose-1st Group continued to show a clinically significant response. Likewise, these percentages for the HAM-A were 76% and 24%, respectively, for the High-Dose 1st Group and Low-Dose-1st Group 5 weeks after Session 1, and 83% for the High-Dose-1st at 6 months.
- An analogous pattern of results was shown for symptom remission to normal range (i.e. ⩾50% decrease relative to Baseline and a score of ⩽7 on GRIDHAMD-17 or HAM-A), with rates of symptom remission of 60% and 52% for depression and anxiety, respectively, 5 weeks after the high psilocybin dose in Session 1, and with rates of 71% and 63%, respectively, sustained at 6 months. Collapsing across the two dose sequence groups, the overall rate of clinical response at 6 months was 78% and 83% for depression and anxiety, respectively, and the overall rate of symptom remission at 6 months for all participants was 65% and 57%, respectively.
- Participants attributed to the high-dose session positive changes in attitudes about life, self, mood, relationships and spirituality, with over 80% endorsing moderately or higher increased well-being or life satisfaction. These positive effects were reflected in significant corresponding changes in ratings by community observers (friends, family, work colleagues) of participant attitudes and behaviour.
- Community observer ratings showed significant positive changes in participants' attitudes and behaviour at the two post-psilocybin assessment time-points. All three measures of spirituality showed similar increases. The high dose produced significantly greater ratings of positive persisting effects on attitudes about life and self, mood changes, social effects, behaviour, and spirituality. These effects were sustained at 6-month follow-up. Negative ratings of these dimensions were low and not significantly different between conditions. The high-dose experiences were rated as producing significantly greater personal meaning, spiritual significance and increased well-being or life satisfaction, with differences sustained at 6 months.
- The immediate postsession mystical experience score (MEQ30) was linearly correlated with therapeutic efficacy measured via measurements of meaningfulness, spiritual significance, life satisfaction, GRID-HAMD, HADS Depression, HADS Total, HADS Anxiety, HAM-A, BSI, MQOL-meaningful existence and LAP-R Coherence).

Discussion:
- The study showed that psilocybin could be safely administered to a screened group of patients suffering from a depressive- or anxiety disordered and had a life-threatening cancer diagnosis.

- It demonstrated the efficacy of a high dose of psilocybin administered under supportive conditions, measured through 17 therapeutically relevant measures.
- Psilocybin produced large and significant decreases in clinician-rated and self-rated measures of depression, anxiety or mood disturbance, and increases in measures of quality of life, life meaning, death acceptance, and optimism.
- These effects were sustained at 6 months follow-up. For the clinician-rated measures of depression and anxiety, respectively, the overall rate of clinical response at 6 months was 78% and 83% and the overall rate of symptom remission was 65% and 57%. These findings are consistent with previous studies on the subject.
- The significant association of mystical-type experience (MEQ30) during Session 1 with most of the enduring changes in therapeutic outcome measures 5 weeks later were too consistent with previous findings showing that such experiences on session days predict long-term positive changes in attitudes, mood, behaviour, and spirituality (Garcia-Romeu et al., 2014; Griffiths et al., 2008, 2011).
- Griffiths et al (2016) wrote that this suggested that mystical-type experience per se has an important role apart from overall intensity of drug effect. Finally, a mediation analysis further suggested that mystical-type experience has a mediating role in positive therapeutic response.
- Participants were crossed over to the alternative dose condition after 5 weeks. Although this allowed assessment of acute and persisting effects of psilocybin in all study participants, it precluded double-blind assessment of efficacy of the high dose of psilocybin based on across group comparisons after 5 weeks.
- Although the study found significant decreases in depression and anxiety symptoms on both participant-rated and clinician-rated measures is a strength, the inclusion of blinded clinician ratings would further strengthen the study.
- Finally, it is important to note that the overall approach of treating cancer-related psychological distress with psilocybin is limited by a variety of exclusion criteria and by the significant time and cost of professional support provided before, during, and after the psilocybin session. Patients may also be reluctant to participate in such an intervention because high doses of psilocybin have sometimes been associated with transient episodes of psychological distress or anxiety in patients.

Conclusions:
When administered under psychologically supportive, double-blind conditions, a single dose of psilocybin produced substantial and enduring

decreases in depressed mood and anxiety along with increases in quality of life and decreases in death anxiety in patients with a life-threatening cancer diagnosis. Ratings by patients themselves, clinicians, and community observers suggested these effects endured at least 6 months. The overall rate of clinical response at 6 months on clinician-rated depression and anxiety was 78% and 83%, respectively.

A multisite study in a larger patient population should be conducted to establish the generality and safety of psilocybin treatment of psychological distress associated with life-threatening cancer.

Ross et al (2016). Rapid and sustained symptom reduction following psilocybin treatment for anxiety and depression in patients with life-threatening cancer: a randomized controlled trial.

Methods:

Ross et al (2016) recruited 29 participants (18 women) for a randomised, blinded, controlled, crossover, study in order to investigate the efficacy of a single psilocybin dosing session (0.3 mg/kg) versus one dosing session of an active control (niacin 250 mg), administered in conjunction with psychotherapy, to treat clinically significant anxiety or depression in patients with life-threatening cancer (breast or reproductive (59%); gastrointestinal (17%); hematologic (14%); other (10%)). All participants carried an anxiety-related diagnosis with the majority meeting criteria for an adjustment disorder (26, 90%) and the rest for generalised anxiety disorder (three, 10%). Nearly two-thirds (59%) had previously been treated with anti-depressants.

The trial employed a two-session, double-blind, crossover (7 weeks after administration of dose 1) design to compare groups. Participants were randomly assigned to two oral dosing session sequences: psilocybin (0.3 mg/kg) first then niacin (250 mg) second, or niacin (250 mg) first then psilocybin (0.3 mg/kg) second

Drug administration dose 1 (psilocybin or control) occurred 2–4 weeks (mean 18 days) after baseline assessments and the crossover occurred 7 weeks (mean 52 days) after dose 1, at which point drug administration dose 2 occurred.

The practical aspects of the study and the education of the participants was carried out according to the principles described in the beginning of this chapter (Johnson et al, 2008). The sessions took place in a environment similar to the one described by Johnson et al (2008), and the psychiatric and somatic screening were according to the recommendations by Johnson et al (2008).

Various self-report inventories and questionnaires were administered at baseline (2–4 weeks prior to dose 1), 1 day prior to dose 1, day of dose 1 (7 hours post-dose), 1 day after dose 1, 2 weeks after dose 1, 6 weeks after dose 1, 7 weeks after dose 1 (1 day prior to dose 2), day of dose 2 (7 hours post-dose), 1 day after dose 2, 6 weeks after dose 2, and 26 weeks after dose 2.

Results:
Adverse Effects:
- Somatic AE were elevated HR and BP, headaches/migraines (28%) and nausea (14%).
- Psychiatric AEs were transient anxiety (17%) and transient psychotic-like symptoms (7%: one case of transient paranoid ideation and one case of transient thought disorder).
- All AE were self containing and didn't require medical intervention.

Effects:
- For each of the six primary outcome measures (HADS T, HADS A, HADS D, BDI, STAI S, STAI T), there were significant differences between the experimental and control groups (prior to the crossover at 7 weeks post-dose 1) with the psilocybin group (compared to the active control) demonstrating immediate, substantial, and sustained (up to 7 weeks post-dosing) clinical benefits in terms of reduction of anxiety and depression symptoms.
- The magnitude of differences between the psilocybin and control groups (Cohen's d effect sizes) was large across the primary outcome measures, assessed at 1 day/2 weeks/ 6 weeks/7 weeks post-dose 1.
- For every primary outcome measures, the psilocybin first group demonstrated significant within-group reductions (compared to baseline at each post-baseline assessment point) in anxiety and depression immediately after receiving psilocybin. These reductions remained significant at each time point, including the final point at 26 weeks post-dose 2 (approximately 8 months), post-psilocybin dosing. Prior to the crossover, the niacin first group demonstrated either no significant within-group reductions or a transient reduction that became non-significant prior to dose 2. For the majority (five/six) of the measures, the niacin first group demonstrated significant within-group reductions in anxiety and depression immediately after receiving the psilocybin dose (dosing session 2), and these statistically significant improvements persisted until the end of the study (approximately 6.5 months post-psilocybin dosing, 26 weeks post-dose 2, for this group).
- Psilocybin produced immediate and enduring anxiolytic and anti-

depressant response rates, as well as significant anti-depressant remission rates (measured by the HADS D and BDI). For example, 7 weeks after dose 1, 83% of participants in the psilocybin first group (vs. 14% in the niacin first group) met criteria for anti-depressant response (with the BDI) and 58% (in the psilocybin first group) for anxiolytic response using the HAD A, compared to 14% in the niacin first group. At the 6.5-month follow-up (after both groups received psilocybin), anti-depressant or anxiolytic response rates were approximately 60–80%.
- In the short-term (2 weeks postdose 1), psilocybin (compared to control) produced decreases in cancer-related demoralization and hopelessness, while improving spiritual wellbeing and quality of life (physical, psychological, environmental domains). These effects were sustained at the final 6.5 month follow-up. Regarding anxiety and attitudes towards death, the data were mixed.
- In the short-term (2 weeks post-dose 1), psilocybin was not significantly associated with decreased death anxiety or increased death transcendence. However, at the 26-week post-dose 2 final follow-up assessment, while death anxiety (as measured by the DAS) continued to demonstrate no significant reductions, there was a significant improvement in attitudes and adaptations towards death (as measured by the DTS) in the psilocybin first group compared to the niacin first group (assessed at 2 weeks post-dose 1).
- Prior to the crossover, psilocybin produced significantly greater ratings (compared to the niacin first group assessed at 2 weeks post-dose 1) of positive persisting effects on: attitudes about life and self, mood changes, social effects (e.g. increased altruism), behavior, and spirituality. After the crossover, these effects were sustained at the final 6.5-month follow-up. When all participants were asked (26 weeks post-session 2) to reflect on what they thought was their psilocybin session, 52% and 70% rated the psilocybin experience as the singular or top 5 most spiritually significant, or the singular or top 5 most personally meaningful experience of their entire lives, respectively; while 87% reported increased life satisfaction or wellbeing attributed to the experience.
- Total mystical experience scores (MEQ 30) at the end of dose 1 (e.g. 7 hours post-drug administration) correlated with change scores (baseline to 6 weeks after dose 1) on four out of six primary outcome measures: HADS T; HADS A; HADS D; BDI; STAI S; STAI T.

Discussion:
- As in previous research on the topic, no serious AEs, either medical or psychiatric were observed in the trial.
- Single moderate-dose psilocybin, in conjunction with psychotherapy, produced rapid, robust, and sustained clinical benefits in terms of

reduction of anxiety and depression in patients with life threatening cancer. This pharmacological finding is novel in psychiatry in terms of a single dose of a medication leading to immediate anti-depressant and anxiolytic effects with enduring (e.g. weeks to months) clinical benefits. Ross et al (2016) wrote that the post-crossover data analyses of the two dosing sequences suggest that the clinical benefits, in terms of reduction of cancer-related anxiety and depression, of single-dose psilocybin (in conjunction with psychotherapy) may be sustained for longer than 7 weeks post-dosing, and that they may endure for as long as 8 months post-dosing.

- The within-group analyses for the primary outcome measures demonstrate that immediately after receiving psilocybin there were a marked reduction in anxiety and depression scores for both the psilocybin first and niacin first groups. Also, the magnitude of psilocybin-induced change across each participant's active psilocybin treatment session did not differ across treatment group for any of the primary outcome measures.
- Together, this suggests that the pharmacological/psilocybin intervention produced rapid anti-depressant and anxiolytic clinical benefits. Both groups demonstrated significant clinical improvements in anxiety/depression from baseline relative to the final assessment. It is unclear from the data whether the sustained benefits in clinical outcomes were due to psilocybin alone or some interactive effect of psilocybin plus the targeted psychotherapy.
- Ross et al (2016) recommended future research should examine the various therapeutic contributions of psilocybin versus psychotherapy.
- Psilocybin was associated with substantial anti-depressant response rates (as high as approximately 80% at 6.5 months follow-up). There have been several meta-analyses of placebo controlled trials exploring the efficacy of anti-depressants in the treatment of cancer-related depression and they have generally failed to show a clear effect of anti-depressant treatment over placebo (Iovieno et al., 2011; Laoutidis and Mathiak, 2013; Ostuzzi et al., 2015). In a meta-analyses of anti-depressants for major depressive disorder in patients with comorbid medical disorders (including cancer), anti-depressants were more effective than placebo in some medical conditions (e.g. HIV/AIDS, poststroke) but not in cancer patients, where the anti-depressants performed about as well as the approximately 40% placebo response rate (Iovieno et al., 2011).
- Psilocybin decreased cancer-related demoralisation (e.g. loss of meaning/hope/purpose, desire for hastened death) and hopelessness, while improving spiritual wellbeing, general life satisfaction, and quality of life. While a minority of patients with advanced or terminal cancer experience clinically relevant existential/spiritual distress, when it occurs

its effects are highly consequential (e.g. decreased quality of life, increased depressive and anxiety symptoms, increased desire for hastened death, increased suicidal ideation and behaviors) (Puchalski, 2012) and improving spiritual wellbeing (e.g. through a pharmacological-psychosocial intervention) could serve as a buffer against these negative clinical outcomes.
- Although affect/anxiety towards death did not improve in the short-term or longer-term follow-up period, psilocybin was associated with improved attitudes and adaptations to death at the 6.5-month follow-up.
- Psilocybin experiences were reported as highly meaningful and spiritual, and associated with positive cognitive, affective, spiritual, and behavioural effects lasting weeks to months. This finding is consistent with prior research administering psilocybin to healthy volunteers (Doblin, 1991; Griffiths et al., 2006, 2008, 2011; Pahnke, 1963).

Conclusion:

Single moderate-dose psilocybin (in conjunction with psychotherapy) was safely administered to a cohort of participants with cancer-related psychological distress (e.g. anxiety, depression). It produced rapid and sustained anxiolytic and anti-depressant effects (for at least 7 weeks but potentially as long as 8 months), decreased cancer-related existential distress, increased spiritual wellbeing and quality of life, and was associated with improved attitudes towards death.

The psilocybin-induced mystical experience mediated the anxiolytic and anti-depressant effects of psilocybin. Psilocybin, administered in conjunction with appropriate psychotherapy, could become a novel pharmacological-psychosocial treatment modality for cancer-related psychological and existential distress. Further empirical research is needed definitively to establish its safety and efficacy.

Ayahuasca and DMT

Ayahuasca, meaning "vine of the soul" or "vine of the dead" in the Quecha language, is a traditional Amazonian decoction also known by the names of hoasca or oasca (the Portuguese transliteration), caapi or kahpi, daime (which means "give me" in Portuguese), yajé or yage, cipó, natema or natem, dapa, mihi, or vegetal (Halpern, 2008; Kjellgren, 2009). The psychoactive drink is made from the stem bark of the *Banisteriopsis caapi* vine, rich in beta-carboline harmala alkaloids, usually in combination with N,N-dimethyltryptamine (DMT)- containing leaves of the *Psychotria viridis* bush (Gable, 2007). The harmala alkaloids harmine and harmaline are monoamine oxidase inhibitors (MAOIs), without which the DMT would be inactivated by the gut and liver MAOs, while tetrahydroharmine acts as a weak serotonin reuptake inhibitor without any MAOI action (Callaway et al, 1999). The combined action of the two plants has been empirically understood by Amazonian indigenous populations for at least 3000 years (Mabit, 2007). Originally used by Amazonian shamans in ritual ceremonies and by folk healers for a variety of psychosomatic complaints (de Rios, 1971), worldwide interest in ayahuasca has been rising. It is now being used as a sacrament by three Brazilian churches, by tourists seeking a spiritual experience, and by recreational users all over the world. With growing interest and increasing use of ayahuasca, it is important to understand the safety, behavioral effects, and potential clinical uses. Research into medical use of ayahuasca indicates potential as a treatment in addictions, depression and anxiety (dos Santos et al, 2016), with a variety of other possible medical uses, though these require more research.

DMT

A brief history of Ayahuasca:
According to Hamill et al (2018) who summed the history of ayahuasca up in their review, do the use of ayahuasca dates back to the earliest aboriginal inhabitants of the Amazonian basin, where it was used by indigenous shamans for communication with spirits, magical experiences, rites of initiation, and healing rituals (Grob et al, 1996). Ayahuasca was held in high regard among these populations, particularly for religious and healing purposes. These were small private ceremonies where the patient and the shaman, and perhaps 1 or 2 others, would consume ayahuasca. Shortly after consumption, vomiting and often intense diarrhea occured, but after this, visions begin to appear, and the nature of the disease and curative plants were revealed to the shaman and the patient (Demarchelier, 1996). During the past several hundred years, the use of ayahuasca spread into Peru, Colombia, and Ecuador among indigenous Mestizo populations where it was integrated into folk medicine (Grob et al, 1996). These practices evolved during the early 1930s (McKenna, 2007) for use as a sacrament in three Brazilian syncretic churches which combine indigenous and Christian traditions, the União do Vegetal (the largest, more meditative), the Santo Daime (the oldest, livelier, with music), and Barquinha (an Afro-Brazilian church), during twice monthly ceremonies lasting approximately four hours (Kjellgren, 2009; Callaway, 1999; Barbosa, 2005; Labate, 2011; Riba et al, 2003).

In 1970, DMT was classified as a Schedule I drug under the US Controlled Substances Act (Araujo, 2015). The International Narcotics Control Board is currently the control body in charge of implementing the conventions (Blainey, 2015; Tupper, 2012). Not until 1987 was the use of ayahuasca in a religious context protected by Brazilian law (Grob, 1996; Ott, 1999). Members of the American ayahuasca churches kept their use quiet until 1999 when the United States' Drug Enforcement Administration (DEA) confiscated ayahuasca that had been smuggled in. The UDV began a federal lawsuit in 2000 (Groisman et al, 2007), where under the Religious Freedom Restoration Act of 1993, they argued they could use ayahuasca on the basis of religious freedom, and the courts agreed (Halpern, 2008). The federal government appealed the decision several times until, in 2006, the US Supreme Court unanimously decided to allow the ceremonial use of ayahuasca in the UDV church, as they were unable to demonstrate that it had any detrimental effects (Gable, 2007; Bullis, 2008). The Santo Daime religion fought a similar battle in Oregon, likely benefitting from the precedent set by the UDV church, and won an injunction allowing ceremonial use of ayahuasca in 2009. Even before that, the Oregon State Board of Pharmacy concluded in 2000 that in the Santo Daime religion, ayahuasca had a "non-drug" use, and was not subject to state regulation (Halpern, 2008). A Canadian branch of the Brazilian Santo Daime church in Montreal, called the Céu do Montreal, sought an exemption from the Canadian Controlled Drugs and Sub- stances Act in 2001, and in 2006, Health Canada authorised the church to import ayahuasca in the form of tea (Tupper, 2011).

Ayahuasca therapy has been used by witch doctors in treating addictions, and Lemlij (1978) describes a group therapy model where participants come as many weeks as they need and may make a voluntary monetary contribution at the end. In recent time had the drink become more popular in North America, Europe and beyond for religious, spiritual, and recreational use (Kjellgren *et al,* 2009). Cardenas and Gomez (2004) examined motives for modern urban use by 40 residents of Bogota, Colombia. They found that subjects used ayahuasca to achieve mental well-being and also to enhance their ability to solve personal problems; in another study, the participants cited "healing" and "equilibrium" as reasons for use (Barbosa et al, 2009). Kjellgren *et al.* (2009) found similar motives among northern European users, including exploring their inner world, personal development, increasing self-awareness, examining psychological patterns, and enhancing creativity. Fiedler *et al.* (2011) studied motives for use among Santo Daime members, and found that reasons were consistently religious or spiritual, as well as self- treatment.

In recent times many Westerners had too travelled to the South Americas in search of a transformative hallucinogenic experience, which is referred to in the literature as drug tourism, spiritual tourism, or modern shamanic tourism. Ayahuasca tourism is growing in popularity, and most often this involves non-indigenous tourists going on all-inclusive trips to the Amazon to partake in a shaman-led ayahuasca ceremony (Holman, 2011). Modern shamanic tourism is discussed in a dissertation by Fotiou (2011) and in articles by Winkelman et al (2005) and Arrevalo et al (2005), both of whom collected data showing that motivations to participate in such an experience are usually not excuses for drug experimentation, but are genuinely sought out as spiritual pilgrimages. Kavenska and Simonova (2005) also examined the motivations, perceptions, and personality traits of 77 study participants who had gone to South America to use ayahuasca. Motivations included "curiosity, desire to treat mental health problems, need for self-knowledge, interest in psychedelic medicine, spiritual development, and finding direction in life". Reported benefits included self-knowledge, improved interpersonal relations, and gaining new perspectives on life. Participants scored significantly above average on the PSSI scales of "intuition, optimism, ambition, charm, and helpful- ness and significantly lower on the scales of distrust and quietness".

Chemical composition:

Ayahuasca's psychedelic effect originates largely from DMT and beta-carbolines: DMT is a serotonin-like psychedelic structurally resembling other indolealkylamines, including melatonin and psychedelic tryptamines such as psilocybin, which it share its activity as a 5-HT_{2A} receptor agonist (Cakic et al, 2010; Carbonaro et al, 2016). DMT is found in fungi, marine sponges, tunicates, frogs, legumes, and grasses and has been reported to be formed endogenously in human and rat brains (Saavedra et al, 1972) as well as to be found in human urine, blood, and CSF. DMT has affinity for 5-$HT_{1A/1B/1D/2A/2B/2C/6/7}$ receptors, with proven partial agonist activity at the 5-$HT_{1A/2A/2C}$ receptors (Freedland et al, 1999; Riba et al, 2012; Fontanilla et al, 2009; Keiser et al, 2009). Further, Carbonaro *et al.* (2005) proposed that the mGluR2 glutamate receptors may have some involvement in DMT's psychedelic effect.

Beta-carbolines are tricyclic indole alkaloids resembling tryptamines (McKenna et al, 2007). 6-Methoxy-tetrahydro-β-carboline has been found in the human pineal gland (Langer et al, 1984) Several beta- carbolines are found in the *B. caapi* vine, including harmine, harmaline, and tetrahydroharmine. The first two act as selective and reversible monoamine oxidase A inhibitors (MAO- AIs), while tetrahydroharmine acts as a weak serotonin reuptake inhibitor without any MAO-AI action (Callaway, 1999). Beta- carbolines are found naturally in wheat, rice, corn, barley and throughout different body tissues (Louis et al, 2002). They elicit their effects through several mechanisms. Beta-carbolines without DMT have been shown to produce psychological and physiologic effects. The effects, including nausea, vomiting (Carbonaro et al, 2015), hallucinations, ataxia, confusion, and agitation are attributed to CNS stimulation by MAOI activity as well as the serotonin reuptake inhibition by tetrahydroharmine. Frison *et al.* (2008) suggested that the hallucinogenic effects could be a result of the affinity of harmine and harmaline for 5-HT receptors. The

DMT in ayahuasca is from the *Psychotria viridis* or *Diplopterys cabrerana* vines, and ranges in concentration from 0.1% to 0.66% of the dry plant weight (Riba et al, 2012; Gable et al, 2007). The beta-carbolines come from *Banisteriopsis caapi*. These compounds represent 0.05% to 1.95% of the dry plant weight, and are much more concentrated in the seeds and roots than in stems and leaves (Gable et al, 2007). DMT, a hallucinogen, can be smoked, ingested orally, given IV, or insufflated (Gable et al, 2007). As mentioned earlier, is a MAO-inhibitor needed when consumed orally, to prevent degradation of the DMT by gut and liver and lengthen its action in the CNS (Gaujac, 2012; Herraiz, 2010). In ayahuasca, DMT is taken in combination with beta-carbolines which act as reversible inhibitors of monoamine oxidase A (MAO- A), protecting the DMT from degradation (Callaway, 2005).

The chemical composition of ayahuasca differs from brew to brew, all depending on the ratio of the plants and differences in preparation methods. In a review on ayahuasca, Gable (2007) looked at previous data on the composition of one serving of various studies' brews, and found a range of 8.8 mg to 42 mg for DMT, 17 mg to 280 mg harmine, 4.6 mg to 28 mg harmaline, and 4.2 to 150 mg for tetrahydroharmine. Another study on ayahuasca samples from Brazilian religious groups found DMT concentrations ranging from 0.17-1.14 g/L (Gaujac, 2012), which, assuming an average serving size similar to previous studies being around 150 mL, would give a dose ranging from 25.5 to 171 mg of DMT per serving.

The toxic dose of ayahuasca would be approximately 7.8 litres for a 75 kg person, and given its highly unpleasant taste, it is unlikely anyone would ever reach this dose. In addition, vomiting and diarrhea occur long before this limit is reached (Mabit, 2005).

Physiological safety:
Experimental studies of acute ayahuasca administration to healthy volunteers (Riba
et al. 2001; Riba et al, 2003; Riba et al, 2006; dos Santos et al. 2011; dos Santos et al, 2012; de Araujo et al. 2012; Palhano-Fontes et al. 2015; McKenna and Riba, 2016) and mental health assessments of long-term ayahuasca consumers (Grob et al. 1996; Barbosa et al 2005; Barbosa et al, 2009; Barbosa et al, 2012; da Silveira et al. 2005; Halpern et al. 2008; Fábregas et al. 2010; Bouso et al. 2012; Bouso et al, 2015; dos Santos, 2013) suggest that the preparation is quite safe.

Even though, risk have been reported from non-clinical use of ayahuasca. These are the risk as summed up by Malcolm et al (2017):

Ayahuasca is not well tolerated physically and frequently results in non-significant but possible unpleasant reactions as nausea, vomiting, and diarrhea, as well as other somatic disturbances collectively known as purging or la purga. From the perspective of indigenous cultures, these adverse effects are considered to be cleansing and normal. Although a specific mechanism has not been established, these effects are consistent with mild serotonin toxicity. The frequency of vomiting reported with ayahuasca as well as being in an acutely altered state may increase risk of aspiration events (Malcolm et al, 2017).
Mild and transient increases in cardiovascular parameters, such as increases in diastolic blood pressure of approximately 10 mmHg, as well as the somatic disturbances outlined above are common in the clinical litterature (Riba et al, 2003). Neuroendocrine activity, including transient increases in cortisol (12 lg/dL) and prolactin (14 ng/mL) that persist for approximately 6 hours with consequent immunomodulatory changes, has been identified (dos Santos et al, 2011). Many studies have been limited to healthy people with ayahuasca experience at baseline, which may skew reports on tolerability or objective or subjective effects. Few studies have included ayahuasca-naive patients or patients diagnosed with a psychiatric illness (Osório et al, 2015; Barbossa et al, 2009; Sanches et al, 2016).

There have been several reports of death, including an alleged homicide during an ayahuasca ceremony (dos Santos et al, 2013 and Plucinska, 2015). Circumstances around deaths are generally unclear and may be related to shamans adding additional plants with increased toxicity to brews or inappropriately screening patients for drug interactions. There has never been a death observed during a clinical study (dos Santos et al, 2013). Szmulewicz et al 2015 published a case report of a switch to mania in a patient with bipolar disorder who consumed ritual ayahuasca during a depressive episode. Ayahuasca does not appear to increase the risk of precipitating psychosis or schizophrenia among young adults with reported rates in the UDV being equal or less than that of the general population (Gable et al, 2007). One case report by suggested that repeated use of smoked DMT may precipitate psychosis. Other persistent psychotic-like reactions have been described (dos Santos et al, 2013). Riba et al (2002) reported reduced P50 sensory gating suppression with ayahuasca use and decreased P50 sensory gating is associated with schizophrenia. Given the paucity of data, ayahuasca may best be avoided in patients with a history of mania or psychosis (Malcolm et al, 2017).

Drug and dietary interactions
According to Malcolm et al (2017) following drug-interactions should require special attention:

Due to MAO inhibition by harmala alkaloids, ayahuasca carries a higher risk of drug interactions than other psychedelics. Ayahuasca has previously been recognized to have interaction potential with selective serotonin reuptake inhibitors (SSRI) (Callaway et al, 1998). Ayahuasca should also be avoided with other serotonergic agents, including tricyclic antidepressants (TCA), serotonin norepinephrine reuptake inhibitors, trazodone, and St John's wort. Non-antidepressants, such as lithium, triptans, metoclopramide, levodopa, phentermine, pseudoephedrine, linezolid, methadone, and dextromethorphan, may also have serotonergic effects (Volpi-Abadie, 2013). Psychoactive drugs, such as phenylethylamines (MDMA, mescaline, 2C compounds), methcathinones or "bath salts" (mephedrone, methylone), and tryptamines (LSD, 5-MeO-DMT, psilocybin) are high-risk combinations as fatalities have been reported when combined with harmala alkaloids in a recreational setting (Lanaro et al, 2015; Wiltshire et al, 2015; Ott et al, 1999; Santos et al, 2013). Alternative combinations of extracted harmala alkaloids with DMT as well as other tryptamines was described by Ott as "Pharmauasca" and likely pose similar or greater druginteraction risks than ayahuasca (Ott et al, 1999). Harmine is also a substrate and inhibitor of CYP2D6 (Brierley et al, 2012 and Callaway et al, 2005). Pharmacokinetic data of ayahausca users suggested genetic polymorphisms of CYP2D6 to play a significant role in harmine metabolism. However, similar DMT concentrations remained despite higher concentrations of harmala alkaloids, which indicates alternative metabolic routes for DMT apart from MAO (Callaway et al, 2005)

Effects of tyramine intake in subjects taking ayahuasca have not been described although extrapolation from pharmaceutical MAOIs suggest an increased risk of hypertensive crisis. Although not necessarily designed to minimize tyramine content, Amazonian dietas used in preparation of ritual ayahuasca involve bland foods that do not involve alcohol, cheese, or other fermented food items (Malcolm et al, 2017).

Psychedelic drug effects:
The ayahuasca experience begins approximately 40 min following ingestion, peaking between 60 and 120 min, with subjective effects fading by approximately 4 hours. The DMT-experience do in comparison only last a few minutes, with effects subsiding almost completely in half an hour (Strassman et al, 1992). Mabit et al (2007) reports that ayahuasca users do not lose consciousness but experience alterations in it, while Strassman (1992) reported that with IV DMT injection, users experience a transient loss of their normal awareness.

Some of the psychological effects during ayahuasca ingestion include a powerful sense of self-confidence, a new perspective and reinterpretation of intrapsychic conflicts; users may reveal intimate truths, and ayahuasca may be powerful in facilitating psychotherapy (Mabit et al, 2007.

Kjellgren *et al (2009)* described the "transcendental circle", a cycle of experiences consistent among different users following ayahuasca ingestion. Approximately 30 minutes after ingestion, subjects noted changing perceptions and shaking, and felt vulnerable and easily influenced. Shortly after, participants developed feelings of confusion, paranoia and fear; psychological defences were diminished and participants experienced traumatic memories and gained new insight into personal matters (Bresnick et al, 2006). This terrifying state peaks with intense vomiting, after which most participants noted an abrupt shift into an expansive state. Participants describe a transcendental experience in a spiritual world, encountering plant and animal spirits and even contact with a higher power, feelings of oneness with the universe, profound peace and ecstasy, and newly gained understandings of death and what comes after. Sense of time is altered, and users experience feelings of timelessness, time speeding up or slowing down, or traveling in time (Shanon et al, 2001; Riba et al, 2001). Users remain aware of their surroundings and are able to speak (Gable et al, 2007). Beyer (2009) refers to a similar pattern and describes three phases, the first with visual imagery and sometimes nausea or vomiting; the second phase is contact with a spiritual world in which users report useful lessons from spirit teachers, and the third phase involves fading visuals and feeling physically drained.

With regard to visual effects, objects appear to vibrate or increase in brightness, colours intensify, moving geometric patterns and intricate images occur with eyes closed or open (Gable et al, 2007) ; kaleidoscopic imagery or visions of people, beautiful scenery, or snakes or jungle animals are common (Brosnick, 2006; Metzner, 1998; Strassman, 1994). Visual creativity may be heightened for some time even after acute effects wear off, and visual phenomena tend to linger even after acute effects subside (Rhodium Archive. 2009). Synesthesia, and particularly auditory to visual synesthetic effects are common, and usually they are associated with music. The tempo and feel of the music are often reflected in the movements of the visions and how often the images change (Shanon, 2007). Shanon (2007) also noted enhanced improvisation and improvements in their ability to play their instruments by the musicians during Santo Daime rituals, as well as in himself at the piano.

Abuse and dependence
Morgenstern *et al* (1994) reported that almost no hallucinogen users had

difficulty cutting down or controlling use, unlike the situation with many other drugs. In a study of rhesus monkeys, Fantegrossi *et al.* (2004)) found reinforcing effects of the hallucinogens DMT, mescaline, and psilocybin, and suggest that the patterns of self-administration demonstrate weak reinforcing effects, and possibly mixed reinforcing and aversive effects. Ayahuasca does not seem to have the negative psychosocial implications caused by many other drugs of abuse (Fabregas, 2010). Mixed results were found in studies of drug tolerance in animal studies (Cole et al, 1973; Gillin et al, 1973; Kovacic, 1976) as well as in human studies (Gable, 2017), particularly to the psychoactive effects, which is unique among other known hallucinogens. Callaway *et al.* (1994) found that some physical tolerance may develop in humans with regular use. In a study by dos Santos *et al.* (dos Santos, 2012), acute tolerance failed to develop for any measures aside from growth hormone (GH), which showed decreased release on second administration, as well as a slightly lower response in the systolic blood pressure (SBP) and heart rate (HR). Another study similarly showed tolerance with heart rate, adrenocorticotropic hormone (ACTH) and prolactin (Strassman, 1994). Another study found that there was little to no tolerance with DMT in cats (Gillin, 1973).

Beta-carbolines can induce tremor in mice, thought to be due to the interaction of these compounds with tryptamine binding receptors (Airaksinen et al, 1987). An experiment by Louis *et al.* (2002) suggests we should be cautious with beta-carbolines, as they are found endogenously in higher levels in essential tremor patients, and that harmine and harmane may be tremorigenic. Bouso et. al. (2013) compared two groups of ayahuasca users, one with long-term experience and the other with occasional use. The study found that acute use does impair working memory, but having greater prior exposure was associated with less incapacitation during administration, and detrimental effects on cognition were mainly seen in the occasional use group. Those findings suggest there may be neuromodulatory or compensatory effects induced by long-term use.

Ayahuasca for major depression disorder:

Possible biological mechanisms in the treatment of major depression disorder:
Hamilla et al (2018) summed up on the possible biological mechanism of ayahuasca on depression:
DMT activates sigma-1 receptors, and most antidepressants of the SSRI, MAOI and TCA classes have been found to do so as well. These receptors are found throughout the nervous system, and are concentrated in the

hippocampus, frontal cortex, and olfactory bulb, consistent with a possible role in depression (Urani et al, 2001). Past experiments have shown an antidepressant-like effect in mice administered sigma-1 receptor agonists (Wang et al, 2007) and attenuation of these effects with sigma receptor antagonists (Samoylenko et al, 2010). Agonists of the sigma receptor are being studied as potential antidepressant drugs (Urani et al, 2001). More work into the functions of sigma receptors and their role in depression treatment is needed. A possible connection lies in the inhibitory effect of DMT on the NMDA receptor through sigma receptor activation (Schenberg et al, 2013).

Both I1 and I2 imidazoline receptors have been associated with the pathology of depression. I1 sites are decreased in brains of depressed suicide victims, notably in the hippocampus and prefrontal cortex (Piletz et al, 2000). I1 binding sites are found throughout the human brain, and the highest density areas includes the striatum, pallidum, hippocampus, amygdala, and substantia nigra (Finn et al, 2003). I1 receptors are thought to be involved in the central inhibition of sympathetic outflow, which can be altered in depression (Halaris et al, 2003). I1 binding sites have been reported to be increased on platelets of patients experiencing depression and premenstrual dysphoric disorder, and in studies a return to normal levels following treatment with fluoxetine, citalopram, bupropion, desipramine, clomipramine, imipramine, and lithium have been observed (Halaris et al, 2003). A downregulation of I2 binding sites has been found in frontal cortices and hippocampi of depressed humans post-mortem. Harmine and harmaline have high affinity for the I2 binding site in rat brains [188]. In terms of clinical use, the selective I2 ligand BU224 showed antidepressant-like activity in rats and increased 5-HT levels in the frontal cortex and hypothalamus (Finn et al, 2003) and antidepressant treatment caused upregulation of I2 sites in rat brains (Paterson et al, 187). Most I2 selective ligands have been found to be allosteric inhibitors of both MAO-A and MAO-B (Garcia-Sevilla et al, 1999).

Several studies of harmine have shown an antidepressant effect (Farzin et al, 2006; Fortunate et al, 2009; Fortunate et al, 2010a; Fortunate et al, 2010b; Osório et al, 2011). One known mechanism through which harmine and harmaline may exert an antidepressant effect is reversible inhibition of MAO-A (Samoylenko et al, 2010), resulting in increased neurotransmission. Their reversibility for MAO-A inhibition makes them safer than the traditional non-selective, irreversible MAOIs [10]. Fortunato et al. (2010a and 2010b) conducted animal studies of harmine, and found it to have an anti depressive effect.

Evidence is suggesting that reactive oxygen species may be involved in the pathogenesis of depression and anxiety (Bouayed et al, 2009). Harmine has shown to be of benefit as it increased levels of both superoxide dismutase and catalase enzymes, and attenuated oxidative stress parameters of lipid and protein oxidation in rat brain hippocampus, a structure involved in mood regulation (Reus et al, 2010).

Previous research:
Ayahuasca weren't investigated in the pre-prohibition times.

Current research:
These are the papers who have currently been published on the clinical use of ayahuasca for the treatment of major depression disorder.

Osório et al (2014). Antidepressant effects of a single dose of ayahuasca in patients with recurrent depression: a preliminary report (2014).

Methods:
Osório et al (2014) recruited six patients (four women) with a diagnosis of recurrent major depression disorder for an open-label study exploring ayahuasca as a possible treatment of depression. Within this group, two volunteers were experiencing a current mild depressive episode, three were experiencing a moderate episode, and one was experiencing a severe depressive episode. None were experiencing psychotic symptoms and none took any psychopharmaceutical medication. Major somatic illness and a personal or family history of major psychiatric illness were a exclusion criteria. The participants were educated about ayahuasca and and the general psychological effects of psychedelics. Ayahuasca were prepared by members of the Santo Daime community, consisting of the stalks of B. caapi combined with the washed leaves of P. viridis, boiled and concentrated for several hours. The resulting brew was stored in a refrigerator until the day of the experimental session. The batch used in the experiment contained 0.8 mg/mL DMT, 0.21 mg/mL harmine, and no harmaline.

Participants were admitted to an inpatient psychiatric unit for 2 weeks prior to ayahuasca administration as part of the open-label trial. During this time, participants were not under the influence of any psychiatric medication or recreational drugs. The experimental session, which was performed individually, lasted on average 4 h. Each participant drank 120-200 mL of ayahuasca (2.2 mL/kg body weight), followed by administration of the psychological rating scales. During measurements, volunteers remained seated in a comfortable recliner in a quiet, dimly lit room. After the end of the session, patients remained under observation for 24 h; if no complications were observed, they were discharged. The BPRS, YMRS, HAM-D and MADRS scales were completed by a psychiatrist with clinical experience and training in the use of these scales, at the following time points: 10 minutes (-10) before AYA administration (baseline); 40 min (+40), 80 min (+80), 140 min (+140), and 180 min (+180) after AYA administration; and on days 1 (D1), 7 (D7), 14 (D14), and 21 (D21) after ayahuasca administration.

Results:
Adverse effects:
- Ayahuasca was well tolerated by all participants. With the exception of vomiting, participants did not spontaneously report any other adverse effect. Vomiting was reported by 50% of the participant, and this emetic effect was considered by participants as an integral part of the effects produced by ayahuasca, and none did consider vomiting as causing severe discomfort.
- Participants considered the effects of ayahuasca on thought content and sensory perception mild and short-lived, and none reported dysphoric manifestations associated with the psychoactive effects of ayahuasca.
- Blood pressure increased moderately and nonsignificantly.

Effects:
- The average baseline HAM-D (Hamilton Rating Scale for Depression) score of the volunteers was 17.56 (a moderate level of depression). At D1, there was a 62% decrease in the mean score, which was statistically significant. This decrease was even more pronounced by D7 (72%, $p = 0.01$). However, on D14, the level of symptoms increased, and although the symptom score remained 45% below baseline, this difference was not statistically significant ($p = 0.11$). On D21, there was a further significant decrease in depressive symptoms ($p = 0.01$).
- The greatest score changes were observed for items related to depressed mood, feelings of guilt, suicidal ideation, and difficulties at work/activities, i.e., those associated with typical depressive symptoms.
- Regarding Montgomery-Åsberg Depression Rating Scale (MADRS) scores, results were similar to those observed for the HAM-D scale. The average baseline score of the volunteers was 23.5 points. At +180, there was a significant decrease in MADRS scores (38%, $p = 0.01$). On D1, a more robust decrease was observed ($p = 0.003$), and the average score on D7 was 82% below baseline ($p = 0.009$). On D14, a significant increase in symptoms was observed ($p = 0.001$), although a subsequent

significant decrease occurred on D21 (p = 0.002).
- As observed with the HAM-D scale, the most significant score changes were observed for items related to apparent and expressed sadness, pessimistic thinking, suicidal ideation, and difficulty concentrating.
- Regarding the Brief Psychiatric Rating Scale (BPRS), participants were generally asymptomatic on the withdrawal-retardation (BPRS-WR), thinking disorder (BPRS-TD), and activation (BPRS-A) subscales at baseline. Ayahuasca administration produced nonsignificant increases in the scores of these subscales, with effect peaking at 80 min. Although nonsignificant, the increase in the scores suggests that ayahuasca produced mild psychoactive effects.
- On the Anxious-Depression BPRS subscale (BPRSAD), participants demonstrated higher scores at baseline, likely due to the presence of depressed mood, feelings of guilt, and psychic anxiety, which are typical symptoms of the underlying psychopathology. Throughout the experiment, the presence of these symptoms varied, but values remained lower as compared to baseline. At +140, these symptoms were significantly reduced (p = 0.02) and remained so (72% below baseline) until D7, when they began to increase but still remained significantly lower than baseline values.
- Regarding the YMRS scale, participants exhibited no significant changes in symptoms throughout the treatment.

Discussion:
- Ayahuasca was well tolerated by all patients, suggesting that it can be safely administered to depressed patients. This result corroborates previous studies reporting a good tolerability profile for ayahuasca administration to healthy volunteers. The nonsignificant increases in blood pressure and high prevalence of vomiting replicate previous findings in human studies (Riba et al, 2001; Riba et al, 2003; dos Santos et al, 2011; dos Santos et al, 2012; Riba et al, 2006; dos Santos et al, 2013; dos Santos et al, 2007; Riba et al, 2005).
- In future studies, it could be be interesting to try to reduce the emetic effect of ayahuasca by premedicating with an antiemetic. However, this possibility should be explored with caution, considering that ayahuasca alkaloids could interact with antiemetic drugs. Another possibility could be to administer ayahuasca in different formulations. Freeze-dried ayahuasca appears to produce less vomiting than oral (Riba et al, 2001 and Riba et al, 2003)
- Osório et al (2014) concluded that ayahuasca had significant and impressive anti depressive effects, since score reductions were observed in both the HAM-D and MADRS scales on D1 and D7, and these effects lasted for several days.Furthermore these changes showed a

profile that was very similar across participants, regardless of the prior level of depression, i.e., the severity of the current depressive episode. This were consistent with the findings of dos Santos et al (2007).
- The statistically significant reductions in BPRS-AD scores from D1 to D21 suggest that ayahuasca produced antidepressive and anxiolytic effects. This is too consistent with the findings in dos Santos et al (2007).
- The absence of statistically significant effects on BPRS-TD scores could be explained by the DMT concentration found in the ayahuasca batch (0.08 mg/mL), which was lower than DMT doses used in previous studies that reported significant psychotropic effects of ayahuasca (0.53 mg/ mL DMT) (Riba et al, 2003 and Riba et al, 2006). The nonsignificant effects of ayahuasca on the BPRS-TD subscale suggest that changes in sensory perception and thought content may not be essential for therapeutic effects.
- Considering currently available antidepressive medications which often takes several weeks to show an effect, do the fast-acting antidepressant action of ayahuasca seem impressive.
- Early academic research on classical psychedelics was designed considering the powerful influences of set and setting (see chapter one) on the effects of this class of substances. Considering this background, the researchers carried out the study in a friendly environment, which may have reduced the probability of dysphoric reactions.
- An important limitations of the present open-label study include the small sample size, the absence of a systematic inquiry about side effects, and the lack of placebo and control groups. Although patients did not spontaneously report adverse effects other than vomiting, the lack of a systematic assessment of adverse effects may have reduced the likelihood of registering more subtle effects, such as impacts on cognition.
- Osório et al (2014) recommended that future studies should assess the possible adverse effects of ayahuasca in clinical populations by using other subjective measures, such as visual analogue scales and other scales that measure hallucinogenic effects, explore other variables that could be modified by ayahuasca administration, and include a control group.

Conclusion:
Osório et al (2014) concluded that the findings of this preliminary study demonstrated the potential antidepressant and anxiolytic effects of ayahuasca. These findings suggest that ayahuasca may represent a powerful new substance for the treatment of depressive and anxiety symptoms.

Sanches et al (2016). Antidepressant Effects of a Single Dose of

Edited by Dr. Oliver Rumle Hovmand

Ayahuasca in Patients With Recurrent Depression A SPECT Study.

Methods:

Sanches et al (2016) were conducted by the same team that published Osório et al (2014). They recruited seventeen participants (14 women) with a diagnosis of recurrent major depression disorder, for an open-label study investigating the antidepressive properties of ayahuasca. Three participants were experiencing a current mild depressive episode, 13 a current moderate episode, and 1 a current severe depressive episode. All did not present a therapeutic response to their current antidepressive drug and were thus without any psychopharmacological medication. Participants were educated about ayahuasca. Participants were free of current somatic illness or pregnancy, as assessed by medical interview, physical examination, and laboratory tests. A diagnosis of bipolar or psychotic disorder, presence of active psychotic symptoms, and a previous history of mania or hypomania induced by antidepressant or substance use were considered exclusion criteria.

The ayahuasca were obtained from the Brazilian religious organization Santo Daime, and were the same used in Osório et al (2014) and contained 0.8 mg/mL DMT, 0.21 mg/mL harmine, and no harmaline. Each participant drank a single dose of 120 to 200 mL of ayahuasca (2.2 ml/kg), which were a dose commonly used in the Santo Daime and União do Vegetal churches. Thus, the range of alkaloid content in individual doses was 96 to 160 mg DMT and 25 to 42 mg harmine.

Participants were admitted to an inpatient psychiatric unit for two weeks prior to ayahuasca administration. During this time they did not take any psychiatric medication or recreational drugs. Except for the initial information on the effects of ayahuasca, there was no formal preparation sessions prior to drug administration. Non-drug factors that are commonly present in ritualized and religious contexts, such as singing or listening to music, were excluded from the session. Ayahuasca was administered in a quiet dimly lit room, where volunteers remained seated in a comfortable reclining chair. The session was performed individually and lasted 4 h, and no psychological intervention was included after drug effects had subsided. Patients remained under observation for 24 h after drug intake, and if no complications were noticed they were discharged.

Depressive symptoms were assessed with the Hamilton Depression Rating Scale (HAM-D) and the Montgomery-Åsberg Depression Rating Scale (MADRS), maniac symptoms with the Young Mania Rating Scale (YMRS), general psychiatric symptoms with the Brief Psychiatric Rating Scale

(BPRS), and dissociative symptoms with the Clinician Administered Dissociative States Scale (CADSS). Scales were completed 10 minutes before ayahuasca administration (baseline) and 40, 80, 140, and 180 minutes after drug intake. The HAM-D, MADRS, and BPRS scales were also completed 1 (D1), 7 (D7), 14 (D14), and 21 (D21) days after ayahuasca administration. The effects of ayahuasca on regional cerebral blood flow were assessed by single photon emission tomography (SPECT) imaging performed before drug intake and eight hours after treatment. Adverse effects were recorded by spontaneous verbal reports, and blood pressure and heart rate were measured 10 minutes before ayahuasca administration and 40, 80, 140, and 180 minutes after drug intake.

Results:
Adverse effects:
- Blood pressure and heart rate were nonsignificantly increased. Vomiting, reported by 47% of the volunteers, was the only adverse effect recorded. No dysphoric effects were reported. Volunteers were calm and relaxed during acute drug effects, and considered the ayahuasca session as a pleasant experience.

Effects:
- Average baseline score in the HAM-D scale was 19.24 (SD = 5.52), (a moderate level of depression), and 25.6 points (SD = 7.6) in the MADRS scale. Administration of ayahuasca was associated with significant HAM-D and MADRS score decreases from 80 to 180 minutes ($P < 0.01$) and from D1 to D21 ($P = 0.000$). At D21, average score in the HAM-D scale was 7.56 (SD = 4.7) (a mild level of depression).
- Significant score increases in the CADSS scale were observed from 40 to 80 minutes ($P < 0.01$) after ayahuasca intake, while no significant changes in YMRS scores were observed. Ayahuasca administration was also associated with significant score decreases in the Anxious-Depression (from 40 to 180 minutes, $P < 0.01$; and from D1 to D21, $P = 0.000$), Thinking Disorder (180 minutes, $P < 0.05$; and at D1, D14, and D21, $P < 0.05$), and Withdrawal-Retardation (from D1 to D21, $P < 0.05$) subscales of the BPRS.
- Ayahuasca administration was associated with significant ($P < 0.01$) activation of the left nucleus accumbens, right insula and left subgenual area.

Discussion:
- Ayahuasca was well tolerated. No significant cardiovascular effects were observed after ayahuasca intake, and vomiting was the only adverse

effect recorded. However, patients did not consider vomiting as causing severe discomfort. Moreover, ayahuasca psychoactive effects were considered mild and short-lived, and no dysphoric effects were reported. Indeed, volunteers were calm and relaxed under the effects of ayahuasca, and considered it as a pleasant experience.
- Administration of ayahuasca was associated with rapid and sustained antidepressive effects. Results were similar across volunteers, regardless of the severity of the current depressive episode.
- Significant score decreases in HAM-D, MADRS, and Anxious-Depression BPRS subscale scores were observed during acute drug effects and from D1 to D21 and were related to depressed mood, sadness, anxiety, feelings of guilt, suicidal ideation, difficulties at work/activities, pessimistic thinking, and difficulty concentrating. Improvements in emotional withdrawal and blunted affect were (Thinking Disorder and Withdrawal-Retardation BPRS subscales) were also observed.
- Ayahuasca induced significant score increases in the CADSS scale at 40 to 80 minutes, suggesting increased psychoactivity in the same time point previously associated with peak ayahuasca psychoactive effects and DMT plasma levels (Riba et al, 2003; Riba et al, 2006; McKenna et al 2015).
- No significant changes in YMRS and Activation BPRS subscale scores were observed after ayahuasca intake, suggesting an absence of maniac-like effects.
- A major limitation of the study were the lack of a randomized or double-blinded protocol, and a placebo or other comparator group. Moreover, it is important to note that the controlled clinical setting in which the experiments took place is different from the typical ritual context of ayahuasca consumption, which may impact the generalizability of the findings (Moreno et al, 1998 and Tupper et al, 2014).
- Sanches et al (2016) suggested future research should utilise a randomized, double-blind, placebo-controlled design, and investigate whether or how a ceremonial/ritual context may impact therapeutic outcomes.
- Ayahuasca administration was also associated with increased blood perfusion in the nucleus accumbens, insula, and subgenual area, brain regions involved in the regulation of mood and emotional states. Hypoactivation of these brain regions is usually associated with depression, while increased activation is usually associated with antidepressive effects (Pizzagalli et al, 2009; Fitzgerald et al, 2008; Bewernick, 2010; Merkl et al, 2013; Drevets et al, 2008). Interestingly, ayahuasca increased blood perfusion in the anterior insula of healthy

volunteers, but no significant changes were observed in the subgenual area or nucleus accumbens (Riba et al, 2006). These data suggested that Sanches et als (2016) results may be specific to depressive patients.

Ayahuasca for substance dependence:

Anecdotal clinician reports as well as naturalistic studies suggest ayahuasca may have positive effects on substance use disorders, and when used appropriately does not appear to carry risks of abuse or dependence (Halpern et al, 2008; Fabregas et al, 2010; Loizaga-Velde et al, 2014; Doering-Silveira et al, 2005; Da Silveira et al, 2005; Morgenstern et al, 1994). Ayahuasca may enable sustained abstinence from alcohol, barbiturates, sedatives, cocaine, amphetamines, and solvents, though most continue to use marijuana (Fabregas et al, 2010). Hamill et al (2018) did in their paper make the case of ayahuasca in the treatment of addiction:

Compared to matched controls, regular participants in Brazilian ayahuasca church ceremonies scored significantly lower on the Addictions Severity Index subscales of Alcohol Use and Psychiatric Status (Fabregas et al, 2010). Doering-Silveira *et al (2005)* found that adolescents from a Brazilian ayahuasca-using church had less recent alcohol use (32.5%) compared to adolescents who had never used ayahuasca (65.1%). It is off course hard to separate whether these effects were from the ayahuasca, involvement in a supportive community, or both (Fabregas et al, 2010). Barbosa et al (2009) suggested that based on their findings, administration of hallucinogens in both clinical settings and religious settings can provide benefits.

Possible biological mechanism in the treatment of dependence:

Liester & Prickett (2012) did in their paper suggest two hypotheses to explain ayahuasca's possible anti-addictive properties:

1. Ayahuasca reduces brain dopamine levels or activity in the mesolimbic dopamine pathway, decreasing the reward associated with an addictive substance. DMT is a known 5-HT_{2A} receptor agonist and 5-HT_{2A} receptor agonism is known to inhibit dopamine release in the mesolimbic, nigrostriatal, and mesocortical pathways. Reduced brain dopamine also fits with elevated prolactin levels with ayahuasca use (Callaway et al, 1999). The opposite is also true as illustrated by atypical antipsychotics, which have 5-HT_{2A} receptor antagonist activity and exhibit reduced dopamine blockade (70-80% blockade) compared to typical antipsychotics (90%) which have little action at serotonin receptors (Stahl et al, 2008).

2. Reduced dopamine in reward pathways impairs the synaptic plasticity involved in addiction development and maintenance.
3. The introspection, self-realizations, and healing of past traumas afforded by an ayahuasca experience offer better understanding of consequences and improved decision- making, empowering the individual to abstain.
4. Ayahuasca facilitates transcendent experiences; the authors give the example of Bill Wilson, founder of Alcoholics Anonymous, having such an experience (not ayahuasca- induced) and being able to give up alcohol.

Possible psychological mechanism in the treatment of addiction:
Liester & Prickett (2012) did in their paper also suggest two hypotheses to explain ayahuasca's possible anti-addictive properties on a psychological level:

1. The introspection, self-realisations, and healing of past traumas afforded by an ayahuasca experience offer better understanding of consequences and improved decision-making, empowering the individual to abstain.
2. Ayahuasca facilitates transcendent experiences; the authors give the example of Bill Wilson, founder of Alcoholics Anonymous, having such an experience, although not ayahuasca- induced, and being able to give up alcohol.

Previous clinical research:
No clinical research have been conducted on the subject. But Thomas et al (2013) carried out a preliminary observational study (n=12) of the "Working with Addiction and Stress" retreats in Canada, which combined four days of group counselling with two expert-led ayahuasca ceremonies. Statistically significant ($p < 0.05$) improvements were demonstrated for scales assessing hopefulness, empowerment, mindfulness, and quality of life meaning and outlook subscales. Self-reported alcohol, tobacco and cocaine use declined, although cannabis and opiate use did not; reported reductions in problematic cocaine use were statistically significant. All study participants reported positive and lasting changes from participating in the retreats, which included six months follow-up.

MDMA

MDMA, also known as the street drug Ecstasy or Molly, is a psychoactive compound with structural similarities to both amphetamine and the hallucinogenic phenethylamine mescaline (Grob and Poland, 1995).
When discussing use of MDMA is it important to distinguish between use of MDMA (a known substance) and use of the street-drug labelled Ecstasy or Molly which might contain only MDMA, but might be anything from rat-poison to methamfetaimne. In this text MDMA refers to MDMA used in controlled studies, where the researchers know they are working with MDMA, and Ecstasy refers to drugs in studies where none knows which drug it actually is (often self-reported data).
MDMA is a laboratory-synthesized compound that does not exist on its own in nature. Even though MDMA has been illegal in the United States since the mid-1980s, there were 0.8 million past-year initiates who reported first-time Ecstasy use in 2013 (Substance Abuse and Mental Health Services Administration, 2014).

MDMA

A brief history of MDMA:
The following is the history as summed up by Danforth et al (2015): MDMA was developed as a byproduct of a styptic compound at Merck in Germany in 1912. University and industry based medicinal chemists started conducting initial scientific investigations during the 1970s after chemist Alexander Shulgin began exploring MDMA's potential to create controllable altered states of consciousness. Despite reported therapeutic potential (Greer and Tolbert, 1986; Grinspoon and Bakalar, 1986), concerns about potential neurotoxicity resulted in suppression of FDA-approved research with human subjects in clinical investigations. Gross errors in reporting on MDMA's effects, side effects, and risk factors in non-human primate studies (e.g., Ricaurte et al., 2003), in addition to problems with interspecies scaling algorithms leading to overdosing by an order of magnitude in animal studies (Baumann et al., 2007), have contributed to confusion about which policies and approaches are optimal regarding regulation and research.

Early investigators noted MDMA's capacity to help people talk openly and honestly about themselves and their relationships, without defensive conditioning intervening (Greer and Tolbert, 1986; Stolaroff, 2004). For several hours, anxiety and fear appeared to decrease, even in subjects who were chronically constricted and apprehensive.
Proponents saw the therapeutical-benefits of MDMA, compared to classic hallucinogens, making it uniquely suited as an adjunct to therapy. It was comparatively mild, shorter acting, and induced
an enhanced ability to facilitate heightened states of introspection, all without distracting cognitive distortions and alterations in perception, body image, and sense of self commonly seen with classic hallucinogens, such as LSD, psilocybin, and mescaline. Users were reported as losing defensive anxiety and feeling more emotionally open thus giving them access to feelings and thoughts not ordinarily available to them. In informal settings, MDMA was reported to be useful in treating a wide range of conditions, including post-traumatic stress, phobias, psychosomatic disorders, depression, suicidality, drug addiction, relationship difficulties and the psychological distress of terminal illness (Adamson and Metzner, 1988; Downing, 1986; Greer and Tolbert, 1986; Grinspoon and Bakalar, 1986; Riedlinger and Riedlinger, 1994). Lasting improvement was often reported in patients' self-esteem, ability to communicate with significant others, capacity for achieving empathic rapport, interest in and capacity for insight, strengthened capacity for
trust and intimacy, and enhanced therapeutic alliance (Grinspoon and Bakalar, 1986).

Formal hearings commenced in 1985 to determine MDMA's legal status. Weighing the interests of the therapeutic community against the growing perception of MDMA's abuse liability and the threat it posed to public health and safety, the U.S. Drug Enforcement Administration (DEA) eventually ordered that it be placed in the most restrictive category, Schedule I, in 1986 (Lawn, 1986).
In the decades following the DEA scheduling, discord and divisiveness escalated in the research world. At the center of the debate was the question of whether or not MDMA use caused neurotoxicity resulting in brain damage. Histopathological findings in animal studies with repeated "binge administration" injections demonstrated that distal serotonergic axonal degeneration could result with doses much higher than recreational users consume (Sumnall, 2006). Implications of such pre-clinical findings are further confounded by observations of proximal axonal regeneration, cell body sparing, and absence of standard laboratory markers of neurotoxicity. Some studies suggested that even modest use could lead to irreparable organic and psychiatric damage, which included emotional and memory deficits, although these reports were often marred by flawed research methodologies, questionable data analyses, and biased conclusions (Danforth and Grob, 2009; Grob, 2000, Grob 2005; LeVay, 2008)

Pharmacology:
MDMA is primarily a potent releaser of serotonin, and an inhibitor of presynaptic serotonin, dopamine, and norepinephrine (de la Torre et al., 2004). In addition MDMA also produces a robust increase in the neurohormone oxytocin (OT) (Dumont et al., 2009). Pharmacologically it shares many effects with amphetamine type drugs, with a chemical structure that also resembles the classic hallucinogen mescaline. The primary mode of action of MDMA is as an indirect serotonergic agonist, increasing the amount of serotonin released into the synaptic space. MDMA interacts with the serotonin transporter, and is transported into the nerve terminal, facilitating the release of serotonin. After oral ingestion, MDMA is readily absorbed from the gastrointestinal tract.

At doses of at least 1 mg/kg (or approximately 70 mg) and higher, active doses of MDMA alter mood and cognition and produce slight alterations in perception (Dumont and Verkes, 2006; Liechti et al., 2001). Its onset of action is within 30–45 min of intake, and effects peak 90 to 120 min after oral administration, and they are near to or at pre-drug levels 3 to 6 h later (Lamers et al., 2003; Tancer and Johanson, 2001; Vollenweider, 1998). Sub-acute effects may occur one to three days after drug administration, but are no longer apparent seven to 14 days later (Harris et al., 2002; Huxster et al.,

2006; Pirona and Morgan, 2010). The elimination half-life is approximately 7 h. MDMA's primary metabolite, 3-4 methylenedioxyamphetamine (MDA), has a longer half-life of approximately 16–38 h. Primary enzymatic activity responsible for the metabolism of MDMA occurs at the hepatic cytochrome P45 CYP2D6 enzyme. MDMA is metabolized in a non-linear manner with relatively small increases in dose causing disproportionate elevation in MDMA plasma concentration, consequently necessitating vigilance for the development of signs of acute adverse reactions (Harris et al., 2002; Mas et al., 1999).

Physiological safety:
MDMA appears to be physiologically safe when administered in a clinical setting to healthy individuals (e.g., Mithoefer et al., 2011, Mithoefer et al, 2013; Oehen et al., 2013, Grob, 1998; Grob et al., 1996; Lieb et al., 2002, Check, 2004; Doblin, 2002; Hysek et al., 2012; Lieb et al., 2002; von Sydow et al., 2002).
MDMA had been administered to more than 1133 research subjects, in both Phase 1 and Phase 2 studies. Only one expected severe adverse effect that was probably drug-related has been reported, which was an increase in frequency of premature ventricular contractions experienced during treatment, which resolved with full recovery to baseline after the effects of MDMA ceased. No acute cardiac damage occurred, and hospitalization during this event was a cautionary measure. No unexpected, life-threatening severe adverse effect have occurred in published or ongoing research studies (Danforth et al, 2015).

Even through, some possible risk are associated with the use of MDMA, which require further discussion: These were summed up by Danforth et al (2015) in their review:

MDMA acutely increases cortisol, prolactin, adrenocorticotropic hormone and neurohormone oxytocin concentrations in a dose-dependent manner (Farré et al., 2004; Grob et al., 1996; Harris et al., 2002; Mas et al., 1999; Parrott et al., 2008, Dumont et al., 2009). Oxytocin is considered a crucial effect of the therapeutic effects of MDMA, since it is a neuropeptide associated with pair bonding and social affiliation in mammals, that too attenuates amygdalar response to anxiogenic stimuli (Adolphs et al., 2005; Bartz and Hollander, 2006). Exogenous oxytocin administration is associated with increased interpersonal trust and changes in social perception, including attenuated reactivity to threatening faces (Domes et al., 2007a, Domes et al 2007b; Kosfeld et al., 2005). Oxytocin administration also improves empathic accuracy in some individuals who are shy or lack adequate social skills (Guastella et al., 2010). Alterations in oxytocin signaling have also been proposed as a potential mechanism for the underlying neurological basis for the core social differences in autism and have been implicated as a possible novel therapy for enhancing social adaptability (Bartz and Hollander, 2006). MDMA elevates oxytocin in peripheral blood (Dumont et al., 2009; Hysek et al., 2012; Wolff et al., 2006), which is an imperfect but somewhat reliable indicator of elevated oxytocin in the brain (Bartz and Hollander, 2006). Findings of an association between elevated oxytocin and detectable MDMA in peripheral blood were first reported in a naturalistic study of London nightclub attendees with and without detectable plasma MDMA levels (Wolff et al., 2006). Dumont et al (2009) reproduced these results in humans and found that MDMA significantly elevated peripheral plasma OT levels in a placebo-controlled study in healthy volunteers, in addition to a positive association between elevated levels of oxytocin and prosocial feelings. Hysek et al (2012) replicated these results and further reported that administering of a SSRI attenuated the effects of MDMA on oxytocin levels, suggesting a serotonergic mechanism in producing elevated (Hysek et al., 2012). The effects of MDMA on oxytocin could be partially responsible for changes in empathy (Bedi et al, 2010). However, the multi-level effects of MDMA on monoaminergic signaling and oxytocin, combined with a therapeutic setting focused on enhancing functional skills, are more likely to provide the opportunity for a corrective emotional experience greater than oxytocin alone, and could be useful in the treatment of social anxiety in autistic adults (Danforth et al, 2015).

Hyperthermia has occurred in people using Ecstasy in unsupervised and non-medical conditions -often involving vigorous dancing in hot, underventilated spaces without adequate access to water. Although rare, it is one of the most frequently reported severe adverse effect occurring in Ecstasy users (Henry and Rella, 2001; Liechti et al., 2005). The opposite can also be a problem. In rare but sometimes lethal cases, naïve Ecstasy-users have consumed too much water without ingesting required amounts of electrolytes, leading to water intoxication (hyponatremia) (Milroy, 2011).

Taking MDMA with monoamine oxidase inhibitors (MAOIs) or with certain antiretroviral medications can induce a life-threatening hypertensive crisis (Harrington et al., 1999; Smilkstein et al., 1987).

MDMA produces sympathomimetic effects that include elevation in blood pressure and heart rate. Elevation in blood pressure above 140/ 110 or higher occurred in approximately 5% of research participants receiving at least 100 mg MDMA in research studies, but were self-limiting (Downing, 1986; Grob, 1998; Grob et al., 1996; Lester et al., 2000; Liechti et al., 2001;

Mas et al., 1999; Vollenweider et al., 1998). This can lead to risks and complications, and first-time users with congenital heart defects are especially vulnerable to cardiac events (Hall and Henry, 2006). Due to properly conducted medical screening, there have been no such events to date in any clinical trial of MDMA.

Hepatotoxicity (liver disease or damage) was reported in approximately 16% of 199 case reports from non-medical, uncontrolled Ecstasy users, making it the third most adverse effects reported in the literature (Baggott et al., 2001). No cases of liver disease or hepatotoxicity have occurred clinical trials with MDMA.

Subjective Effects:
MDMA facilitates states of positive mood as well as transient anxiety (Camí et al., 2000; Harris et al., 2002; Liechti et al., 2001; Tancer & Johanson, 2001). MDMA users report feeling more talkative and friendly after receiving MDMA, and at least one research team informally reported increased feelings of closeness to others (Vollenweider et al., 1998). However, subjects have also reported feeling anxious and undergoing negatively experienced derealization, including increased anxiety related to loss of control and experiences of racing or blocked thoughts (Camí et al., 2000; Liechti et al., 2001; Vollenweider et al., 1998). Subjects receiving MDMA experienced euphoria, positive mood, vigor and positively experienced derealization, and they also experienced anxiety, tension and dysphoria, as concern over losing control over the self (Camí et al., 2000; Harris et al., 2002; Tancer & Johanson, 2001; Liechti et al., 2001). Available data is unclear regarding whether the increases in positive and negative mood occur simultaneously or occur at different times throughout the duration of MDMA effects; data in reports from two different teams suggest that peaks in negative mood may precede peaks for positive mood (Tancer & Johanson 2001; Liechti and Vollenweider, 2000).

Vollenweider et al (1998) reported that MDMA produced acute "increased responsiveness to emotions, a heightened openness, and a sense of closeness to other people". When combined with psychotherapy that supports one or more of these effects, MDMA permits individuals to confront and consider emotionally intense memories, thoughts or feelings and perhaps through changes in mood and perception increases empathy and compassion for others and one's self (Bouso et al., 2008; Greer and Tolbert, 1986; Mithoefer et al., 2011).

Abuse and dependence:
MDMA is not considered physically addictive, but there have been reports

of both acute and chronic psychological reactions in vulnerable individuals (Parrott, 2007). Nevertheless, these cases generally have been in the context of frequent polydrug use, Ecstasy use of dubious quality, adverse environmental settings, and significant underlying psychological vulnerability (Grob, 2005).

Even though Ecstasy is considered a drug of abuse, pure MDMA is not considered a drug of dependence on the order of opioids, amphetamines, methamphetamines, and cocaine. This lack of dependence is evidenced by rodents and nonhuman primates self-administering MDMA at much lower rates than the aforementioned drugs (De La Garza et al., 2007; Schenk, 2009), and even heavy Ecstasy users fail to report the intensive patterns of use seen with other stimulants. Hence, MDMA possesses moderate abuse liability that is greater than that for serotonergic hallucinogens but less than that for stimulants. Nutt et al. (2010) have studied the relative harm of a variety of drugs and have identified MDMA as being among the least dangerous recreational compounds.

Conducting MDMA-mediated therapy:

The following section is based on the Manual for MDMA-Assisted Psychotherapy in the Treatment of Posttraumatic Stress Disorder by Mithoefer (2017). It represents a modification of earlier work with psychedelics (Grof, 2001; Pahnke et al., 1971), which was subsequently adapted for use with MDMA (Greer and Tolbert, 1998; Metzner and Adamson, 2001).

The basic premise of this treatment approach is that the therapeutic effect is not due simply to the physiological effects of the medicine; rather, it is the result of an interaction between the effects of the medicine, the therapeutic setting and the mindsets of the participant and the therapists. As explained earlier, MDMA produces an experience that appears to temporarily reduce fear, increase the range of positive emotions toward self and others, and increase interpersonal trust without clouding the sensorium or inhibiting access to emotions. The hypothesis then is that MDMA may catalyze therapeutic processing by allowing participants to stay emotionally engaged while revisiting traumatic experiences without being overwhelmed by anxiety or other painful emotions.

In the pre-prohibition literature and the emerging modern clinical research, participants are able to experience and express fear, anger, and grief as part of the therapeutic process with less likelihood of either feeling overwhelmed by these emotions or of avoiding them by dissociation or emotional numbing. In addition, MDMA can enable a heightened state of empathic rapport that facilitates the therapeutic process and allows for a corrective experience of secure attachment and collaboration with the therapists.

At some point during the MDMA experience, feelings of empathy, love, and deep appreciation often emerge in conjunction with a clearer perspective of the trauma as a past event and a heightened awareness of the support and safety that exist in the present.
Research participants have said that being able to successfully process painful emotions during MDMA-assisted psychotherapy has given them a template for feeling and expressing pain that has changed their relationship to their emotions. MDMA may also provide access to meaningful spiritual experiences and other transpersonal experiences, release of tensions in the body, and a sense of healing on a non-verbal level that are incompletely understood, but are considered important by many participants.

The therapists work with the participant to establish a sense of safety, trust, and openness, as well as to emphasize the value of trusting the wisdom of the participant's innate capacity to heal the wounds of trauma. Greer and Tolbert suggested that "the relationship should be oriented toward a general healing for the client, who should feel safe enough in the therapists' presence to open fully to new and challenging experiences." Establishing these conditions requires that the therapists carefully set the parameters of treatment and prepare the participant before each MDMA-assisted session, and then provide appropriate support following the session so that the experience can be successfully integrated.

Who might be fit for MDMA use in a clinical setting?
Danforth et al (2015) listed the following criteria for enrolment in their clinical studies:
Participants must be able to safely discontinue any psychotropic medications they are currently being prescribed. They must also have healthy cardiovascular function, as per electrocardiogram and medical history, and not suffer from diabetes, glaucoma, seizures, hypertension, liver disease, glaucoma or any other condition that the investigator or medical monitor believes might interfere with subject participation and safety.
Participants must be without active substance use disorders, and without family history in first-degree relatives of schizophrenia or bipolar I disorder, or participant diagnoses of active or past psychotic disorder, borderline personality disorder, dissociative identity disorder, eating disorder or active suicidal ideation. Prior to treatment, all participants must have a physical examination, EKG, normal BP, negative pregnancy test and normal blood-works.

Preparation of the MDMA session:
Prior to the first treatment session, all participants receive several

preparatory psychotherapy sessions, where the structure of treatment and range of possible effects will be discussed, as will any past or current salient issues in the subject's life. These preparatory sessions also focus on establishing effective rapport between the participant and the treatment team.

Participants can with benefit receive core mindfulness skills training as part of their therapy (Linehan, 1993). An anticipated advantage of this intervention is according to Danforth et al (2015) it will provide vocabulary, concepts, and skills that support research subjects with transitioning into MDMA-influenced cognitive and affective states as well as communicating with others during a novel, often ineffable, altered state of consciousness.

The therapeutic approach:

MDMA-mediated therapy employs a non-directive approach. The overall approach does include some instances of more directive communication from the therapists, but the essence of what is meant by "non-directive" rests in the timing of interventions. It is not a prohibition against more active engagement under appropriate circumstances. In fact, there are occasions when failure to offer direction in a sensitive way would be problematic, just as being overly directive is problematic.

The therapist should allow the participant's own process to unfold spontaneously. Therapists must allow ample time for this unfolding before offering direction. For example, if a participant is feeling stuck, the initial approach should be to encourage them to experience and express this stuck feeling as fully as possible, trusting that their own so-called "inner healing intelligence" will guide their response.

"Inner healing intelligence" is a concept used throughout Dr. Mithoefers manual, to help put the participant in touch with their innate ability to heal and grow. He uses the following analogy to explain the concept:
"The body knows how to heal itself. If someone goes to the emergency room with a laceration, a doctor can remove obstacles to healing (e.g. remove foreign bodies, infection, etc.) and can help create favorable conditions for healing (e.g. sew the edges of the wound close together), but the doctor does not direct or cause the healing that ensues. The body initiates a remarkably complex and sophisticated healing process and always spontaneously attempts to move toward healing. The psyche too exhibits an innate healing intelligence and capacity"

Likewise, if a participant seems to be avoiding an important subject, the therapists should take note, but should not immediately intervene, allowing time for the possibility that the participant will acknowledge and address the avoidance themselves, which will likely have a more powerful impact coming from the participant rather than as an observation from the therapists. In this way, delaying an intervention may make the intervention unnecessary.

Later in the session, if feelings of being stuck, avoidance, or other significant unresolved aspects of the process persist, it can be helpful for the therapists to offer direction so long as it is done in the spirit of collaborative inquiry and invitation, ultimately leaving the decision whether or not to follow suggestions up to the participant.

The concept of Empathetic Presence and Listening is central to MDMA-mediated therapy. Listening with empathic presence means that the therapists provide a non-judgmental environment that offers the participant permission to talk openly and honestly. It requires that therapists listen beyond spoken words for deeper meanings, acknowledging the participant's suffering, and validate their feelings. Empathic presence also involves appreciating and even rejoicing in the participant's accomplishments and conveying that appreciation. Empathic presence decreases feelings of abandonment and isolation. Empathetic listeners are relaxed but engaged, asking questions and exploring without prying. The listener maintains appropriate eye contact and offers reassuring, appropriate touches if culturally acceptable and agreed upon by participants. Empathic listeners are not hesitant to admit they don't have answers.

They employ means such as minimal encouragement, verbal and non-verbal Invitation rather than direction, paraphrasing, reflecting, emotional labeling, validating, reassurance and waiting and allowing participants to come to conclusions themselves.

They use non-directive communication using invitation rather than direction. For example: "We encourage you to ..."

Preparation of the MDMA session:

The screening and preparation phase begins with informed consent. This period also provides adequate time in non-drug therapy sessions to begin establishing a safe and positive therapeutic alliance, which is an absolute prerequisite for treatment, and will continue to develop throughout the sessions.

During the initial visits, the therapists introduce themselves, explain their interest in this work, and describe their experience in treating PTSD. This interaction establishes a basis for the participants to develop trust in the therapists' experience and their commitment and ability to support the participant throughout the process. Greer and Tolbert note that self-disclosure on the part of the therapist creates a context for collaboration, intimacy, and trust. It also can give the participant a sense of shared identification with the therapists, which can increase personal comfort as

the participant enters a state of heightened vulnerability.
The therapists and the participant should also discuss the participant's previous experiences with MDMA, psychedelic drug use, or other non-ordinary states of consciousness.

The therapists describe the kinds of experience that can be expected during MDMA-assisted session. They enquire further about the participant's expectations, motivations, and concerns, and emphasize their own commitment to support the participant's innate capacity to heal the wounds of the trauma. The therapists may liken the effect of the MDMA to an opportunity to step inside a safe container in which it will be easier for the participant to remain present with their inner experience. The participant should be encouraged to cultivate an attitude of trust in the wisdom and timing of the inner healing process that is catalyzed by this approach.

Rarely, there may be an experimental session in which the participant's traumatic experiences do not come up spontaneously. Therapists should ask for a prior agreement that, if this is the case, they may inquire about the trauma at some point in the session. This agreement applies only to sessions in which the participant is regularly talking to the therapists about their ongoing experiences. If a participant is spending much of the session in a deep non-verbal process that they appear to be handling well but is not inclined to talk about at that time, the therapists should not interrupt the process by requiring discussion about the content. After this kind of experimental session, the participant will typically describe their experience at the end of the day, or during follow-up integrative sessions. It is likely that processing trauma will turn out to have been an important part of the experience.

Office visits as well as treatment sessions will take place in a specially prepared room, which has been designed to minimise sensory distress (e.g., soft lighting, comfortable seating, minimal noise) and to resemble a comfortable living room-like. It should be aesthetically pleasing, with fresh flowers and artwork. Images with powerful negative or disturbing connotations should be avoided.
To whatever degree possible, the setting should be more similar to a comfortably furnished living room than a medical facility. However, the participant should be aware of all safety measures and equipment in place to respond to the unlikely possibility of a medical complication.

Maintaining physical safety includes providing access to treatment for possible reactions to the medicine during or immediately after each treatment session. Most reactions can be dealt with through supportive care, but some, such as a cardiovascular complication, could require additional intervention. Although there have not been any emergencies requiring medical intervention during any MDMA-mediated psychotherapy should be done in a setting where Basic Cardiac Life Support (BCLS) is immediately available and Advanced Cardiac Life Support (ACLS) can be summoned reasonably quickly in the unlikely event of an acute medical problem. The facility should have a means of readily assessing blood pressure and heart rate during the MDMA-assisted session.

Water intake should be monitored to avoid dehydration or water intoxication, and optional snacks and a light meal should be made available two hours after the study drug is administered. The therapists should ensure adequate fluid intake but also make sure that participants do not consume more than 3 L over the course of the MDMA-assisted session. Therapists may also wish to provide electrolyte-containing beverages such as juices instead of water as a means of reducing risk of hyponatremia.

The therapists should inquire about the participant's social support network. Before any MDMA-mediated treatment session, the therapists and participant should consider ways in which the members of the participant's support system could be of help during the time between therapy sessions. The therapists should explain the potential value of sharing information about the treatment sessions with selected individuals, as well as the potential pitfalls of doing so and the importance of using discretion about whom to talk to about their deep personal experience. Some people may have preconceived notions about the use of drugs like MDMA because of its illegal use as "Ecstasy" and they may not understand that "non-ordinary states" may be beneficial in a therapeutic setting. Participants should be advised to consider this possibility before discussing their experiences, especially immediately following experimental sessions when they may be emotionally vulnerable and may feel particularly open and eager to talk about their experience in the session and about their trauma.
It is usually helpful for the participant to have a period of quiet time alone after the MDMA-assisted session for journaling or introspection. Participants should be encouraged to make allowances for this so they don't become overly engaged in social interaction and receiving outside feedback. Taking time alone at this stage can be a valuable beginning of the integration process, and can provide a template for fostering the continued unfolding of the healing process that is expected to occur over the ensuing days and even weeks.

Music should selected to support emotional experience while minimizing suggestion. During MDMA-mediated sessions, the participant is provided with eye shades, headphones, and a preselected program of music. The participant may elect to forgo eyeshades and/or headphones at any time. This choice is not uncommon among people with PTSD, who, at least in the early stages of their participation in the study, may not feel safe if they can't maintain a certain level of vigilance. The participant also has the option to request periods of silence and the therapists have the option to make adjustments in the musical program to fit the unfolding experience. Therapists use music to support the experience without being intrusive. Music selections should be culturally appropriate to the population participating in a particular study. The individual selections within a program of music should vary in tempo and overall volume, so that the program has relatively quiet and tranquil sections as well as relatively active and dramatic sections. The sets can be a progression from music that is relaxing at first, then in succession more active, more emotionally evocative and later quieter and more meditative. The order of play can be changed as needed to fit the general mood and flow of the session. It is important for at least one of the therapy team members to be very familiar with the music so it can be used effectively to support each individual's process. It may be helpful to have some multi-hour playlists prepared, providing a semi-standardized music set. Instrumental music is generally preferable to music with lyrics in a language that the participant understands, but this is not a hard-and-fast rule. There should be a variety of music on hand in case a change is needed from the pre-recorded set. Participants should be told that they are welcome to ask for periods of silence or for a change in music if a piece of music is distracting or doesn't fit well with their process. However, they should be discouraged from devoting ongoing attention to managing the music.

Conduct of the MDMA session:

On the days of the treatment sessions, participants will typically arrive at the clinical research center early in the morning, accompanied by a partner, who has previously committed to driving the subject to and from research sessions, as well as to and from day-after integrative sessions.

When the MDMA is administered, it should be offered to the participant in a bowl or other small container for the participant to pick up themselves and swallow with water. This presentation symbolises the nature of the therapeutic relationship in which the therapists are offering the participant a tool and the participant retains the ability to choose whether to use it. Shortly after MDMA administration, the participant is guided towards a relaxed state and may find it helpful to focus on abdominal breathing. Within approximately 15 minutes of ingesting the MDMA, the participant is encouraged to recline on the futon, use eye shades and headphones, if they are comfortable doing so, and relax into the music selected for the session. The therapist softly reminds the participant to be open to whatever unfolds and trust their innate healing capacity and to ask for whatever they need. From this point on, the MDMA-assisted session consists of periods of inner focus during which the participant attends to their intrapsychic experience without talking, alternating with periods of interaction with the therapists. The ratio of inner focus to interaction is typically approximately 50:50, but varies considerably from session to session. During the periods of inner focus, the therapists maintain a clear empathic presence to support the process. In some cases, the participant may become anxious at the onset of the MDMA.

Diaphragmatic breathing could be used to aid relaxation ("stress inoculation") near the beginning of the MDMA-assisted session if anxiety comes up during the onset of the MDMA effect. In preparatory sessions, the therapists explain that some people feel anxious during this time and others do not. For those who do, the anxiety will be transient and it can be eased by use of the breath to release tension from the body and, as much as possible, to relax into the experience. Later in the MDMA-assisted session, if anxiety or any other intense emotion comes up, rather than trying to relax, it is often most helpful to use the breath to "breathe into" the experience and stay as present with it as possible in order to fully experience, process, and move through it.

The therapists check-in with the participant after 60 minutes if the participant has not talked since the administration of the medication. This check-in reminds the participant of the therapists' presence and provides the therapists with a sense of the participant's inner state. Based on this information, the therapists either encourage the participant to return to an inner focus or to share more about their inner experience. To check-in with the participant at 60 minutes, one of the therapists may put a hand gently on the participant's shoulder (if the participant has previously given permission to be touched in this way) and ask softly. Consider the following example: Therapist: "It's been an hour and we're just checking in to see how you're doing."

As the session progresses, the participant is likely to experience a positive mood and a sense of trust in both self and others. During some sessions, this shift, often accompanied by a sense of gratitude and helpful insights about current life situations, occurs relatively early in the session, before the trauma comes up. These experiences seem to provide a platform from which the participant is then later able to approach the emergence of traumatic memories and painful emotions with a greater sense of strength

and safety that comes with an empathic shift in consciousness.
This expansion in consciousness allows the participant to develop a new sense of mastery over the trauma and the accompanying painful emotions. During other sessions, participants are confronted by traumatic memories relatively early in the session before they have affirming experiences. In this case, affirming experiences are likely to come later in that session, or even in subsequent sessions, and contribute to a sense of resolution and healing and a shift in perspective about the world. What Grof said of work with LSD also applies to MDMA: the medicine functions to some extent as a "nonspecific amplifier" of mental processes. What is usually experienced as difficult, may come to feel intensely sad, frightening, or enraging. What is typically pleasant or affirming, may become associated with intense joy.

MDMA-assisted psychotherapy helps the participant face traumatic memories and process associated thoughts and emotions. As illustrated above, there are often insights about longstanding emotional and behavioural patterns based on early protective responses to underlying rage, grief, and shame. With more self-acceptance and less self-criticism, the participant gains clarity and self-confidence, a sense of self-efficacy, and a less fearful, more open and curious, relationship to unfolding memories, thoughts, and feelings. A sense of inner calm, rather than extreme arousal, on confronting trauma-related material is expected to help the participant examine memories and thoughts more closely and objectively, while at the same time, allowing powerful emotions to surface.

The sense of safety may work in concert with facilitated recall to allow deeper exploration of trauma-related events and their effects on relationships and other aspects of the participant's life. This mechanism is consistent with observations from other methods of therapy that require trauma processing, which to be effective, must be accompanied by a degree of emotional engagement or "fear activation," while avoiding dissociation or overwhelming emotion. This strategy has been referred to as working within the "optimal arousal zone" or "window of tolerance"

As the participant experiences a greater sense of closeness to others, with more trust and intimacy, they may also feel empathy and forgiveness for self and others. Ideally, this progression leads the participant to feel worthy despite the shame or distress caused by the traumatic event or events. Such insights may also help the participant develop greater trust in the therapists and make it easier to talk about inner experience. The participant may also be more likely to comply with any suggestions intended to improve the therapeutic experience or to help the participant stay engaged with a particular element of the experience, such as a difficult memory, feeling, or insight.

During the drug-assisted treatment sessions, both structured and unstructured tasks can be employed, including but not limited to listening to preselected music, working with art supplies, writing in journals, silent introspection, and engaging in rapport building interactions with therapists. Two therapist should be present. The co-therapists, preferably one male and one female to manage potential transference during therapy, will emphasise creating and communicating a setting of safety and support for the participant during periods of inner focus.

The therapists should be prepared to help participants address somatic manifestations of their trauma by becoming aware of, expressing and releasing any blocks, pains or tensions in the body that may arise. This concept should be introduced during the integrative sessions and built upon subsequently. There are many methods that can be used. The following is a discussion of some methods for dealing with somatic manifestations including nurturing touch, focused bodywork, and breathing techniques. The therapists may employ other methods from their own backgrounds that are compatible with this therapeutic approach.
In MDMA-assisted psychotherapy, mindful use of touch can be an important catalyst to healing during both the MDMA-assisted sessions and the follow-up therapy. Touch must always be used with a high level of attention and care, with proper preparation and communication, and with great respect for the participant's needs and vulnerabilities. Any touch that has sexual connotations or is driven by the therapist's needs, rather than the participant's, has no place in therapy and can be counter-therapeutic or even abusive. By the same token, withholding nurturing touch when it is indicated can be counter-therapeutic and, especially in therapy involving non-ordinary states of consciousness, may even be perceived by the participant as abuse by neglect. If the participant wants to touch one of the therapists, the therapist allows for and/or provides touch as long as it is appropriate and nonsexual. Nurturing touch that occurs when the participant is deeply re-connecting with times in life when they needed and did not get it can provide an important corrective experience. Another kind of touch that can be therapeutic is focused bodywork, usually in the form of giving resistance for the participant to push against.

As the effects of the MDMA subside, the therapists may talk with the participant more extensively about what they experienced during the session. The therapists ask if the participant would like to give more detailed feedback on their emotional and psychosomatic status. However, there should be no pressure to do so at this point; it may be left for follow-up sessions.
The therapists encourage the participant to reflect on and accept the validity

of the experience, including any new insights. If the participant expresses any regrets or self-judgment about what occurred during the experimental session the therapists help them to normalise these feelings and provide reassurance.

As the MDMA-assisted session draws to a close, the participant may invite a significant other into the consultation room to join in their integration process. This visit should be discussed and planned for well in advance of the MDMA-assisted sessions. The therapists should meet with the participant and significant other so they can assess the quality of the relationship and the level of the significant other's ability to be appropriately supportive without being directive or intrusive. If there is reason to believe that a visit at this time would interfere with rather than support the integration process, the therapists should advise against contact with the significant other until the next day.

If a significant other is invited to visit, there should be an agreement that they will wait in the waiting room until one of the therapists comes out to talk to them. If, as is sometimes but not usually the case, the significant other has been asked to come before most of the MDMA effects have worn off, the participant should be prepared to wait until the therapists and participant decide it is a good time to invite them into the session room. The participant should be encouraged not to take it personally if, because of the nature of the session, they are not invited in until later than anticipated. When the significant other arrives, one of the therapists (with prior permission from the participant) should meet briefly with them outside the session room to explain the participant's present condition, to ask about any concerns or questions the significant other may have, and to assess their capacity to be empathically present with the participant in their current state of mind.

Toward the end of the session, the therapists discuss with both the participant and significant other some of the after-effects of the MDMA experience and what might be expected over the course of time as the healing process unfolds. This point can be a good time to review understandings about how they may best support each other during this time.

Participants can be discharged when all subjective effects of the drug have remitted, and when the participant feels ready to be without health-professionals.Thus, For the therapy session to conclude effectively, the therapists and participant must agree that the participant is in a safe and stable condition.

The participant can either be discharged to their own home, or be offered to stay at the facility. If the participant leaves the facility is it important that he or she is with someone they trust during the night and following day. The participant should be informed that, though the acute effects of the MDMA have worn off, the effects of the MDMA-assisted session inevitably continue to unfold over the hours and days following the session. Often, the participant is encouraged to write about their experience and/or create artwork with materials provided as ways of continuing to explore and express their unfolding experience. The participant is also encouraged to pay attention to and write down any dreams they remember in the days following the session. The participant is also assured that the therapists will continue to provide support and help in working through and resolving any difficulties. Before leaving, the therapists may review and assist the participant in practicing relaxation and self-soothing techniques that were taught in the introductory sessions. If the participant's distress is not sufficiently decreased by the above measures, the therapists should consider focused bodywork. A "rescue medication" may be administered if significant anxiety persists and all other interventions have failed to reduce anxiety to a tolerable level.

Post-session follow-up:
The day following each of the two experimental treatment sessions, participants will return to the study location for an integrative session, where the content of the previous day's experience will be examined and methods for adjusting back to daily life after treatment will be reviewed. Additional in-person integrative psychotherapy sessions should be scheduled at two week intervals for one month and then again at the six-month follow-up point. Telephone safety checks should occur daily for the week following treatment sessions, overlapping with the 3–4 days for the drug to be excreted from the body.

The ultimate goals of MDMA-assisted psychotherapy are to eliminate symptoms and attain an improved level of wellbeing and functioning. The process of accomplishing these goals continues well beyond the MDMA-assisted sessions themselves and is supported by the follow-up integrative sessions. The importance of integration is emphasised during the introductory therapy sessions, when the participant and therapists discuss the likely trajectory of the therapeutic process. The challenges during the integration stage are to facilitate continued emotional processing and address any difficulties that arise as the experience from the session continues to unfold, and at the same time to help the participant apply any benefits gained in the MDMA-assisted sessions to daily life. These benefits are likely to include valuable insights and perspectives, a broader emotional range, greater resilience, and deepened interpersonal skills. The therapists help the participant weave all aspects of the therapeutic experience into a new relationship with self, with others, and with their traumatic history. This phase of treatment brings these elements together in a cohesive, harmonious way.

Since it is difficult to predict how much difficulty a given participant will have with the integration process, it is important to be alert to possible problems, such as shame and selfjudgment about having revealed secrets or challenging shifts in relationships and family systems as the participant heals and changes. Conversely, the therapists should be open to the possibility of an easy integration that requires minimal intervention beyond empathic listening and sharing appreciation for the participant's healing and growth.

During follow-up integrative sessions, the therapists are present to answer any questions the participant may have, as well as to offer support and encouragement as the participant processes the emotional responses and new perceptions resulting from the MDMA-assisted session. The therapists take a supportive and validating stance toward the participant's experience. They help the participant further explore and develop new insights about their trauma, new perspectives about life and relationships, shifts in their relationship to their own emotions, and the clearing of old thought patterns and reactions that may have outlived their usefulness. They discuss the meaning of the memories, thoughts, feelings, and insights experienced during the MDMA- assisted sessions and how this new meaning will be manifested in daily living. The therapists may offer insights or interpretations regarding the participant's experience, but this should be minimised. Participants should be encouraged to exercise their own judgment about whether any given comment by the therapists may or may not resonate for them and to apply their own discernment about what may be applicable to them and useful for understanding their experience.

MDMA for treatment resistant PTSD:

Possible biological models of psychedelic treatment of PTSD:
This model of treatment is different to most pharmacological interventions, in that its effectiveness appears to be mediated through pharmacological effects augmenting meaningful psychotherapeutic experiences. MDMA might attenuate response to anxiety-provoking thoughts or feelings during recall of trauma memories by reducing activity in the amygdala (Carhart-Harris et al, 2015; Gamma et al, 2000) and insular cortex (Walpola et al, 2017), and simultaneously improve top-down modulation of thoughts and emotions by increasing activity in the prefrontal cortex (Gamma et al, 2000).

Increased functional connectivity between the amygdala and hippocampus during MDMA administration (Carhart-Harris et al, 2015) suggests that reconsolidation of traumatic memories might occur, rendering them less activating during ordinary states (Feduccia et al, 2018). Conversely, veterans with symptomatic PTSD have shown decreased resting state functional connectivity between the amygdala and hippocampus (Sripada et al, 2012). MDMA modulates emotional memory circuits dysfunctional in PTSD (Fredman et al, 2011), and engages neural networks illustrated to be important for other trauma processing therapies (Cisler et al, 2014).

Other proposed models include an explicit role for experiential "regression" and re-examination of past experiences, and non-ordinary or transpersonal experiences in MDMA-assisted psychotherapy (Passie, 2012). MDMA-stimulated decrease in amygdala (Carhart-Harris et al., 2015; Gamma et al., 2000) and insular cortex activity (Walpola et al., 2017) may allow for emotional engagement without overwhelming anxiety during processing of painful traumatic memories. In healthy humans, MDMA acutely modulates brain circuitry important for memory and affective processing, and implicated in the pathophysiology of PTSD (Lanius et al., 2010), including increased resting state functional connectivity between the hippocampus and amygdala and decreased coupling of the medial prefrontal cortex with the hippocampus and posterior cingulate cortex (Carhart-Harris et al., 2015). Given that MDMA modulates emotional memory, neural pathways, fear extinction and memory reconsolidation might play a role in the underlying mechanisms for the positive treatment response (Feduccia and Mithoefer, 2018).

Possible psychological models of psychedelic treatment of PTSD:
Possible mechanisms for the treatment effect demonstrated in the following clinical studies are theorised based on the pharmacological effects of MDMA and its actions in the context of psychotherapy. Subjective effects of MDMA that bolster prosocial feelings and behaviours (Bedi et al., 2010; Hysek et al., 2014; Kamilar-Britt and Bedi, 2015) make unpleasant memories more tolerable (Carhart-Harris et al., 2014), and enhance empathy, self-compassion, (Baggott et al., 2015; Kamboj et al., 2015), and trusting in the pace of processing the experience, could all be beneficial in promoting a strong therapeutic alliance and inducing an optimal state of engagement for effectively processing traumatic memories. Healthy volunteers also report that MDMA can change the significance or meaning of perceptions (Liechti et al., 2001). MDMA-assisted psychotherapy is meant to maintain the optional "window of tolerance" (Mithoefer, 2016; Ogden et al., 2006). An enhanced therapeutic alliance combined with reduced anxiety or discomfort around difficult memories, increased self-

compassion, and openness to expanding meaning of thoughts, feelings or experiences may all contribute toward therapeutic effects. Thus, by increasing prosocial and empathetic feelings, MDMA might improve therapeutic alliance and engagement with difficult psychological material. Similar therapeutic procedures that include attention to setting, a pair of therapists offering non-directive, supportive care and substances that alter consciousness, are also used in psilocybin and ayahuasca research in people with depression (Carhart-Harris et al., 2018; Sanches et al., 2016).

Previous research:
MDMA weren't studied specifically for PTSD in the pre-prohibition era, but in the 1970s, psychotherapists used MDMA-assisted psychotherapy to treat psychological disorders, including anxiety [66]. A few uncontrolled human studies of MDMA in a psychotherapeutic context occurred in the 1980s (Downing et al, 1986; Greer et al, 1986).

Contemporary research:
At the time of writing the following papers have been published on the subject:

Marcela et al (2018). 3,4-Methylenedioxymethamphetamineassisted psychotherapy for treatment of chronic posttraumatic stress disorder: A randomized phase 2 controlled trial.

Methods:
Marcela et al (2018) recruited and randomised 28 participants (19 female) with treatment resistant-PTSD. Most had experienced two or more traumatic events, such as childhood sexual or physical abuse, combat, ritual abuse, assaults, accidents or witnessing a crime. All but one met the criteria for PTSD on the CAPS-IV (all had a score of $\geqslant 50$ on the CAPS-IV), and the average duration of PTSD before enrollment was 29.4 years. All participants had undergone at least one form of psychotherapy, 20 participants had been prescribed drugs for depression, and 15 participants had been prescribed drugs for anxiety. Nearly half of the participants (42.9%) had been diagnosed with major depression disorder, and another quarter with depression. Self-injurious behavior prior to enrollment was reported by 10 participants (35.7%). 27/28 (96.4%) of participants had suicidal ideation and 8/28 (28.6%) reported suicidal behaviour.

All underwent at screening in-person psychological assessment, ECG, and physical examinations. Inclusion criteria required PTSD for at least six months, and a score of $\geqslant 50$ on the Clinician Administered PTSD Scale (CAPS-IV). Candidates had failed to respond to at least one course of pharmacotherapy and/or psychotherapy. Participants were otherwise physically healthy and free of psychiatric or medical contraindications for receiving MDMA. Women could not be pregnant or lactating.

After enrolment patient were assessed by the research-team. To establish a safe setting and therapeutic alliance before MDMA sessions, participants underwent three 90-minute preparatory sessions with a male/ female therapy team. Psychiatric medications were tapered by the study physician and discontinued at least five half-lives before MDMA administration. Each participant was assigned to one of nine therapy teams, and randomized to receive an active (125 or 100 mg) or a active placebo (40 mg) dose of MDMA during two doubleblind eight-hour experimental sessions spaced a month apart. A supplemental dose half the quantity of the initial dose (62.5, 50 or 20 mg) was available approximately 90 min after the first dose, if not contraindicated.

The study utilised the manualized therapeutic approach by Mithoefer et al (2016), which is explored in-depht earlier in this chapter.
On the morning following each experimental session, the first of three integrative sessions was conducted. The purpose of this session was to assess the participant's mental state and stability, and to facilitate assimilation of experiences and insights gained during the experimental session. Daily 15–60-minute telephone contact occurred for seven days following each experimental session. Two more integrative sessions took place before the next experimental session.

At the primary endpoint, one month after the second blinded experimental session, each participant was assessed by the same blinded independent rater and completed self-report measures, after which the blind was broken. Participants in the 40 mg group then crossed over to have one preparatory session and three open-label sessions (100–125 mg MDMA) with associated integrative sessions. Participants in the 100 mg and 125 mg groups underwent a third, open-label session (100–125 mg MDMA). Outcome measures were administered a month after the second open-label session and two months after the third open-label session. A 12-month follow-up assessment occurred 12 months (±one month) after the final active dose MDMA session.
In total, 27 completed the primary assessment, and 25 were assessed at 12-month follow-up.

Results:
Adverse Effects:
- Adverse effects during the sessions were anxiety and jaw clenching/tight

jaw, headache, muscle tension, dizziness, fatigue, and low mood. The most commonly reported reactions on one or more of the seven days following blinded MDMA sessions, included sleep-related reactions (insomnia, need more sleep) and low mood, increased irritability, and ruminations. Most were mild to moderate, with frequency decreasing across the week following the experimental sessions. No adverse effects required treatment and all were self limiting.
- A small increase in HR and blood pressure were observed during the treatment.

Effects:
- In the intention to treat (ITT) set, the active dose groups had the largest reduction in PTSD symptom severity with mean (SD) CAPS-IV changes of −26.3 (29.5) for 125 mg, −24.4 (24.2) for 100 mg, and −11.5 (21.2) for 40 mg, but the overall effect failed to show significance (p=0.52). Cohen's d effect sizes with 40 mg subtracted was 0.42 (−0.57, 1.42) for 125 mg and 0.37 (−0.57, 1.42) for 100 mg.
- In the Per-protocol (PP) set, there was a significant main effect in change of CAPS-IV total scores (p=0.03). Compared to the 40 mg group (mean change (SD) −4.0 (11.9)), the 125 mg group had a significant reduction (−37.0 (20.9), p=0.01) and the 100 mg group trended towards significance (−24.4 (24.2), p=0.10). Cohen's d effect sizes with 40 mg subtracted was 1.12 (−0.10, 2.35) for 125 mg and 0.73 (−0.45, 1.90) for 100 mg.
- In the ITT set, more participants in the active dose groups did not meet PTSD diagnostic criteria according to the CAPS-IV at the primary endpoint (33.3% (40 mg), 44.4% (100 mg), and 41.7% (125 mg)). As a measure of clinical significance, the percentage of participants who attained a ⩾30% decrease in CAPS-IV total scores was substantially greater for active dose groups (16.7% (40 mg), 55.6% (100 mg), and 50.0% (125 mg)).
- In the ITT set, change in depressive symptoms as determined by the BDI-II, was approximately equivalent across groups (p=0.97).
- Two months after the final open-label session, CAPS-IV total scores significantly declined compared to the primary endpoint for both groups, and four additional participants no longer met criteria for PTSD, indicating that the third MDMA session further improved treatment outcomes in this sample.
- After two blinded sessions, the 40 mg group crossed over for three open-label MDMA (100–125 mg) sessions. One month after the second open-label session, PTSD symptom severity improved significantly compared to the primary endpoint, as did symptoms of depression Scores did not significantly change further two-months after the third

openlabel session for this group
- Twelve months after the last active dose of MDMA, PTSD symptom severity was evaluated again. CAPS-IV total scores for the ITT set at baseline and 12-month follow-up mean (SD) were 92.0 (18.0) and 31.0 (24.2), respectively. PTSD severity was significantly lower compared to baseline ($t24=11.30$, $p<0.0001$). CAPS-IV total scores declined on average -9.6 (19.5) from treatment exit to the 12-month assessment.
- The majority (76%) did not meet PTSD diagnostic criteria, demonstrating enduring positive effects of MDMA-assisted psychotherapy. Analysis of secondary outcomes also found significant improvement at the 12-month follow-up compared to baseline for depression (BDI-II: $t23=8.15$, $p<0.0001$), sleep quality (PSQI: $t22=6.46$, $p<0.0001$), and dissociation (DES-II: $t22=5.7$, $p<0.0001$), indicating sustained gains well after the active treatment period ended.

Discussion:
- Consistent with prior research, this study shows that MDMA-assisted psychotherapy can be safe and efficacious in individuals with treatment-resistant PTSD. Vital signs generally increased in a dose-dependent manner to values similar during moderate exercise, and were well tolerated in these participants. There were no significant adverse effects.
- Although significant group differences were detected only in the PP set for the primary outcome, over half of participants in the ITT set who received active MDMA doses reached a 30% or greater drop in CAPS-IV total scores compared to 16.7% in the 40 mg group.
- After two blinded MDMA sessions, active dose groups had the largest reductions in CAPS-IV total scores with more participants attaining clinically significant improvements in PTSD symptoms relative to the 40 mg group, supporting a dose response.
- To understand if three experimental sessions were more beneficial than two sessions, outcomes were evaluated again two months after the third (last) MDMA session. After the third experimental session, both the 100 mg and 125 mg groups showed further reductions in CAPS-IV scores, providing evidence that an additional session significantly improved PTSD outcomes.
- On the other hand, after the 40 mg group crossed over, a large treatment response resulted after two open-label sessions with little change after the third. The difference in time to respond is likely due to individual variation in the small samples, although there may have been a small additional therapeutic effect from the initial two low-dose sessions.
- Importantly, the gains were maintained over a 12-month follow-up after all groups had received active doses of MDMA in either blinded or open-label sessions, with 76% (n=25) of individuals not meeting the

criteria for a diagnosis of PTSD.
- The fact that CAPS scores continued to improve between the two-month and 12-month follow-up visits lends support to the hypothesis that MDMA helps to catalyze a therapeutic process that continues long after the last drug administration. Moreover, the secondary outcome measures (depression, sleep, and dissociation) all showed significant reduction of symptoms at 12 months compared to baseline.
- At the 12-month visit, only one participant was taking a medication for PTSD; nine others were taking medications for insomnia, depression, generalized anxiety disorder, attention deficit/hyperactivity disorder (ADHD), and anxiety. These findings are noteworthy given that participants had moderate to extreme PTSD and had previously failed to benefit from psychotherapy, including approaches thought to be relatively effective (cognitive behavioral therapy (CBT) and eye movement desensitization reprocessing (EMDR)), and pharmacological treatment, including medications for depression and anxiety.
- At baseline, 96.4% of participants reported suicidal thinking at some point in the past; for 46.4% the suicidal ideations were serious, and 28.6% reported a history of suicidal behaviour. Thus, the participants were severely impacted by symptoms before study participation, and the sample was not restricted to exclude people who had previously experienced suicidal thinking.
- Frequency and intensity of adverse events, reactions, and suicidal ideation were similar to previous reports (Mithoefer et al., 2011, Mithoefer et al, 2018; Oehen et al., 2013). The greater number of psychiatric symptoms in active dose groups, such as anxiety, depression, or suicidal ideation, could be caused by the psychotherapeutic process of recalling and discussing experiences, thoughts, and emotions related to traumatic events, and also possibly be a direct pharmacological effect of MDMA. It is likely due to the MDMA-stimulated release of cortisol (Baggott et al., 2016; Dolder et al., 2018; Kirkpatrick et al., 2014b; Liechti et al., 2001).
- The most common time for mild to moderate anxiety related to drug onset to occur is in the first hour after administration; anxiety associated with painful or stressful memories typically occurred later in the session. Therapists encourage diaphragmatic breathing and other stress inoculation techniques that are discussed during the non-drug preparatory sessions. Participants may be able to continue the therapeutic processing of trauma memories, even when facing anxiety, because of the support of two therapists, and reduced amygdalar activity (Gamma et al., 2000) through the pharmacological effects of MDMA.
- Possible mechanisms for the treatment effect demonstrated in this sample are theorized based on the pharmacological effects of MDMA

and its actions in the context of psychotherapy. Subjective effects of MDMA that bolster prosocial feelings and behaviors (Bedi et al., 2010; Hysek et al., 2014; Kamilar-Britt and Bedi, 2015) make unpleasant memories more tolerable (Carhart-Harris et al., 2014), and enhance empathy, self-compassion, (Baggott et al., 2015; Kamboj et al., 2015), and trusting in the pace of processing the experience, could all be beneficial in promoting a strong therapeutic alliance and inducing an optimal state of engagement for effectively processing traumatic memories.

- Healthy volunteers also report that MDMA can change the significance or meaning of perceptions (Liechti et al., 2001). MDMA-assisted psychotherapy is meant to maintain the optional "window of tolerance" (Mithoefer, 2016; Ogden et al., 2006). An enhanced therapeutic alliance combined with reduced anxiety or discomfort around difficult memories, increased self-compassion, and openness to expanding meaning of thoughts, feelings or experiences may all contribute toward therapeutic effects.
- Other proposed models include an explicit role for experiential "regression" and re-examination of past experiences, and non-ordinary or transpersonal experiences in MDMA-assisted psychotherapy (Passie, 2012). MDMA-stimulated decrease in amygdala (Carhart-Harris et al., 2015; Gamma et al., 2000) and insular cortex activity (Walpola et al., 2017) may allow for emotional engagement without overwhelming anxiety during processing of painful traumatic memories. In healthy humans, MDMA acutely modulates brain circuitry important for memory and affective processing, and implicated in the pathophysiology of PTSD (Lanius et al., 2010), including increased resting state functional connectivity between the hippocampus and amygdala and decreased coupling of the medial prefrontal cortex with the hippocampus and posterior cingulate cortex (Carhart-Harris et al., 2015). Given that MDMA modulates emotional memory, neural pathways, fear extinction and memory reconsolidation might play a role in the underlying mechanisms for the positive treatment response (Feduccia and Mithoefer, 2018).
- Limitations of the study includes the participants being relatively homogeneous, with the majority being predominantly female (68%) and White (93%). In addition to this the relatively small sample size and establishing an effective blind for MDMA is difficult.

Conclusion:

Both short-term (one and two month) and long-term (12 month) follow-up results were positive across numerous therapy teams, demonstrating generalizability of the approach. The treatment was safe and well-tolerated.

More research is needed to determine the optimal number of MDMA sessions needed to achieve symptom remission. Upcoming phase 3 trials, with a planned enrollment of 200–300 participants will evaluate the time to response and other factors that influence outcomes. If findings are replicated in phase 3 trials, MDMA-assisted psychotherapy will become an available treatment option for people suffering with PTSD.

Bouso et al (2008). MDMA-Assisted Psychotherapy Using Low Doses in a Small Sample of Women with Chronic Posttraumatic Stress Disorder.

Methods:

Bouso et al (2008) recruited six women with chronic, treatment-resistant PTSD (ages 29- 49), who had failed to respond to standard treatment. All participants were in good physical health and non-pregnant, confirmed by medical history, laboratory tests, ECG, and urinalysis, and had no other psychiatric disorder (except for PTSD and comorbid symptoms), as assessed by the structured psychiatric interview for the DSM-IV.

The study was originally designed to assess the safety of a single dose of MDMA in women with chronic PTSD secondary to a sexual assault, studying five increasing doses of MDMA, ranging from 50 to 150 mg, in 29 women assigned to five different groups in a double-blind, ascending-dose study, randomized and placebo-controlled manner.
Groups 1 (group of 50 mg) and 5 (group of 150 mg) were composed of four subjects each, three receiving the MDMA dose and one receiving a placebo dose. Groups 2 (group of 75 mg), 3 (group of 100 mg) and 4 (group of 125 mg) were composed of seven subjects each, with five women receiving the MDMA dose and two women the placebo in each group. In this way, they planned to have 21 subjects receiving an MDMA dose and eight subjects receiving a placebo. But the study was suddenly shut down as a result of political pressure when only six participants had been treated, why the data presented here were gathered from those six participants. Participant 2 and 6 received placebo; participant 1, 3 and 4 received a 50 mg dose of MDMA; and participant 5 received a dose of 75 mg of MDMA.
All participants had six nondrug psychotherapy sessions with two therapists (a man and a woman), three before the experimental session (sessions 1, 2 and 3) where they were educated about MDMA and worked out specific objectives of the session, and the other three (sessions 5, 6 and 7) after the experimental session (session 4). The psychotherapy before the experimental sessions consisted of preparing subjects for the possibility of an MDMA experience, and therapy sessions after the experimentalsession consisted of discussing the events and material from the experimental

session with participants so that they could understand and integrate the MDMA experience into everyday life. Each nondrug session was 90 minutes long, while the experimental sessions lasted six hours plus another two hours of rest.

The experimental session was intended to offer subjects a deep psychological experience where they could re-experience the traumatic event without being emotionally overwhelmed, and where they would perceive emotional control as internally rather than externally situated. Immediately after the administration of MDMA/placebo, the patient was invited to wait for the first psychological effects while lying in the bed with eyes closed while listening to music.

The therapists remained with the subject throughout the experimental session, supporting her while she confronted the traumatic event. There was little dialogue between the subject and therapists at this time. After approximately two hours, the therapists invited the subject to sit in a chair and share her experience with them. During the remainder of the session, the therapists and subject worked together to go deeper into the experience and to put it into words in order to keep the experience fixed in the subject's consciousness. Relevant narratives regarding the traumatic event and new insights were intensively discussed, trying to enable the subject to experience as much as possible, emphasizing the importance of organizing new thoughts and emotions.

At hour 8, all subjects went home accompanied by a relative or by a close friend. One psychotherapy session took place the day following the experimental session; this session was designed to help the subject further explore and integrate the experiences that took place during the experimental session. The rest of the sessions took place with a five to seven day interval. Participants filled out a Therapeutic Alliance questionnaire after each session, and a questionnaire of subjective effects after the experimental session. They also filled out a questionnaire assessing side effects 24 hours and again five to seven days after the experimental session. Participants also completed a battery of psychological tests at the beginning and at the end of the treatment, administered by an independent evaluator(a woman) who was blind to the treatment assignment. Followups were planned at one, three, six, nine and 12 months after the treatment though none of the subjects could be reached for all of the follow-ups. Participant 1, 3, 4 and 5 underwent the first follow-up, participant 4 and 5 completed the second follow-up, and only participant 4 completed the third follow-up. No one was reached for the final follow-up at month 12.

Results:
Adverse Effects:
- Because only six subjects were treated in this clinical trial, it was not possible to perform any statistical analysis comparing between groups, so the present analysis is only descriptive.
- Side effects following the MDMA-experience included headache, increased fatigability, sleepiness and inner unrest. All were self-limiting and didn't require medical attention.
- A slight increase in BP and P were observed during the MDMA-experience. It dint require medical intervention and were self-limiting.

Effects:
- MDMA induced higher subjective effects in participant 5 (75 mg) than in the any of the 50 mg group, and an improvement in almost all the outcome scales. In the Severity of Symptoms Scale for Post-traumatic Stress Disorder results they found that at the post-treatment phase participant 5 improved seven points more as compared with the 50 mg group, while the 50 mg group improved 4.5 points as compared to the placebo group, who improved 4.5 points. The total improvement for participant 5 was 16 points between pre- and post-treatment, 17 points between pre-treatment and the first follow up (vs. 12.3 points for the 50 mg group), and 20 points between pre-treatment and the second follow up.
- By comparison, the total improvement for the placebo group at the post-treatment was 4.5 points, and for the 50 mg group 9 points, and 12.3 points between pre-treatment and the first follow-up.
- Participant 5 also showed greater improvement than the 50 mg group and the placebo group on the first and second follow-ups in the STAI/S. Participant 5 attained lower scores than the placebo and the 50 mg group subjects on post-treatment and follow-up measures on both depression scales (BDI and HAM-D), and in the MFS III.
- The 50 mg group scored lower than the placebo group in all PTSD symptoms, and higher on subjective effects. The 50 mg group scored better than subject 5 on the MS, and both 50 mg group subjects and subject 5 scored better than the placebo group. This is because subject 3 (50mg) had a dramatic reduction in her scores, destabilizing the mean value for the 50 mg group.
- All subjects except subject 6 had a higher therapeutic alliance, indicated via higher HAq scores post-treatment when compared with pretreatment scores.

Discussion:
- Bouso et al (2008) created the first post-prohibition controlled study on

- MDMA to investigate the safety of administering MDMA to a patient population.
- Due to political-circumstances, only six subjects could be treated before sudden termination of the study (Caudevilla 2006; Caudevilla 2003; Bouso 2003; Bouso & Gómez-Jarabo 2003; Doblin 2002).
- Blood pressure, heart rate and other somatic side effects were also assessed and showed no significant elevation, again suggesting that the doses administered were physiologically safe.
- The subjective effects of MDMA were greater in the subject who received 75 mg as compared to subjects who received 50 mg, and this subject obtained the greatest reduction in almost all the outcome scales employed, including the PTSD scale.
- The finding that the 75 mg subject obtained better scores on outcome measures as compared to the 50 mg group, and that the 50 mg group improved more than the placebo group, supports greater efficacy as doses increase, at least within the range studied here.
- As is true of psychotherapies involving exposure to traumatic memories or trauma-associated items, one of the main risks of MDMA psychotherapy for the treatment of PTSD is that the re-experiencing of the traumatic event could induce retraumatizations. It is interesting to note that none of the subjects in this study showed increased scores in the reexperiencing subscale at the post-treatment phase or at the follow-ups. It is also interesting to note that subject 5 had the highest score on the PTSD scale at the pretreatment phase yet she experienced the greatest improvement of all the subjects.
- Given these findings, it would be important to explore the effects of higher doses of MDMA in order to see what dose exhibits the best outcomes with the fewest side effects.
- Ongoing and planned studies of MDMA-assisted therapy are administering a 125 mg dose of MDMA, and severalstudies will include the possibility of administering a supplemental dose of 62.5 mg.

Conclusion:
Low doses of MDMA administered as an adjunct to psychotherapy were found to be safe for the six subjects with chronic PTSD, and there were promising signs of efficacy and reduced PTSD symptomatology. Further studies with a larger sample size and with the administration of higher doses of MDMA are clearly needed in order to clarify both the safety and the efficacy of MDMA-assisted psychotherapy in patient populations.

Mithoefer et al (2011). The safety and efficacy of ±3,4-methylenedioxymethamphetamine-assisted psychotherapy in subjects with chronic, treatment-resistant posttraumatic stress

disorder: the first randomized controlled pilot study.

Methods:

Mithoefer et al (2011) recruited 23 participants (17 female) who were randomized in a double-blind fashion, to receive two experimental sessions of either psychotherapy with concomitant MDMA administration (n=15) or the same psychotherapy accompanied by inactive placebo (lactose) administration (psychotherapy-only) (n=8). Two participants from the MDMA-group dropped out before after the first MDMA-session, and were thus omitted from the analysis. One dropped out due to relapse of depression and the other due to being unwilling to travel.

Assessments Study entry screening consisted of a Structured Clinical Interview for Axis I Diagnosis (SCID) (First et al., 1994), the SCID II for personality disorder (First et al., 1997), CAPS, medical history, physical examination, serum chemistry profile, complete blood count, thyroid-stimulation hormone (TSH), free thyroxine, HIV serology, urinalysis, and electrocardiogram (ECG). Subjects were required to meet DSM-IV-R criteria for the diagnosis of crime or war-related chronic PTSD, and to have treatment-resistant symptoms, defined as a CAPS score of 50 (signifying moderate to severe symptoms) following at least 3 months of prior SSRI or serotonin–norepinephrine reuptake inhibitor (SNRI) treatment in addition to at least 6 months of psychotherapy.

Exclusion criteria required freedom from any major medical conditions. In addition, psychiatric exclusion criteria included Borderline Personality Disorder or any current Axis I disorder with the following exceptions which were allowed: anxiety disorders, affective disorders other than bipolar disorder type 1, substance abuse or dependence in remission for 60 days, and eating disorder without active purging.

Urine testing for pregnancy and urine drug testing for cocaine, marijuana, amphetamines, MDMA, opiates and benzodiazepines was performed during initial screening and immediately before each experimental session. All screens were negative in all subjects.

After screening and enrollment, participants completed baseline psychological and neurocognitive measures. Outcome measures were repeated approximately 4 days after each of two 8-h experimental sessions and 2 months after the second experimental session. Participants completed neurocognitive measures at baseline and again 2 months after the second experimental session.

The blind was broken for each subject after the follow-up visit 2 months after the second experimental session. All subjects who initially received placebo were offered participation in an open label crossover segment ('Stage 2'). After the 2-month follow-up, nine subjects were given a third session of MDMA with psychotherapy, as allowed in a protocol amendment. However, because not all subjects received a third session and placebo subjects received only two sessions, data related to the third session were omitted from analysis.

Stage 2 Placebo participants who enrolled in the open-label arm completed outcome measures 2 months after their last experimental session. The schedule of visits in Stage 2 was nearly identical to the schedule in Stage 1. After preliminary evidence of safety and efficacy had been established, a protocol amendment was approved allowing the last nine subjects to receive a supplemental dose of MDMA or placebo in all experimental sessions. The purpose of this supplemental dose, half the initial dose administered 2 h afterwards, was to prolong the therapeutic window of MDMA effects and gather pilot data about dose for design of future clinical trials.

Participants were required to taper and abstain from all psychotropic medication during study participation except sedative hypnotics or anxiolytics used as-needed between MDMA or placebo sessions (referred to as 'rescue medications').

The practical and therapeutic aspects of the study were carried out similar as described in the manual by Mithoefer (2015), and as described in the beginning of this chapter.

Results:
Adverse effects:
- No medical treatment was required during any experimental sessions. No serious drug-related adverse effects occurred.
- Elevations of blood pressure, pulse, and body temperature were greater in the MDMA group, and spontaneously returned to baseline at session end in both groups. There were no resulting medical complications or pharmacologic interventions.
- The most common side effects that occurred more frequently in the MDMA group on the day of experimental sessions were: jaw tightness, nausea, feeling cold, dizziness, loss of appetite, and impaired balance. Equally or more common in the placebo group on the day of experimental sessions were: anxiety, insomnia, headache and fatigue. In the week following experimental sessions, some of the most common side effects were reported at similar incidence by both groups: fatigue, anxiety, low mood, headache and nausea, with anxiety being slightly more frequent in the MDMA group and low mood slightly more frequent in the placebo group. During this week, irritability and loss of appetite were more frequently reported in the MDMA group and

insomnia was reported more often in the placebo group. Side effects typically resolved over a period of hours or days, usually spontaneously; sometimes with short-term symptomatic treatment such as sedative hypnotics or NSAID following experimental sessions.
- At baseline, there were no significant group differences on any of the cognitive measures including the RBANS total score, PASAT Trial 1, PASAT Trial 2 and the Rey-Osterrieth Figure 30-minute delay. To test whether the experimental condition had an adverse impact on cognition, between-group comparisons were performed at the study follow-up 2 months after the second experimental session. There were still no significant group differences on any of the major index scores.
- Zolpidem was administered following 31 of 51 MDMA-assisted sessions (60.7%) and after 11 of 16 psychotherapyonly sessions (68.8%) (p=0.77). Benzodiazepines were administered following (though usually not the same day as) 24 of 51 MDMA-assisted sessions (47.0%) and after six of 16 psychotherapy-only sessions (37.5%) (p=0.579)
- Seventeen of 20 subjects, the majority of whom had pre-existing sleep disturbance related to PTSD, received zolpidem for insomnia during study participation. In five cases this was limited to one or two nights following MDMA or placebo sessions. Fourteen subjects received benzodiazepines during study participation. Eleven of 14 reported taking benzodiazepines before enrollment. Two of the three who had not taken benzodiazepines before study enrollment did so for 1 and 7 days, respectively.

Effects:
- PTSD symptoms, as measured by CAPS, improved over time in both groups (Time: $F(3, 17) = 40.292$, $p < 0.0005$).
- The MDMA group showed significantly greater improvement (Time*Group interaction $F(1, 17) = 7.173$, $p=0.015$).
- Mean differences between 'group time' were examined using independent t-tests with Holm's sequential Bonferroni correction (α) for multiplicity. Statistical significance (*) is indicated where $p < \alpha$: Time 1 $p=0.966$, $\alpha=0.050$, Time 2* $p=0.013$, $\alpha=0.017$, Time 3* $p=0.002$, $\alpha=0.012$, Time 4* $p=0.013$, $\alpha=0.025$.
- PTSD symptoms, as measured by IES-R, improved over time in both groups (Time: $F(3, 17) = 11.003$, $p = < 0.0005$), but the MDMA group showed significantly greater improvement (Time*Group interaction $F(1, 17) = 3.290$, $p=0.027$). Mean differences between 'group- time' were examined using independent t-tests with Holm's sequential Bonferroni correction (α) for multiplicity. Statistically significance (*) is indicated where $p < \alpha$: Time 1 $p=0.976$, $\alpha=0.050$, Time 2* $p= 0.016$, $\alpha=0.017$, Time 3* $p=0.006$, $\alpha=0.012$, Time 4 $p=0.038$, $\alpha=0.025$.

- The CAPS scores of the two subjects who dropped out, both of whom were randomized to receive MDMA, fell from 110 and 107, respectively, at baseline, to 17 and 27, respectively, 4 days after their only MDMA-assisted psychotherapy session. These data are not included in the analysis.
- Seven of the eight placebo participants chose to enroll in the open-label crossover arm. One of the placebo responders, whose CAPS score had fallen from 67 to 15 after placebo, elected not to enroll in the crossover because she was satisfied with her improvement.
- The other placebo responder had a transient decline in CAPS from 54 to 15 after placebo, but her CAPS increased to 64 in the 3 months prior to enrollment in Stage 2. Paired t-tests were used to analyze change in outcome measures from Time 1c to Time 4c in the crossover arm.
- For the seven placebo subjects who completed the open-label crossover, there were significant decreases in CAPS and IES-R scores (mean IES-R decrease = 15.9, SD=12.1, p=0.013) from end of the control trial to 4–6 weeks after two MDMA sessions were completed. These decreases were similar in magnitude to the CAPS and IES-R decreases in the subjects initially randomized to full-dose MDMA.
- Clinical response was defined as >30% reduction from baseline in CAPS total severity score. In Stage 1, the clinical response was 83.3% (10/12) in the MDMA group versus 25% (2/8) in the placebo group.
- Likewise, 10 of the MDMA group no longer met DSM-IV criteria for PTSD compared with two of the placebo group. In Stage 2, the clinical response rate was 100% in the seven subjects, six of whom had failed to respond to placebo and one of whom had relapsed after an initial placebo response.
- All three subjects who reported being unable to work due to PTSD were able to return to work.

Discussion:
- The study demonstrated that MDMA-assisted psychotherapy can be used with acceptable and short-lived side effects in a carefully screened group of subjects with chronic, treatment-resistant PTSD.
- There were no drug-related serious adverse events and no evidence of impaired cognitive function as measured by neuropsychological testing.
- Compared with the same psychotherapy with inactive placebo, MDMA produced clinically and statistically significant improvements in PTSD symptoms as measured by standard symptom scales. This difference was immediate and was maintained throughout the time period.
- The betweengroup effect size (1.24) of the study drug compares favorably with other treatment modalities for PTSD (Foa et al., 2009), particularly given the treatment-refractory nature of the current sample.

- The clinical significance of the symptom reductions is indicated by the high percentage of subjects attaining a >30% reduction in CAPS scores and no longer meeting criteria for PTSD 2 months after MDMA-assisted psychotherapy, and by the report that all three subjects who had been unable to work because of PTSD were able to return to work.
- The strengths of this study are its prospective, doubleblind, crossover design, the use of a standardized primary outcome measure (CAPS) that is widely used for PTSD research, enrollment of chronic, treatment-resistant subjects who had moderate to severe PTSD, and the use of a blinded, independent rater. Subjects met welldefined inclusion and exclusion criteria.
- Groups were well matched; at baseline, subjects in both groups had nearly identical CAPS scores.
- The study had several limitations and should be considered only a preliminary step toward exploring MDMA as a possible therapeutic adjunct. Sample size were small, as is appropriate in a Phase II pilot study. The majority of participants were female.
- At baseline, the placebo group had a history of more prior psychotherapy than the MDMA group, which could mean that the placebo group was more treatment-resistant; however, this covariate proved non-significant. Furthermore, in the open-label phase, the placebo group had a response comparable to the MDMA group, so in fact, the placebo group proved not to be more resistant to MDMA-assisted psychotherapy.
- Another important weakness of this study is the transparency of the blinding. The authors chose to use an inactive placebo in this initial trial in order to compare side effects of MDMA with those of placebo in this patient population. Although the independent rater remained effectively blinded because he was not present during experimental sessions, the novel subjective experience was a strong clue for the subjects, as was the subjects' increase in pulse and blood pressure for the investigators.

Mithoefer et al (2013). Durability of improvement in post-traumatic stress disorder symptoms and absence of harmful effects or drug dependency after 3,4-methylenedioxymethamphetamine-assisted psychotherapy: a prospective long-term follow-up study.

Mithoefer et al (2013) reported follow up data on the participants enrolled in Mithoefer et al (2011). All 20 subjects from the initial study were recruited for LTFU and participated in the data collected herein. All 20 subjects completed the LTFU questionnaire, and 17 (14 women) completed the Clinician-Administered PTSD Scale (CAPS) and Impact of Events Scale-Revised (IES-R) as well.

The data from the one subject who never received MDMA was excluded from the data analysis, but were reported. Results thus focused on the 19 subjects (16 women) who received MDMA-assisted treatment, 16 of whom had also completed CAPS and IES-R measures.

There were three subjects who did not complete the measures: one moved and so was lost to follow-up after answering the LTFU questionnaire, but before completing the IES-R or scheduling administration of the CAPS; while the other two declined to repeat these two measures. Of the latter, one subject, who had previously shown the smallest reduction in CAPS score at the 2-month follow-up, was concerned that testing might trigger more symptoms and the other subject, who had responded well during the original study, declined to complete the measures again, citing stressful family matters as the reason for not devoting time nor attention to our current study.

LTFU ranged from 17–74 months (mean=45.4; SD=17.3; n=17) after the final MDMA session for the CAPS and IES-R administration, and 10–74 months (mean=40.8; SD=19.2; n=20) after completion for the questionnaire.

Results:
Effects:
- Mean CAPS and IES-R scores at LTFU for the 16 study completers were not statistically different from their 2-month (short-term) mean scores.
- At LTFU, two subjects had CAPS scores above 50 (13%), which indicates relapse with moderate-to-severe PTSD symptoms, which is above the cut-off for original study entry. Using an intent-to-treat analysis, the three subjects who did not complete the CAPS were treated as negative outcomes, as were the two who relapsed. Thus, the intent-to-treat analysis produced 5 out of 19 (26%) PTSD subjects with negative outcomes, as compared to 2 out of 16 (13%) CAPS completers with negative outcomes.
- The single participant who chose not to continue to the crossover arm to receive MDMA-assisted treatment sessions had a strong, sustained response to psychotherapy plus placebo (2-month CAPS = 14; LTFU CAPS = 16 and 2-month IES-R = 5; LTFU IES-R = 15).
- At the time of enrollment, 16 of 19 (84%) subjects were in active psychotherapy. At LTFU, only 8 of 19 (42%) were in psychotherapy.
- The percentage of subjects taking psychiatric medication did not change from the baseline 58% (12/19). The mean number of medicines taken fell from 1.7 to 1.3.
- Only one participant, who had received two MDMA-assisted

psychotherapy sessions, reported the subsequent use of "ecstasy" in a quasi-therapeutic setting.
- All participants answered "Yes" to the question, "Do you believe more MDMA sessions would have been helpful?" for further treatment of PTSD, set either "at a later time point" or "soon after the last one."
- 15 wrote comments. Participants described the experimental treatment as being helpful, sometimes dramatically so ("The therapy made it possible for me to live"), but also as being difficult at times ("one of the toughest things I have ever done"). Several participants described it as a step in an "ongoing process" rather than simply a completed cure. Some comments shed light on the participants' understanding of the way MDMA affected the therapeutic process ("It increased my ability to stay with and handle getting through emotions." "The MDMA provided a dialogue with myself I am not often able to have, and there is the long-term effect of an increased sense of well-being." "I was always too frightened to look below the sadness. The MDMA and the support allowed me to pull off the controls, and I ... knew how and what and how fast or slow I needed to see my pain").

Discussion:
- The evidence we report in this LTFU study, conducted on the average of nearly 3 ½ years after the prior study's exit date, indicates that there was an enduring, clinically meaningful benefit from MDMA-assisted psychotherapy to PTSD patients. The fact that 3 of the 19 subjects did not complete the CAPS and IES-R must be taken into consideration in interpreting these data. These three "CAPS non-completers" did complete the LTFU Questionnaire, where they reported nearly the degree of benefit and the same degree of persistence of benefit as those who had completed the CAPS. Therefore, it may be the case that up to 89% (17/19) of those who received MDMA had long-term improvement in their PTSD symptoms. However, these three "CAPS non-completers" should be assumed to have had higher CAPS scores than the others. An intent-to-treat analysis, that made the assumption that each of these three individuals had relapsed, concluded that 74% (14/19) of these previously treatment-resistant subjects demonstrated meaningful, sustained reductions in their CAPS scores at LTFU.
- At LTFU, two of the subjects who completed the CAPS had relapsed, with CAPS scores above the cutoff (≥ 50) that was the original study entry criterion.
- The LTFU data supports that MDMA can be administered in a clinical setting with minimal risk that the participants will subsequently seek out and self-administer "street ecstasy," or other drugs.
- This is consistent with the comments from many study subjects, who

expressed the strong opinion that the therapeutic setting and close follow-up were essential elements of the treatment, and they did not think MDMA should be used without this level of clinical monitoring and therapeutic support.

- Favorable reports about cognitive function, memory, and concentration on the LTFU Questionnaire were consistent with findings from formal measures of cognitive function that were taken before and after psychotherapy with MDMA versus placebo
- The lack of evidence of neurocognitive decline associated with MDMA in the initial study, as well as in the LTFU self-reports are consistent with the most well-controlled studies of recreational ecstasy use and neurocognitive performance, which report largely negative findings (Halpern et al., 2004; Hoshi et al., 2007; Roiser et al., 2007; Bedi and Redman, 2008; Hanson and Luciana, 2010; Halpern et al., 2011).
- No subjects reported any harm from study participation. All of them reported some degree of benefit and many experienced benefits beyond decreased PTSD symptoms. Some of the improved domains include increased self-awareness, improved relationships, an enhanced spiritual life, and more involvement in the community or world.
- The benefits endorsed and described extend beyond the realm of symptom reduction. Many participants reported deeply meaningful therapeutic experiences and ensuing improvements in their lives. A majority of participants endorsed benefits such as, "increased self-awareness and understanding" and "enhanced spiritual life." These responses and many of the individual comments on the Questionnaire point to a subjectively authentic process of psychological and spiritual exploration and growth that could logically be expected to facilitate trauma processing and symptom reduction, and to promote healthy psychological development.
- Improvements of this kind could reasonably be expected to persist for a year or more, as was endorsed by 80% of the subjects, and even to "last and continue to grow," as endorsed by 40% of subjects. In addition, several participants wrote comments describing an incomplete but ongoing process of improvement, referring to an "ongoing journey" or having "gained tools" while "still struggling in many areas." Since these comments were usually accompanied by persistently low CAPS scores, the authors believed that they represented additional evidence for a meaningful, ongoing, therapeutic process that was originally catalysed by MDMA-assisted psychotherapy and was likely leading to important benefits in addition to PTSD symptom reduction.
- There are several limitations of the study design to be taken into account in interpreting the data. Only 16 out of 19 subjects completed the LTFU CAPS or IES-R, though this issue was addressed with the intent-to-treat

analysis and with the information gathered from all 19 MDMA subjects who did complete the Questionnaire.
- While the randomised control group design, along with the crossover arm in the original trial, went a long way toward ruling out the possibility that there was only a placebo response, there was no meaningful control group for our LTFU, because all but one subject ultimately received active treatment in the initial study.
- It is possible that the favourable results of this LTFU study were caused by resolution of symptoms due to natural history (Price et al., 2008) or to other variables that were not controlled for after the original 2-month follow-up. An important argument against this is that the cohort was originally screened specifically to have treatment-refractory PTSD and their mean duration of symptoms had been more than 19 years.
- The long follow-up period allowed the researchers to identify relapses that would not have been identified within a shorter follow-up period. On the other hand, the longer the time elapsed between the experimental intervention and follow-up, the more likely it is that life events will have intervened and had their own effect on outcome, either positive or negative.
- Perhaps the most important factor confounding the attribution of the persistence of therapeutic benefits entirely to the authors existence, were that at LTFU, 8 of 19 subjects were still in psychotherapy and 12 of 19 were taking psychiatric medicines. Although this did represent a decrease in the use of psychotherapy and psychiatric drugs compared to baseline, it is impossible to know how much these treatments may have influenced the durability of benefits measured at LTFU. Although these confounding factors preclude a definite conclusion about the long-term benefits of the experimental treatment, it is noteworthy that the original sample included only participants with PTSD, usually of many years duration, who had already proven resistant to prior therapy and medication.
- Ongoing treatment could have been targeted at a psychopathology other than PTSD, such as other anxiety disorders or persistent or recurrent mood disorders; and medications could have still been prescribed in the absence of an active Axis I disorder or other well-established indication.
- It may as well be that participants were undergoing psychotherapy to further their personal growth and self-understanding and/or to support expansion and integration of any therapeutic gains made during MDMA-assisted psychotherapy.

Conclusion:
Long-term outcome results in the original cohort demonstred a sustained benefit over time, with no cases of subsequent drug abuse and no reports

of neurocognitive decline. These results indicate that there was a favorable long-term risk/ benefit ratio for PTSD treatment with just a few doses of pure MDMA administered in a supportive setting, in conjunction with psychotherapy. Should further research validate our initial findings, we predict that MDMA-assisted psychotherapy will become an important treatment option for this very challenging clinical and public health problem.

Oehen et al (2013). A randomized, controlled pilot study of MDMA (±3,4-Methylenedioxymethamphetamine)- assisted psychotherapy for treatment of resistant, chronic Post-Traumatic Stress Disorder (PTSD).

Methods:
Oehen et al (2013) recruited 14, of which 10 participants (10 female) completed the study, for a randomized, blinded pilot study of MDMA-assisted psychotherapy in a population of subjects with chronic, treatment-refractory PTSD. Two subjects (one female, one male) discontinued treatment after the first experimental MDMA session.

Pre-enrolment medical evaluation included: a medical history, standard physical examination, ECG, metabolic profile, measurement of thyroid hormones, serum electrolytes, HIV test, urinary drug test and pregnancy test when appropriate. The participants aged older than 40 years, with a positive family history of coronary heart disease and/or presenting risk factors, underwent a stress ECG.
Psychiatric evaluation and confirmation of the PTSD diagnosis were conducted by an independent rater, using CAPS, DSM and SCID I and II. All subjects who were enrolled, met the DSM-IV-text revision (TR) criteria for PTSD with treatment-resistant symptoms, as was indicated by a CAPS score of $\geq$ 50 and having previously undergone at least 6 months of psychotherapy and 3 months of treatment with an SSRI. The mean duration of PTSD symptoms at enrollment was 18.3 years (SD $\pm$ 12). The mean duration of previous psychotherapeutic treatments was 85.8 months (SD $\pm$ 71.4).
Exclusion criteria included significant medical conditions, except for hypothyroidism. Exclusionary psychiatric conditions were: a history of psychotic illness, bipolar disorder type I, borderline personality disorder, dissociative identity disorder, and substance abuse or dependence within 60 days of enrolment. In addition, participants had to taper all all psychotropic medication, before entering the study.
Seven of 12 participants had experienced one or more evidence-based therapies: three participants had CBT, one exposure based therapy was not

specified, one had EMDR, three had unspecified anxiety management and six participants had non-evidence based therapies, such as insight-oriented therapies. Many of the participants had undergone multiple therapies, so it was not possible any more for them to exactly identify in all cases, the specific method that had been applied.

In "Stage 1," eight participants were randomized in a doubleblind manner to the full dose and four to the "active placebo" condition, with their three doses of MDMA administered in three all-day-long MDMA-assisted psychotherapy sessions. The sessions were carried out according to the principles outlined in Mithoefer (2015), and described in the beginning of this chapter.
A full dose consisted of 125 mg followed 2.5 hours later by 62.5 mg MDMA; while the "active placebo" dose consisted of 25 mg, followed 2.5 hours later by 12.5 mg MDMA. The dosages chosen for the low dose condition were selected on the basis of their ability to produce minimal, but detectable subjective effects, and the cumulative dose of 37.5 mg MDMA was not expected to produce a significant reduction in anxiety nor a significant increase in access to emotionally-upsetting material, although this low dosage might produce slight alterations in perception, and increased relaxation or tension.

The CAPS and SCID I substance abuse module were administered at baseline (T0), 3-weeks after MDMA-session #2 (T1); 3-weeks after MDMA-session #3 (T2; end of treatment); and two (T3), six (T4) and 12 (T5) months after the MDMA-session #3 (follow-up). The PDS was administered one day after each MDMA session; 3-weeks after the MDMA-session #3 (T2; end of treatment); and two, six, and 12 months after MDMA-session #3 (T3, T4, T5; long-term follow-up (LTFU)).
The blind was broken following assessment by the independent rater, after the end of Stage 1 treatment. Subjects assigned to the "active placebo" condition were offered an open-label continuation of the study with the fully active dose of MDMA ("Stage 2"), with identical psychotherapy and assessment as in "Stage 1." CAPS scores from the 3-weeks post-MDMA #3 testing served as a baseline for "Stage 2." All subjects in the "active placebo" condition in "Stage 1" chose to proceed to "Stage 2." Follow-up assessments consisting of the CAPS and PDS were completed two (T3), six (T4) and 12 (T5) months after the final MDMA-session #3.
When a preliminary analysis of data showed an insufficient clinical response to the experimental treatment in several full-dose subjects, an amendment to the protocol was obtained, allowing for two additional sessions of MDMA-assisted psychotherapy for any subjects deemed to show insufficient response, which was referred to as "Stage 3" and employed a

dose of 150 mg MDMA and a supplemental dose of 75mg MDMA, unless contraindicated for safety reasons. A response was considered clinically insufficient when all of the three criteria were fulfilled:
- The investigator's and patients' subjective impression of a lack of improvement
- CAPS score changes (baseline to 2 months after the third experimental session ≤ 15 points
- CAPS item #25 ≥ 3 and overall CAPS score still ≥ 50 points at the outcome measurement 2-months after the third MDMA-session served as additional guidelines for the assessment of clinically insufficient response).

Eleven of the 12 subjects who completed the study also participated in the 12-month follow-up. One female subject could not complete the 12-month follow-up, because she died 6 months after finishing the MDMA-assisted treatment, from a brain metastasis arising from a relapse of breast cancer; when chosen for inclusion, this subject had been in breast cancer remission for over 10 years and had not been symptomatic at screening.
Outcome measures included the Clinician-Administered PTSD Scale (CAPS) and The Posttraumatic Diagnostic Scale (PDS).

Results:
Adverse effects:
- There were no serious drug-related adverse events and no medical intervention was required during or following the MDMA sessions.
- The most commonly reported reactions on the day of the experimental session were moderate insomnia, loss of appetite, restlessness and headache. Dizziness and impaired gait/balance were also frequently reported in both groups. Most reactions resolved when the drug effects diminished. Loss of appetite, difficulty concentrating, anxiety and headache persisted beyond this window to 24 hours, but were still self-limiting.
- BP and HR did not change significantly
- Zolpidem for insomnia was offered for the first nights after MDMA sessions, but was administered on only one occasion.
- Lorazepam for anxiety/ distress related to the processing of the traumatic memories was administered in six out of nine subjects, after 10 out of 56 full-dose or 150 mg MDMA sessions, typically during the week after MDMA sessions. Five of these six subjects were on antidepressants and/or benzodiazepines at enrolment. In the "active placebo" group, lorazepam was administered to two of five subjects after three low-dose MDMA sessions. Both had been treated with antidepressants and/or benzodiazepines at enrolment.

Effects:
- The average CAPS scores in the "active placebo" group increased slightly from T1 to T2.
- The three interaction relative treatment effects (RTE) T0-T2 for total CAPS scores in the full dose group showed a distinct decrease in CAPS scores with time, as compared to the active placebo group in the ANOVA, but narrowly missed statistical significance ($p = 0.066$).
- On average, CAPS scores decreased 15.6 points (23.5%) in the full-dose participants. There was a significant simple effect of time in the full dose group ($p = 0.002$), meaning that the time effect was significant only in the full-dose group.
- In contrast, the simple time effect for the active placebo group was not significant ($p = 0.475$). For the other two models, T0 vs. T1 and T1 vs. T2, group and time effects and interactions were not significant.
- PDS scores decreased in the full-dose group, as compared to an increase in the "active placebo" group. There was a significant interaction effect of group and time ($p = 0.014$).
- A Wilcoxon Signed Rank test for paired data was performed to test whether three MDMA sessions were more effective than only two sessions. There was a significant difference in CAPS scores ($p = 0.016$, exact p-value to account for ties) between the two time points T1 and T2.
- The median prior psychotherapy treatment times of the "active placebo" and the full-dose group were 123 and 39.9 months. A comparison of the two distributions, using the two-sample Wilcoxon rank sum test, yielded a two-tailed p value of 0.154.
- Clinical response, as defined above, was observed in four out of eight subjects in the full-dose group, with all of them still fulfilling PTSD criteria, but with a reduction in severity from severe to mild (CAPS score 20–39) (n = 3) or moderate (CAPS score 40–59) (n = 1) PTSD.
- Three full-dosage subjects met criteria for being non-responders and they were enrolled in "Stage 3," receiving either a full or higher dose of MDMA (two full-dose sessions, two high-dose sessions and two high-dose sessions followed by a lower supplemental dose). The dosages were chosen on the basis of clinical judgment. The additional sessions did not lead to any further improvements in CAPS scores (mean CAPS score change of 0.3 points). As a result, no further subjects were enrolled in "Stage 3."
- In the "active placebo" group all four participants failed to respond to the treatment, with two participants showing higher CAPS scores and a slight clinical deterioration. In the "Stage 2" crossover group, all four participants responded to the treatment: two of four participants no

longer fulfilled PTSD criteria and two had improved, but still had moderate PTSD.
- At the one-year follow-up, CAPS scores had decreased by a mean of 24 points (35%) compared to baseline in the full-dose group, while there was a 35-point decrease (52%) in the crossover group, with nine participants showing a significant clinical improvement. During this time, the majority of participants continued with their previous or another psychotherapy or medication.
- Also at LTFU, five of 12 participants no longer met the diagnostic criteria for PTSD, two had switched to having mild PTSD, and four had moderate PTSD, while one had died of a cause not related to the study.
- One of four participants on disability and three who were fit for limited employment at baseline had been able to return to work full-time by the 1-year follow-up.

Discussion:
- This study demonstrated that the treatment can be safely applied in an outpatient setting with no drug-related serious adverse events occurring.
- Cardiovascular effects were similar to those reported in the literature and did not require medical intervention.
- Adverse effects were generally mild and well tolerated. A comparison of the safety profiles between 25 mg and 125 mg doses did support that the 125 mg dose was associated with more reactions, in general.
- Efficacy failed to reach statistical significance ($p = 0.066$) as measured by the primary outcome measure, the CAPS.
- Self-assessment of the subjects' PTSD symptoms, as measured by the self-reporting questionnaire PDS showed a significant reduction ($p = 0.014$). They also found that three experimental MDMA sessions were significantly more effective than only two ($p = 0.016$).
- Further improvement over the one-year follow-up time was unexpected (a CAPS score reduction of 35% in the "Stage 1" full-dose subjects and 52% in the "Stage 2" crossover full-dose subjects, with nine out of 11 subjects showing a clinical response). Because all participants at the 12-month follow-up had received full-dose MDMA in either "Stage 1" or "Stage 2," comparisons by condition were not possible at the 12-month follow-up.
- Four subjects had either changed or begun a new therapy during the follow-up period, two received a SSRI for relapse of depression and one had participated in "Stage 3." It is therefore unclear to which degree these findings at the 12-month follow-up can be attributed to the experimental treatment.
- Additional medication for sleep disorders was needed on only one occasion, which is surprising, given the fact that many of the subjects

experienced chronic insomnia due to their PTSD and had taken sleep medications in the past, noting that insomnia is a common side effect of MDMA.
- In the study, benzodiazepines were used as little as possible, in order to avoid suppressing the ongoing integration process. It is noteworthy that most of the subjects requiring benzodiazepines after the MDMA intervention had been treated with antidepressants with anxiolytic effects and/or benzodiazepines at enrolment, and that only one subject who had been free of any anxiolytic or antidepressant medications at enrolment, received a benzodiazepine during the study.
- The authors postulated that the need for benzodiazepines is more likely to be related to a predisposition for anxiety, rather than to direct MDMA effects, therefore it was not considered a safety concern.
- The authors recommended that future studies include three instead of only two preparatory sessions, to strengthen the therapeutic relationship before administration of MDMA. The observed 100% response rate of the crossover subjects in "Stage 2," as compared to the 50% response rate of the subjects receiving full dose MDMA in "Stage 1," suggested that a strengthening of the therapeutic alliance did contribute to an enhancement of our treatment outcomes.
- It is difficult to interpret the discrepancy between the results of this study and that of Mithoefer and colleagues, in terms of the primary outcome (mean CAPS change score 53.7 under MDMA vs. 20.5 points under placebo ($p = 0.015$), clinical response (> 30% CAPS score reduction) 83% vs. 25%), given that they followed a similar design that employed the same main outcome measure, with only two MDMA sessions and noting the existence of a distinct placebo effect. We presume that other factors could have influenced outcomes, such as: cultural differences, independent rater differences, therapist differences, or the possibility of the sample including more cases with a higher degree of overall severity of the illness, which was not captured by the screening and diagnostic measures employed (i.e. personality structure, attachment style, etc.);however, with the small sample size the difference could also have been due to chance.
- MDMA is not just an augmenting, "add-on" medication, but rather a catalyst that dramatically influences the psychotherapeutic process itself. This makes it virtually impossible to distinguish the purely drug-induced effects from the psychotherapeutic effects.
- The study was underpowered, as is customary in phase-II studies.

Conclusions

In summary, MDMA-assisted psychotherapy was safely administered, with no drug-related serious adverse events, in a small sample of treatment-resistant patients who were suffering from chronic PTSD; however, the approach did not produce significant symptom reductions.

Mithoefer et al (2018). 3,4-methylenedioxymethamphetamine (MDMA)-assisted psychotherapy for post-traumatic stress disorder in military veterans, firefighters, and police officers: a randomised, double-blind, dose-response, phase 2 clinical trial.

Methods:
Mithoefer et al (2018) recruited 26 participants for a randomised, double-blind, dose-response, phase 2 trial at an outpatient psychiatric clinic.

Participants had PTSD with a minimum duration of 6 months or more, as confirmed by the Clinician-Administered PTSD Scale (CAPS-IV), with a total score of 50 or more, and who had failed to respond to or inability to tolerate previous pharmacotherapy or psychotherapy. Participants had moderate-to-severe PTSD, with a mean baseline CAPS-IV total score of 87·1 (SD 16·13).

Participants were required to taper and abstain from psychotropic medications during study participation except for sedative hypnotics or anxiolytics used as needed between MDMA sessions.
Exclusion criteria included major medical conditions except controlled hypertension or adequately treated hypothyroidism, and pregnant or lactating women or women not using effective contraception. Permitted co-morbid disorders were anxiety disorders, affective disorders except bipolar disorder type 1, substance abuse or dependence in remission for 60 days or more, and eating disorders without active purging. Participants were underwent screening using the CAPS-IV and Structured Clinical Interview for DSM-IV Axis I Disorders, and by a physician for assessment of non-psychiatric medical criteria.

Participants were randomly assigned (1:1:2) to three different dose groups of MDMA plus psychotherapy: 30 mg (n=7), 75 mg (n=7), or 125 mg (n=12) of MDMA.
After the primary endpoint, the blind was broken and the study entered the crossover design, which was open-label. Depending on the dose groups, MDMA was administered orally at 30 mg (active placebo), 75 mg, or 125 mg in two blinded experimental sessions spaced 3–5 weeks apart (initial dose followed 1·5–2 h later by an optional supplemental dose of half the initial dose). The first MDMA session was preceded by three 90-min psychotherapy sessions to establish a therapeutic alliance and prepare participants for the MDMA experience, as explained in the beginning of

this chapter and by Mithoefer (2015).

MDMA was administered at the beginning of a 8-h experimental sessions of manualised psychotherapy, followed by an overnight stay onsite, 7 days of telephone contact, and three 90-min psychotherapy sessions aimed at integrating the experience. Overall, a course of treatment included 18 h of non-drug psychotherapy and 16–24 h (2–3 sessions) of MDMA-assisted psychotherapy.

Outcome measures were administered by masked independent raters at baseline and 1 month after the second experimental session (primary endpoint), just before the blind was broken. Subsequently, participants randomly assigned to receive 125 mg of MDMA had one open-label session (within 3–5 weeks of the previous blinded MDMA session) with associated integrative visits and a 2-month follow-up with outcomes assessed (end of stage 1). Participants randomly assigned to receive 30 mg or 75 mg of MDMA crossed over to have one 90-min preparatory session (within 5 months of the primary endpoint), then three open-label sessions spaced a month apart with flexible dosing of MDMA (100–125 mg) followed by the integrative visits and outcome assessments (secondary endpoint, end of stage 2) at corresponding intervals to the blinded segment.

Data were collected during the active treatment period from baseline to 2 months after the final MDMA session, and participants in all three groups were assessed 12 months after the last full dose. A choice between 100 mg and 125 mg (according to the participant's preference and investigators' judgment) was added in the open-label crossover as part of a protocol amendment to gain pilot data about this dose without affecting the blinded stage of the study.

The primary outcome was mean change in the CAPS-IV total score from baseline to 1 month after the second experimental session. Secondary outcomes included the following measures: depression symptoms, measured with the self-reported Beck Depression Inventory-II (BDI-II); self-reported sleep quality, assessed by the Pittsburgh Sleep Quality Index (PSQI); perceived growth following trauma, assessed with the Post-Traumatic Growth Inventory (PTGI); personality factors, assessed via the NeuroticismExtroversion-Openness-Personality Inventory-Revised (NEO-PI-R); symptoms of dissociation, assessed in a subset of participants with the self-reported Dissociative Experiences Scale II (DES-II); and general psychological function, scored by independent raters using the single item Global Assessment of Functioning (GAF).

24 (92%) participants completed treatments through the 1-month follow-

up, and two (8%) completed the baseline assessment (one experimental session, and at least one follow-up assessment). Six (86%) of seven participants who were assigned to the 30 mg group and six (86%) of seven assigned to the 75 mg group completed the crossover open-label sessions and assessments. 24 participants completed the 12-month follow-up assessments.

Results:
- The mean change in the CAPS-IV total score from baseline to 1 month after the second blinded experimental session of MDMA plus psychotherapy was –11·4 (SD 12·7) for the 30 mg group, –58·3 (9·8) for the 75 mg group, and –44·3 (28·7) for the 125 mg group. The 75 mg (p=0·0005) and 125 mg (p=0·004) MDMA groups had significantly greater improvements in PTSD symptom severity than the 30 mg MDMA group (ANOVA for mean change in CAPS-IV total score p=0·001); no significant differences were found between the 75 mg and 125 mg groups (p=0·185).
- Compared with the 30 mg group, Cohen's d effect sizes were large: 2·8 (95% CI 1·19–4·39) for the 75 mg group and 1·1 (0·04–2·08) for the 125 mg group. At the primary endpoint (ie, after the 1-month second blinded experimental session), a larger percentage of participants in the active dose groups did not meet PTSD diagnostic criteria on CAPS-IV compared with the comparator group (six [86%] of seven participants in the 75 mg group and seven [58%] of 12 in the 125 mg group vs two [29%] of seven in the 30 mg group). Additionally, more participants reached a clinically significant decrease of more than 30% in CAPS-IV total score after two active doses of MDMA (all seven [100%] in the 75 mg group, eight [67%] in the 125 mg group, and two [29%] in the 30 mg group).
- A sensitivity analysis adjusting for baseline scores produced similar results. 1 month after the second blinded experimental session, depression symptoms for the 125 mg group were significantly reduced compared with the 30 mg group (mean change in BDI-II score of –24·6 vs –4·6; p=0·0003), while comparison of the 75 mg group with the 30 mg group was not significant (–15·4 vs –4·6; p=0·052; table 2), with the 75 mg group showing a larger average drop from baseline (ANOVA for mean change in BDI-II scores p=0·001). For mean change in PSQI scores, the 75 mg group showed the greatest improvement in sleep quality followed by the 125 mg and 30 mg groups (ANOVA for mean change in PSQI scores p=0·029). t tests indicated superiority in the 75 mg (p=0·014) and 125 mg (p=0·022) groups compared with the 30 mg group. Post-traumatic growth followed a similar trajectory in mean PTGI scores (ANOVA for mean change in PTGI scores p<0·0001), with the

active dose groups reporting significant post-traumatic growth compared with the 30 mg group (p<0·0001).
- Global psychological function improved (ANOVA for mean change in GAF scores p=0·004), with significantly higher functioning in the 75 mg (p=0·004) and 125 mg (p=0·002) groups than the 30 mg group. Similarly, the active dose groups had significant improvement in dissociative symptoms compared with the 30 mg group (p=0·02 for the 75 mg group vs 30 mg group; p=0·01 for the 125 mg group vs 30 mg group; ANOVA for mean change in DES-II scores p=0·026).
- For the NEO-PI-R, only changes in openness produced significant differences between groups (ANOVA for mean change in NEO-PI-R personality scores p=0·025), with the 75 mg group showing qualities of being more open than the 30 mg group (p=0·02).
- 1 month after completing two open-label sessions of 100–125 mg of MDMA in the crossover, the group that received 30 mg during blinded sessions showed reductions in symptom severity, mean change from the primary endpoint was CAPS-IV total score –27·0 (SD 17·5), and two (33%) of six participants did not meet CAPS-IV PTSD diagnostic criteria.
- Within subject t tests comparing scores at primary and secondary endpoints showed significant improvements in mean CAPS-IV total score (p=0·01) and four (67%) of six participants attained a decrease of more than 30% in CAPS-IV total score. The 75 mg group did not have further significant decreases in mean CAPS-IV total score after the two open-label sessions (p=0·81), but all of the participants no longer met CAPS-IV PTSD criteria.
- Although CAPS-IV total scores continued to trend towards further improvement, within-subject comparison of two versus three sessions of MDMA did not yield significant differences for any measures or groups.
- PTSD symptoms were significantly reduced at the 12-month follow-up compared with the baseline for all MDMA groups combined (mean CAPS-IV total score of 38·8 [SD 28·1] vs 87·1 [16·1]; p<0·0001; table 3).
- Of the 24 participants who completed the 12-month follow-up, 16 (67 %) did not meet CAPS-IV PTSD criteria. On the one hand, two participants who did not meet PTSD criteria at treatment exit (after three active doses of the MDMA sessions) met PTSD diagnostic criteria at 12-month follow-up. On the other hand, three participants who met criteria at exit did not meet criteria at the 12-month follow-up.
- Scores on all secondary measures at 12-month follow-up showed improvement compared with baseline. Depression symptom severity as measured on BDI-II was severe at baseline and changed to minimal by 12-month follow-up (p<0·0001). Similarly, sleep quality was vastly

improved at the last endpoint as measured by PSQI (p=0·0002).
- Findings for post-traumatic growth (p<0·0001) and global functioning (p<0·0001) showed marked gains, and severity of dissociative symptoms was reduced (p=0·046). Compared with baseline, all NEO personality traits had significantly improved except conscientiousness (p=0·36; table 3).
- The treatment was well tolerated. The number of participants reporting at least one treatment-emergent adverse event was similar across groups: six (86%) of seven in the 30 mg and 75 mg groups, and eight (67%) of 12 in the 125 mg group. The most frequently reported treatment-emergent adverse events were psychiatric symptoms. The most frequently reported expected adverse reactions during experimental sessions included anxiety, headache, fatigue, and muscle tension. Adverse reactions during 7 contact days included fatigue, anxiety, and insomnia. Most adverse reactions were mild to moderate in severity, with occurrence decreasing across the 7 days following experimental sessions.
- Self-limited elevations in pulse, blood pressure, and body temperature were observed during MDMA sessions and did not require medical intervention.

Discussion:
- MDMA-assisted psychotherapy with 75 mg or 125 mg resulted in marked improvement of PTSD symptoms in veterans and first responders with chronic PTSD who had failed previous treatment.
- Participants in the comparator group of 30 mg receiving the same psychotherapy had significantly less symptom remission than the active dose groups of 75 mg and 125 mg, indicating that adequate doses of MDMA potentiate the effects of psychotherapy. An unexpected finding was that the 75 mg dose led to larger decreases in CAPS-IV total score than the 125 mg dose. This difference might have been due to chance in this small sample size or might be due to other reasons. For example, participants of the 125 mg group had a higher mean baseline depression score than the other groups, and therefore could have been harder to treat. Another possible explanation is that the 75 mg dose might have allowed for more focused processing of traumatic experiences than the 125 mg dose, and might be the optimal dose for at least some patients.
- Severity of depression symptoms was significantly reduced for the 125 mg group compared with the 30 mg group; however, this reduction was not significant for the 75 mg group compared with the 30 mg group. Sleep quality and dissociative symptoms also significantly improved for both active dose groups compared with the control dose group. Additionally, there were gains in psychological, occupational, and social functioning for participants treated with active doses of MDMA, and

similar to the improvements in PTSD symptoms, these gains continued to grow in the year following treatment.
- Increased scores on the PTGI indicate that perceptions of self, others, and life events were reframed during the therapeutic processing, suggesting that treatment effects went beyond reductions in PTSD and mood symptoms to include psychological growth. Compared with the 30 mg group, change in personality traits showed statistically significant reductions in neuroticism in the 125 mg group and increases in openness in the 75 mg group.
- After participants in the 30 mg group crossed over to receive two open-label sessions of 100–125 mg MDMA, mean CAPS-IV total score showed an additional 27-point average decline, suggesting that the same psychotherapy alone was not nearly as effective without a sufficient dose of MDMA.
- The long-term follow-up results showing significant CAPS-IV total score reductions 12 months after the last MDMA-assisted treatment make it unlikely that the more immediate results were simply due to placebo effect or lingering expectancy effects of having received MDMA.
- MDMA was well tolerated with low treatment discontinuation (7·7%) that did not correlate with dose.
- Vital signs transiently increased in a dose-dependent manner during experimental sessions, and returned to approximate baseline values at the session end.
- Incidence of expected reactions and adverse events differed little across groups, although known acute side-effects of MDMA, such as jaw clenching and perspiration, did occur at higher frequency with active doses. Most events were mild to moderate, with many of the psychiatric symptoms possibly attributable to PTSD.
- Participants who were naive to ecstasy before study participation did not report taking ecstasy after receiving MDMA in the trial. Two participants reported taking ecstasy once during the 12-month follow-up, but both had taken the drug before study enrolment.
- Overall safety data support a favourable risk-to-benefit ratio for limited doses of MDMA for treating a population with PTSD.
- This study has limitations regarding the design and small sample size.
- Maintaining the study blind was only partially accomplished by using low-dose MDMA instead of inactive placebo.
- A limitation of the 12-month follow-up results is that after the primary endpoint, the 30 mg dose and 75 mg dose groups crossed over to receive a full dose of MDMA; therefore, no control group for comparison at 12 months existed.

Conclusion:
This trial provides further evidence that MDMA-assisted psychotherapy can be used safely and effectively for treating patients with chronic PTSD. This novel approach to pharmacotherapy offers a means to accelerate substantially the therapeutic process with a short-acting psychoactive compound administered only a few times at monthly intervals in conjunction with a course of psychotherapy designed to maximise the safety and efficacy of drug administration.

Ot'alora et al (2018). 3,4-Methylenedioxymethamphetamine-assisted psychotherapy for treatment of chronic posttraumatic stress disorder: A randomized phase 2 controlled trial.

Methods:
Ot'alora et al (2018) recruited 28 (19 female) participants who were randomised in a double-blind manner. 27 completed the primary assessment, and 25 were assessed at 12-month follow-up.

All participants were screened with ECG and physical examinations. Inclusion criteria required PTSD for at least six months, and a score of $\geqslant 50$ on the Clinician Administered PTSD Scale (CAPS-IV). Participant had failed to respond to at least one course of pharmacotherapy and/or psychotherapy.
Participants should otherwise be physically healthy and free of psychiatric or medical contraindications for receiving MDMA. Women could not be pregnant or lactating.

Each participant was randomised to receive an active (125 or 100 mg) or a comparator active placebo (40 mg) dose of MDMA during two double-blind eight-hour experimental sessions spaced a month apart. A supplemental dose half the quantity of the initial dose (62.5, 50 or 20 mg) was available approximately 90 min after the first dose, if not contraindicated.
Psychotherapy and the practical aspects of the study were carried out according to the manual by Mithoefer (2015), as explained in the beginning of this chapter.

At the primary endpoint, one month after the second blinded experimental session, each participant was assessed by the same blinded independent rater and completed self-report measures, after which the blind was broken. Participants in the 40 mg group crossed over to have one preparatory session and three open-label sessions (100–125 mg MDMA) with associated integrative sessions. Participants in the 100 mg and 125 mg groups underwent a third, open-label session (100–125 mg MDMA). Outcome measures were administered a month after the second open-label session and two months after the third open-label session. A 12-month follow-up assessment occurred 12 months (±one month) after the final active dose MDMA session.

The CAPS-IV served as the primary outcome measure. The dichotomous diagnostic score (Weathers et al., 2001), and ⩾30% drop in CAPS-IV total scores were used to evaluate clinically significant changes in PTSD symptoms. The same blinded independent rater who was not present during any therapy sessions administered the CAPS-IV. Secondary outcome measures assessed symptoms of depression via Beck Depression Inventory-II (BDI-II), dissociation with the Dissociative Experiences Scale-II (DES-II) and sleep quality with the Pittsburgh Sleep Quality Index (PSQI).

Results:
Adverse Effects:
- There were no serious drug-related adverse events and no medical intervention was required during or following the MDMA sessions.
- Heart rate were significant elevated and systolic BP were nearly significantly elevated. No medical interventions were needed for the small to moderate increases in vital signs.
- Adverse effects reported by ⩾40% in any group on day of blinded sessions were anxiety and jaw clenching/tight jaw, followed by headache, muscle tension, dizziness, fatigue, and low mood.
- The most commonly reported reactions on one or more of the seven days following blinded MDMA sessions, included sleep-related reactions (insomnia, need more sleep) and low mood, increased irritability, and ruminations. Most were mild to moderate, with frequency decreasing across the week following the experimental sessions.

Effects:
- In the intention to treat (ITT) set, the active dose groups had the largest reduction in PTSD symptom severity with mean (SD) CAPS changes of −26.3 (29.5) for 125 mg, −24.4 (24.2) for 100 mg, and −11.5 (21.2) for 40 mg.
- Although there was no significant overall effect ($F_{2,26}=0.68$, $p=0.52$). Cohen's d effect sizes with 40 mg subtracted was 0.42 (−0.57, 1.42) for 125 mg and 0.37 (−0.57, 1.42) for 100 mg.
- In the per protocol (PP) set, there was a significant main effect in change of CAPS-IV total scores ($F_{2,22}=4.01$, $p=0.03$). Compared to the 40 mg group (mean change (SD) −4.0 (11.9)), the 125 mg group had a

significant reduction (−37.0 (20.9), p=0.01) and the 100 mg group trended towards significance (−24.4 (24.2), p=0.10). Cohen's d effect sizes with 40 mg subtracted was 1.12 (−0.10, 2.35) for 125 mg and 0.73 (−0.45, 1.90) for 100 mg.
- For the ITT set, did more participants in the active dose groups not meet PTSD diagnostic criteria according to the CAPS-IV at the primary endpoint (33.3% (40 mg), 44.4% (100 mg), and 41.7% (125 mg)). As a measure of clinical significance, the percentage of participants who attained a ⩾30% decrease in CAPS-IV total scores was substantially greater for active dose groups (16.7% (40 mg), 55.6% (100 mg), and 50.0% (125 mg)).
- For the ITT set, change in depressive symptoms, determined by the BDI-II, was approximately equivalent across groups ($F_{2,26}=0.03$, p=0.97). Mean (SD) change in PSQI total scores was −0.8 (2.5) for 40 mg, −3.6 (6.2) for 100 mg, −2.0 (4.7) for 125 mg, indicating some improvement in sleep quality for all groups, yet this failed to reach significance ($F_{2,26}=0.583$, p=0.57). Fewer dissociative experiences were reported by active dose groups (mean (SD) change in DES-II total scores, −13.3 (15.3) for 100 mg, and −5.9 (12.0) for 125 mg) compared to 40 mg −0.2 (6.9), although the difference was not significant ($F_{2,26}=2.09$, p=0.15).
- Two months after the final open-label session, CAPS-IV total scores significantly declined compared to the primary endpoint for both groups (ITT set: blind 100 mg/open-label, $t_8=6.82$, p<0.0001; blind 125 mg/open-label $t_{11}=2.62$, p=0.02), and four additional participants no longer met criteria for PTSD, indicating that the third MDMA session further improved treatment outcomes in this sample.
- Scores also generally improved on other measures, with some reaching significance (BDI-II (blind 100 mg/open-label, $t_8=2.74$, p=0.03; blind 125 mg/open-label $t_{11}=1.14$, p=0.28), PSQI (blind 100 mg/openlabel, $t_8=1.97$, p=0.08; blind 125 mg/open-label $t_8=1.59$, p=0.15), and DES-II (blind 100 mg/open-label, $t_8=2.36$, p=0.046; blind 125 mg/open-label $t_{10}=2.21$, p=0.05)).
- After two blinded sessions, the 40 mg group crossed over for three open-label MDMA (100–125 mg) sessions. One month after the second open-label session, PTSD symptom severity improved significantly compared to the primary endpoint (CAPS-IV total scores ($t_4=4.49$, p=0.01)), as did symptoms of depression (BDI-II scores ($t_4=4.60$, p=0.01)) and dissociation (DES-II scores ($t_4=2.96$, p=0.04)). Sleep quality (PSQI scores ($t_4=1.39$, p=0.24)) presented no significant changes.
- Scores did not significantly change further two-months after the third open label session for this group.

- Twelve months after the last active dose of MDMA, PTSD symptom severity was evaluated again. CAPS-IV total scores for the ITT set at baseline and 12-month follow-up mean (SD) were 92.0 (18.0) and 31.0 (24.2), respectively. PTSD severity was significantly lower compared to baseline ($t24=11.30$, $p<0.0001$). CAPS-IV total scores declined on average -9.6 (19.5) from treatment exit to the 12-month assessment.
- The majority (76%) did not meet PTSD diagnostic criteria, demonstrating enduring positive effects of MDMA-assisted psychotherapy. Analysis of secondary outcomes also found significant improvement at the 12-month follow-up compared to baseline for depression (BDI-II: $t23=8.15$, $p<0.0001$), sleep quality (PSQI: $t22=6.46$, $p<0.0001$), and dissociation (DES-II: $t22=5.7$, $p<0.0001$), indicating sustained gains well after the active treatment period ended.

Discussion:
- Consistent with prior research, this study provides supportive evidence that MDMA-assisted psychotherapy can be safe and efficacious in individuals with chronic PTSD refractory to medication and/or psychotherapy.
- Safety outcomes for MDMA-assisted psychotherapy in a controlled clinical setting strongly suggest a favorable benefit to risk ratio. Frequency and intensity of adverse events, reactions, and suicidal ideation were similar to previous reports (Mithoefer et al., 2011, Mithoefer et al 2018; Oehen et al., 2013).
- Vital signs after MDMA generally increased in a dose-dependent manner to values similar during moderate exercise, and were well tolerated in these participants. There were no SAEs related to the treatment, adding to the evidence that MDMA can safely be administered to patients with PTSD.
- This is the first trial to employ multiple therapy teams with newly trained therapists implementing the manualised approach, which is encouraging regarding the likelihood that other newly-trained providers may replicate these findings in phase 3 trials.
- Although significant group differences were detected only in the PP set for the primary outcome, over half of participants in the ITT set who received active MDMA doses reached a 30% or greater drop in CAPS-IV total scores compared to 16.7% in the 40 mg group.
- After two blinded MDMA sessions, active dose groups had the largest reductions in CAPS-IV total scores with more participants attaining clinically significant improvements in PTSD symptoms relative to the 40 mg group, supporting a dose response.
- To understand if three experimental sessions were more beneficial than two sessions, outcomes were evaluated again two months after the third

(last) MDMA session. After the third experimental session, both the 100 mg and 125 mg groups showed further reductions in CAPS-IV scores, providing evidence that an additional session significantly improved PTSD outcomes.
- On the other hand, after the 40 mg group crossed over, a large treatment response resulted after two open-label sessions with little change after the third. The difference in time to respond is likely due to individual variation in the small samples, although there may have been a small additional therapeutic effect from the initial two low-dose sessions.
- Importantly, the gains were maintained over a 12-month follow-up after all groups had received active doses of MDMA in either blinded or open-label sessions, with 76% (n=25) of individuals not meeting the criteria for a diagnosis of PTSD. The fact that CAPS scores continued to improve between the two-month and 12-month follow-up visits lends support to the hypothesis that MDMA helps to catalyse a therapeutic process that continues long after the last drug administration.
- Moreover, the secondary outcome measures (depression, sleep, and dissociation) all showed significant reduction of symptoms at 12 months compared to baseline. At the 12-month visit, only one participant was taking a medication for PTSD; nine others were taking medications for insomnia, depression, generalised anxiety disorder, attention deficit/hyperactivity disorder (ADHD), and anxiety. These findings are noteworthy given that participants had moderate to extreme PTSD and had previously failed to benefit from psychotherapy, including approaches thought to be relatively effective (cognitive behavioural therapy (CBT) and eye movement desensitisation reprocessing (EMDR)), and pharmacological treatment, including medications for depression and anxiety.
- Certain limitations constrain both the generalisability of findings and the ability to draw inferences concerning interactions among independent variables. The sample was relatively homogeneous, with the majority being predominantly female. In addition, the primary limitation was the relatively small sample size, especially in the low-dose study arm.
- Establishing an effective blind for a psychoactive drug like MDMA is difficult. Previous phase 2 clinical trials used inactive placebo (Mithoefer et al., 2011) and a low dose MDMA as comparator (25 mg or 30 mg) (Mithoefer et al., 2018; Oehen et al., 2013). This study utilised a dose-response design, comparing active doses to 40 mg MDMA, in order to enhance masking of MDMA-stimulated effects.
- A limitation to the openlabel crossover and 12-month follow-up was that the assessments were made under non-blinded conditions and there was no control group for comparison at these time points.

Conclusion:
The promising efficacy and safety results from this dose response study, along with findings from five other phase 2 trials form the basis for expansion into multi-site phase 3 trials. In addition, the FDA granted "Breakthrough therapy" designation for MDMA-assisted psychotherapy for PTSD treatment, which may expedite the drug development process. Both short-term (one and two month) and long-term (12 month) follow-up results were positive, and the treatment was safe and well-tolerated. More research is needed to determine the optimal number of MDMA sessions needed to achieve symptom remission. Upcoming phase 3 trials, with a planned enrolment of 200–300 participants will evaluate the time to response and other factors that influence outcomes. If findings are replicated in phase 3 trials, MDMA-assisted psychotherapy will become an available treatment option for people suffering with PTSD.

MDMA for social anxiety in autistic adults:

Possible biological mechanism in the treatment of social anxiety:
Autism refers to a spectrum of congenital and pervasive neurocognitive variants. Autism presents with myriad manifestations resulting in considerable heterogeneity among individuals with atypical development of social and communication skills. At present, there are no published research data in support of compounds that can influence the course of autism or be a causative agent (Danforth 2013).
There may be underlying biological reasons autistic adults have atypical responses to psychiatric medications commonly prescribed for anxiety, including evidence for fewer benzodiazepine binding sites, atypical GABAergic inhibitory signaling, and atypical serotonin and dopamine transporter binding in autistic brains (Coghlan et al. 2012; King et al. 2009; Nakamura et al. 2010; Uzunova et al. 2016).

In humans, MDMA generates feelings of social affiliation and increases social approach while diminishing negative responses to social rejection (Kamilar-Britt and Bedi 2015)., acting as a potent releaser of serotonin and norepinephrine, and to a lesser extent dopamine (de la Torre et al. 2004; Hysek and Liechti 2012). MDMA also promotes release of the neurohormone oxytocin (OT) (Dumont et al. 2009; Hysek et al. 2012; Kirkpatrick et al. 2014; Kuypers et al. 2017). OT is associated with social affiliation in mammals and attenuates amygdalar response to anxiogenic stimuli (Adolphs et al. 2005; Bartz and Hollander 2006), and OT receptor gene variations may also modulate prosocial effects of MDMA in humans (Bershad et al. 2016; Vizeli and Liechti 2018).
Due to its unique pharmacology, MDMA has shown promise as an adjunct

to psychotherapy for treatment of post-traumatic stress disorder (Mithoefer et al. 2018; Mithoefer et al. 2011; Mithoefer et al. 2013; Oehen et al. 2013, Ot'aulora et a, 2018).

Qualitative data on MDMA/ecstasy use by autistic adults in epidemiological settings supported the selection of social anxiety disorder (SAD) as the primary indication for the exploration of MDMA for this population (Danforth 2013). SAD is characterised by fear of scrutiny and avoidance of social interactions (American Psychiatric Association 2013). Comparative studies suggest that autistic individuals are at greater risk (1:4) of current or lifetime SAD (Bejerot et al. 2014).

Previous research:
MDMA weren't studied specifically for the treatment of social anxiety in autistic adults in the pre-prohibition era.

Contemporary research:
At the time of writing, only the following paper have been published on the subject:

Danforth et al (2018). Reduction in social anxiety after MDMA-assisted psychotherapy with autistic adults: a randomized, double-blind, placebo-controlled pilot study.

Danforth et al (2018) recruited 12 participants (10 male) for a randomised, placebo-controlled, double-blinded phase 2 study, exploring MDMA as a treatment of SAD.
Eligibility was established through clinical interview and administration of diagnostic instruments, including the Structured Clinical Interview for Diagnostic and Statistical Manual of Mental Disorders- Fourth Edition Axis I Research Version (SCID-I-RV), LSAS (Liebowitz et al. 1985), and the Autism Diagnostic Observation Schedule (ADOS-2 Module 4) (Bastiaansen et al. 2011). To be eligible, a global LSAS score of 60 or higher, indicating marked to severe fear and avoidance of specific social situations, was required. Participants were physically healthy, and psychologically stable. The majority of participants had previously received psychotherapy, primarily supportive talk therapy (83.3%). Eight of 12 (66.7%) participants had received pharmacologic treatments, primarily antidepressants (58.3%), stimulants (33.3%), and anxiolytics (25.0%). Baseline LSAS ratings ranged from 69 to 125, indicating marked to very severe SAD symptoms. Based on medical history and confirmed with the SCID, 66.67% of participants had a history of depression, 41.67% had generalised anxiety disorder, and 100% had SAD

Participants were randomised to either MDMA (n = 8) or inactive placebo (n = 4). A dose-finding study design was selected in response to anecdotal data, suggesting that hyper-reactivity to sensory stimulation and emotion regulation challenges associated with autism might indicate the need for a lower, yet therapeutically active, MDMA dose range. Among participants receiving MDMA, the first subgroup (N = 4) received 75mg MDMA at the first session and 100-mg MDMA at the second session. The second subgroup (N = 4) received 100mg MDMA at the first session and 125 mg at the second session.

Participants first received three (In two instances, an additional preparatory session was required to accommodate clinical considerations) 60- to 90-min non-drug preparatory psychotherapy sessions, during which past or current salient issues in the participant's life were discussed. These sessions focused on establishing rapport between the participant and treatment team. They were also educated about mindfulness-based therapies for autistic adults (Spek et al. 2013). Consequently, participants received standardised mindfulness-based therapy adapted from dialectical behavioural therapy (DBT) as part of their treatment (Linehan 1993). DBT was developed to support individuals struggling with interpersonal relationships, emotion regulation, and distress tolerance. In general, these psychosocial domains are challenging for autistic adults with SAD.

A notable advantage of mindfulness-based preparatory psychotherapy was the introduction of vocabulary and skills that helped participants with transitioning into MDMA-influenced cognitive and affective states, as well as with communicating with others during novel, often ineffable, altered states of consciousness.

Participants then received two blinded experimental sessions with MDMA or placebo, spaced approximately 1 month apart.

On the day of the session the participants arrived around 09:30. They were required to refrain from eating after 24:00 (midnight) except for non-alcoholic fluids prior to the session. Study visits took place in a room with a den-like ambiance, which was designed to minimise sensory distress (e.g., soft lighting, noise abatement). Per consultation with members of the autistic community, features such as elements of nature (e.g., fresh flowers), fidget objects for self-regulating through repetitive movement, and suitable décor items were added to support common autistic preferences. Additionally, the room accommodated aesthetic adjustments for comfort (e.g., seating arrangements, temperature) and had an adjacent private lavatory. MDMA/placebo was administered around 10:30 after a guided progressive muscle relaxation exercise (McCallie et al. 2006). Optional snacks and a light meal were made available 3 h after study drug

administration. Sessions concluded in late afternoon, and participants were ready to leave around 17:30 after a brief closing. Participants were then given a contact for urgent assistance from an investigator physician
The morning following each experimental session, participants returned to the center for integrative psychotherapy. Safety data were collected, the content of the previous day's experience was examined, and methods for adjusting back to daily life after treatment were reviewed. Telephone safety checks then occurred each of the 7 days following. Two in-person integrative psychotherapy sessions were scheduled at 2-week intervals for 1 month and again at the 6-month follow-up point, with the option of adding an additional office visit, if needed.

Primary outcome were the Leibowitz Social Anxiety Scale (LSAS) (a 24-item, semi-structured interview evaluating the severity of social anxiety symptoms) (Liebowitz et al. 1985), which were administered at baseline, 1 day, 2 weeks, and 4 weeks after each experimental session and re-administered it before the blind was broken at 6 months. The primary outcome was change from baseline to 1-month post second experimental session in LSAS total scores. At monthly intervals, between the 1-month post-treatment psychotherapy session and the 6-month follow-up visit, participants completed the Beck Depression Inventory (BDI-II) (Beck et al. 1996), Spielberger State-Trait Inventory (STAI Form Y-2) (Spielberger et al. 1983), and Perceived Stress Scale (PSS) (Cohen et al. 1983).

The blind was broken at 6-month follow-up; participants who received placebo in the first treatment phase returned for two optional open-label treatment sessions with MDMA, of which results are not yet reported.

Results:
Adverse Effects:
- No significant adverse event were reported on this study.
- Most commonly reported reactions were anxiety (75.0% MDMA versus 25.0% placebo) and difficulty concentrating (62.5% MDMA versus 25.0% placebo). Fatigue, headache, and sensitivity to cold were also reported (50.0% MDMA versus 0–25.0% placebo). All were self-limiting in the days following the treatment.
- Blood pressure, pulse, and body temperature (BT) were typically, but not always, elevated in the MDMA group versus placebo. This was self-limiting.

Effects:
- Reduction in SAD symptoms as indicated by mean change in LSAS score from baseline to primary endpoint was significantly greater for the

MDMA group than for the placebo group (t(9) = 2.451, P = 0.037, CI 1.92, 47.87). The placebo-subtracted Cohen's d effect size was 1.4 (CI − 0.074, 2.874).
- At 6-month follow-up, the decline in mean LSAS score from baseline was largest for the MDMA group compared to placebo group (t(9) = 2.454, P = 0.036, CI 1.92, 47.01). The placebo-subtracted Cohen's d effect size was 1.1 (CI − 0.31, 2.53).
- Mean (SD) LSAS scores changed minimally from primary endpoint to 6-month follow-up for both groups [MDMA 46.4 (15.2) to 42.9 (20.4), placebo 64.0 (13.3) to 60.0 (17.4)]. Reductions were retained for the MDMA group at 6-month follow-up compared to primary endpoint, supporting durability of improvements (MDMA, t(6) = 1.117, P = 0.307).
- The rate of clinical response was defined as a 20-point reduction in LSAS based on prior studies using the LSAS (Simon et al. 2004). The rate of clinically significant changes in SAD symptoms from Baseline was 6/8 (75%) with MDMA versus 2/4 (50%) with placebo.

Discussion:
- This was the first study to investigate MDMA-assisted psychotherapy to treat generalized social anxiety.
- The primary endpoint, mean change from baseline in LSAS scores was significantly greater for the MDMA group compared to the placebo group. The placebo-subtracted effect size for the changes in LSAS from baseline to the primary endpoint and to 6-month follow-up was very large (d = 1.4 and 1.1, respectively).
- Enrolment required a total score of 60 or greater on the LSAS at baseline, in a range highly suggestive of generalised SAD. Scores in this range are typical of individuals entering treatment and indicate high levels of distress and difficulties with social functioning. In addition, high mean scores on both the social anxiety and social avoidance sub-scales were suggestive of generalised SAD as opposed to specific, focal problems such as public speaking anxiety.
- Mean scores for the placebo group improved at primary endpoint, but not to the degree of the MDMA group. In comparison, mean scores for the MDMA group remained below the enrollment cutoff after treatment and continued to decrease during the 5-month period when participants were not receiving therapy.
- Of seven participants in the MDMA group completing treatment, all dropped two to four levels in severity category, whereas the four participants in the placebo group dropped zero to three levels in severity. In addition, six of seven participants in the MDMA group had a > 20-point drop in LSAS scores compared to two of four participants in the

placebo group.
- Participant self-report on subjective effects was congruent with the marked decrease in LSAS mean scores, with no participant reporting a clinically significant increase in social anxiety or avoidance behaviours post-treatment. Examples of changes that were self-reported included reduced barriers to successful social interactions and increased confidence in school, at work, in friendships, and in romantic relationships. Several participants and SSPs provided accounts of improved interpersonal interactions with family members. Two participants reported being able to initiate dating for the first time, and two reported feeling more comfortable with exploring and expressing gender identity.
- Several participants experienced increased comfort with prolonged eye-contact and enhanced ability to express emotions verbally. Increases in OT levels after MDMA, as reported in healthy individuals, might have enhanced a sense of connection and enriched therapeutic rapport.
- Investigators did not provide psychoeducation or training on how to implement or improve social skills. However, in the majority of cases, they observed emergence of apparently intact latent social skills (e.g., ease of initiating and sustaining conversation) that manifested and became apparent to observers during experimental sessions with MDMA when participants relaxed.
- These improvements persisted to varying degrees through follow-up. Eleven of 12 participants reported marked reductions in anxiety responses to in vivo exposure to triggers previously distressing for them, such as making a presentation, speaking on the telephone, entering new social settings, or interacting with authority figures.
- MDMA were well tolerated and no significant adverse effects were reported. Moderate elevations in blood pressure, heart rate, and temperature were observed during most experimental sessions, as expected.
- Limitations of the study is small sample size and broad range of scores.
- The findings justify the need for future research for treatment of SAD with MDMA-assisted psychotherapy.

Conclusion:
The two primary goals of this study were to establish feasibility and safety of MDMA-assisted psychotherapy in a controlled clinical setting for SAD in autistic adults; both were successfully established. Changes in LSAS scores and subjective observations were consistent with the hypothesis that anxiety interferes with social functioning in autistic adults and can be alleviated with a combination of MDMA and psychotherapy, supportive preparation, and integrative after care.

Medical Psychedelics

KETAMINE

Ketamine:
Ketamine is a dissociative psychedelic like phencyclidine (PCP) and dextromethorphan (DXM), which act primarily as a non-competitive N-methyl-D-aspartate (NMDA) receptor antagonists [Krystal et al. 1994]. Ketamine is used in medicine for inducing and maintaining anaesthesia, and illicitly for its hallucinogenic and dissociative effects. Recently, there has too been a growing interest in its possible antidepressive effects, which this chapter will focus upon.

Pharmacology
Owing to the water and lipid solubility of ketamine, it can be administered by a variety of routes, including intravenous (IV), intramuscular (IM), intranasal (IN) and oral. The bioavailability of ketamine is approximately 90% when given IV or IM, compared with 16% orally, although peak effects occur rapidly with all methods (Craven, 2007).
Whilst oral administration is inevitably more convenient for both patients and staff in clinical use, to date, the majority of clinical research of ketamine has used IV administration.

Ketamine

Ketamine is water soluble and has a short half-life of 1 to 3 hours (White et al, 1982). It is metabolized to dehydronorketamine, norketamine, and hydroxynorketamine (Cheng et al, 2007). Norketamine is an active metabolite with one-third of the analgesic potency of ketamine. The hepatic enzymes responsible for ketamine's biotransformation are CYP3A4, 2B6, and 2C9 (Hijazi et al, 2002).

Ketamine is in most countries sold as a racemic mixture containing equal amounts of two enantiomers, S(+)- and R(-)-ketamine. Hirota et al (2018) describes their differences as follows: S(+)-ketamine has greater potency and higher clearance for anaesthesia and analgesia than R(-)-ketamine (Muller et al, 2016). S(+)-ketamine has about four- and three-fold greater antagonist potency for NMDA21 and m-opioid receptors (Hirota et al, 1999), respectively. In addition, S(+)-ketamine produces better intraoperative amnesia and fewer psychotic emergence reactions and less agitation (Muller et al, 2016). Repeated administration of S(+)-ketamine has been reported to be effective in both bipolar and unipolar depressed patients with pharmacotherapy, psychotherapy, and ECT resistance, suicidal crisis, or both (Andrade et al, 2015). However, several animal studies have shown that R(-)-ketamine produces more potent, safer, and longer-lasting antidepressant actions (Yang et al, 2015). How can R(-)-ketamine induce more beneficial antidepressant effects than S(+)-ketamine? The mechanism remains elusive, but one possible explanation might be as follows: R(-)-ketamine significantly attenuates the reduction in dendritic spine density, BDNF/TrkB signalling, and synaptogenesis in the PFC, hippocampal cornu ammonis-3 (CA3) region and dentate gyrus (Yang et ak, 2015). In addition, a positron emission tomography study suggests that the psychotomimetic and hyperfrontal metabolic actions of ketamine are probably induced by S(+)- ketamine as psychotomimetic doses increase the cerebral metabolic rates of glucose (CMRglu) in the frontal cortex and thalamus; equimolar doses of R(-)-ketamine decreased CMRglu with no psychotic symptoms (Vollenweider et al, 1997).

Physiological safety:
Short et al (2017) published a systematic review of the safety of ketamine in the treatment of depression with single and repeated doses. The most common acute psychiatric side-effect was anxiety followed by agitation or irritability, euphoria or mood elevation, delusions or unusual thoughts, panic, and apathy. The most common psychotomimetic side-effect reported was dissociation, followed by perceptual disturbance, odd or abnormal sensation, derealisation, hallucinations, feeling strange, weird, bizarre, or unreal, and depersonalisation. No long-term psychotomimetic side-effects were reported.

The most common cardiovascular changes were increased blood pressure and increased heart rate. The most common neurological side-effects were headache and dizziness. The most frequently reported other side-effects were blurred vision and nausea.
In general, these side-effects resolve shortly after dose administration. There are no reports regarding chronic adverse reactions of ketamine in this population.

Several studies have been performed on the efficacy of ketamine for treatment of chronic pain (Short et a, 2017; Andrade et al, 2017; Yang et al, 2015; Vollenweider et al, 1997). Occurrence of ketamine-induced adverse reactions is limited and often well tolerated (Amr et al, 2010; Niesters et al, 2014; Sheeby et al, 2017; Jonkman et al, 2017). However, Niesters et al (2014) reported that repetitive or continuous administration of ketamine caused liver enzyme elevations in about 10% of patients, which returned to normal within 3 months of cessation.

In contrast, recreational - which self-report taking illicit obtained ketamine - users often develop urological toxicity, hepatotoxicity, cognitive deficits, and dependency risks. Regarding urological toxicity, cystitis, and bladder dysfunction, an increase in urinary frequency, urgency, dysuria, urge incontinence, occasionally painful haematuria, and secondary renal damage have been reported. More than 20% of recreational ketamine users are estimated to have urinary tract symptoms, although much higher rates have been reported (46% and 90%) (Short et al, 2018). These data indicate severe adverse reactions often occur when used under uncontrolled circumstances. In addition, recreational ketamine users use high doses and simultaneously several illicit drugs with abuse potential. Contamination of ketamine with other substances may also contribute to the adverse reactions (Niesters et al, 2014). It is difficult to be sure if these adverse reactions are directly caused by ketamine per se. Any long-term clinical use will require careful monitoring of patients to detail this profile.

Effects:
The effects of ketamine are largely similar to the classical psychedelics.

Ketamine for the treatment of major depression disorder:

Possible biological mechanism in the treatment of major depression disorder:

Ketamine may affect the glutamatergic system, and has been proposed of major interest in depression since many reports showed a marked antidepressive effect in the very hours following the administration of a single dose (Stahl, 2013; Ghasemi et al., 2014; Dutta et al., 2015).

Ketamine is an antiglutamatergic drug, ketamine. Several brain imaging, genetic and post-mortem studies have showed, that the glutamatergic-system is involved in the pathosyiology of major depression disorder (Manji et al., 2003; Sanacora et al., 2008; Skolnick et al., 2009). The blockade of N-methyl-D-aspartate receptors (NMDA) by ketamine may contribute to antidepressive effects by different mechanisms, recently described by Krystal et al. (2013). Briefly, ketamine might rapidly increase synaptic glutamate release, which may contribute to rapidly increase synaptic connections in the prefrontal cortex (Krystal et al., 2013; **Duman**, 2014). Furthermore, by blocking extrasynaptic NMDA receptors, ketamine could enable the regrowth of dendritic spines by relieving inhibition of BDNF synthesis (Krystal et al., 2013). Furthermore, **Chandley** et al. (2014) found a higher expression levels of the NMDA receptor genes in noradrenergic neurons within the locus coeruleus in patients with major depression, suggesting that glutamate–norepinephrine interactions might contribute to the rapid antidepressive effect of the NMDA antagonist (Ghasemi et al., 2014; Dutta et al., 2015).

Hirota et al (2018) explained in their paper the various mechanism which might explain the andidepressive effect of ketamine:

The NMDA receptor hypothesis:
Although anaesthetic doses of ketamine reduce prefrontal glutamatergic transmission, subanaesthetic doses increase glutamate cycling and as a result, extracellular glutamate increases in the prefrontal cortex (PFC). NMDA receptor blockade of g-aminobutyric acidergic (GABAergic) interneurons inhibits their activity. In addition, ketamine inhibits presynaptic NMDA receptors followed by reduction in presynaptic hyperpolarisation-activated cyclic nucleotidegated channel 1 (HCN1) channel activity, which would lead to increased glutamate release and thereby subsequent postsynaptic glutamate receptor activity (Abdallah et al, 2016; Zang et al, 2016). Postsynaptic a-amino-3-hydroxy-5-methyl-4-isoxazolepropionic acid (AMPA) receptors are activated and extrasynaptic NMDA receptors are inhibited. A combination of AMPA receptor activation and extrasynaptic NMDA receptor inhibition facilitates the postsynaptic activation of neuroplasticity-related signalling pathways involving BDNF and the mammalian target of rapamycin (mTOR). Synaptic NMDA receptor blockade by ketamine leads to suppression of eukaryotic elongation factor-2 (eEF2) kinase. Phosphorylation of eEF2 gradually decreases and Brain-derived neurotrophic factor (BDNF)

translation increases. Upregulation of BDNF translation evokes tyrosine-related kinase-B (TrkB) signalling leading to transphosphorylation and downstream activation of extracellular signalling related kinases (ERKs) and protein kinase-B (Akt/ PKB), and suppression of glycogen synthase kinase-3 (GSK-3). As a result, mTOR is activated to induce synaptogenesis (Muller et al, 2016).

Yang et al (2018) suggests that the rapid antidepressant effects of ketamine may be attributable to blocking of NMDA receptor-dependent bursting activity in lateral habenula neurones, an 'anti-reward centre', to activate a downstream reward centre. These biochemical responses may mediate the rapid and long-term antidepressant effects of ketamine. Interestingly, Williams et al (2018) recently reported that naltrexone markedly diminished ketamine-induced antidepressant effects in patients with treatment-resistant depression. They concluded that opioid system activation, particularly m-opioid receptors, is required to produce the acute antidepressant effect of ketamine. It is likely that the NMDA receptor antagonism potentiates endogenous m-opioid receptor activity to produce the antidepressant actions as clinically relevant concentrations of ketamine induce b-endorphin expression (YaDeau et al, 2003).

Non-NMDA receptor mechanism: Current antidepressants are selective serotonin reuptake inhibitors (SSRIs), serotoninenorepinephrine reuptake inhibitors (SNRIs), noradrenergic and specific serotonergic antidepressants (NaSSAs), and norepinephrine and dopamine reuptake inhibitors (NDRIs). Ketamine can increase monoamine release, including of norepinephrine, dopamine, and serotonin, and inhibits their reuptake (Tso et al, 2004). Ketamine may therefore have more conventional antidepressant actions related to those of SNRIs, NaSSAs, and NDRIs.

However, SSRIs may stimulate serotonin type 3 receptors (5HT3Rs), which are expressed with insulin-like growth factor-1 (IGF-1) in the same neurones in the hippocampal dentate gyrus. IGF-1 has antidepressant effects. Kondo and colleagues (Kondo et al, 2018) found that 5HT3R regulates the hippocampal extracellular levels of IGF-1 levels, which mediates 5HT3R-dependent hippocampal neurogenesis. Expression of IGF-1 is upregulated in response to ketamine in C6 glioma cells (Niwa et al, 2017), and increase in IGF-1 by ketamine may contribute to its antidepressant effects.

Anti-inflammatory actions:
Recent studies strongly indicate a relationship between inflammation and major depression. Several transcription factors such as NF-E2-related factor 2 (Nrf2) and nuclear factor-kB (NF-kB) have been reported to contribute to depressive disorders (Bakunina et al, 2015). In addition,

integrative brain analysis of rat and human PFC transcriptomes demonstrates that a number of convergent genes may be involved in the pathogenesis of depressive disorders as 80% of these genes relate functionally to the stress response signalling cascade involving NF-kB, activator protein 1 (AP1), and ERK/ MAPK (mitogen-activated protein kinase), which are associated with depressive disorder, neuroplasticity, and neurogenesis (Malki et al, 2015). In fact, anti-inflammatory agents such as NSAIDs, statins, and cytokine inhibitors have potential antidepressant properties, whereas pro-inflammatory treatment often induces psychiatric side-effects such as depressive symptoms (Kohler et al, 2016).

In this regard, ketamine has anti-inflammatory effects, which have been confirmed in clinical settings. Dale et al (2012) performed a systematic review and meta-analysis and found that intraoperative ketamine attenuates inflammatory reactivity after surgery as postoperative plasma interleukin (IL)-6 was significantly lower with ketamine. Ketamine can decrease the binding affinity of lipopolysaccharide (LPS) for LPS-binding protein and suppress phosphorylation of several protein kinases and transcription factors including NF-kB and AP-1 via Toll-like receptor (TLR)-mediated signal transduction (Hirota et al, 2011) in the sepsis model. Thus, it is likely that ketamine exerts anti-inflammatory actions not only in systemic inflammation but also in neuroinflammation including depressive disorders.

However, recent clinical trial data do not support the anti-inflammatory effects of ketamine as a single sub-anaesthetic dose (0.5 mg/kg) did not prevent postoperative delirium, which may be attributable to neuroinflammation, in elderly patients undergoing major surgery (Avidan et al, 2017).

In Romeo et al (2015), one results was the given evidence that ketamine contributed to a rapid improvement in both unipolar and bipolar depression, but this effect was sustained over time only in unipolar depression. This observation was in accordance with a differential involvement of the glumatergic system in both disorders. A recent meta-analysis of spectroscopy studies in bipolar and unipolar depression showed that measurements of total glutamate and glutamine in the anterior cingulate cortex could represent a biological marker differentiating both disorders (Taylor, 2014). Indeed, individuals suffering from unipolar depression had a lower level of glutamate– glutamine than healthy controls whereas people with bipolar disorder had a higher level than healthy controls, suggesting that glutamate differentially contributed to both unipolar or bipolar disorders.

Previous research:
At least five meta-analyses on the antidepressive effects of ketamine have been published (Caddy et al., 2014; Fond et al., 2014; McGirr et al., 2015, Romeo et al, 2015; Han et al, 2016). However, two of them failed to assess the time-course of ketamine's effects, which were only assessed for the first day of treatment (Caddy et al., 2014; Fond et al., 2014). The third one assessed the ketamine's effects on the first week following its administration, but analyses were not conducted on depression scores, but on remission rates (McGirr et al., 2015). When considering analyses based on depression scores, results were only given for the first day of treatment (McGirr et al., 2015).
In this test the two most recent meta-analysis are examined in-depth (Romeo et al, 2015 and Han et al, 2016).

Romeo et al (2015). Meta-analysis of short- and mid-term efficacy of ketamine in unipolar and bipolar depression.

Methods:
Romeo et al (2015) made a meta-analysis of the clinical studies examining ketamine as a possible treatment for major depression disorder. They searched december 2013 the major databases for studies utilizing the following inclusion criteria:
(i) they were published in English in a peer-reviewed journal, (ii) they were randomized, doubleblind and placebo-controlled trials of ketamine, (iii) they included patients with the diagnosis of major depressive episode based on DSM, III, IV or V criteria.
Studies that did not fulfill all these three criteria were systematically excluded from analyses. In particular, trials controlled by an active drug, such as midazolam (McGirr et al., 2015; Murrough et al., 2013), or ECT studies (Fond et al., 2014) were not included in the present meta-analysis. In order to obtain additional data, an email alert was created after December 2013 in MEDLINE with the same keywords for detecting putative publications of interest. Finally, a search of unpublished data was conducted by emails to all pharmaceutical laboratories developing psychotropics.

Database searches identified 5 trials (Berman et al., 2000; Zarate et al., 2006, Zarate et al, 2012; Diazgranados et al., 2010; Sos et al., 2013), the email alert identified an additional one (Lapidus et al., 2014) and the search from pharmaceutical laboratories retrieved no unpublished data. Thus, six double blind, randomized, placebo-controlled, cross-over trials fulfilled the inclusion criteria and were included in the present metaanalysis.

A total of 110 patients with a major depressive episode were included in the six selected studies, as follows: 12 suffered from a first depressive episode, 64 from recurrent depressive disorder and 34 from bipolar depression. Among these 110 patients, 103 patients were included in the final analyses described in the selected studies and were thus included in the present meta-analysis. With the exception of the study by Berman et al. (2000) (n=8 patients), all others studies included patients with resistant major depressive episode. Specifically, patients could be included when (i) an adequate antidepressant trial and a prospective trial of a mood stabilizer (either lithium or valproate) failed (Diazgranados et al., 2010; Zarate et al., 2012), (ii) an adequate antidepressant trial failed (Lapidus et al., 2014); (iii) two adequate antidepressant trials failed (Zarate et al., 2006), or (iv) patients were on a stable dose of antidepressant medication for a minimum of three weeks with a MADRS score 420 (Sos et al., 2013).

Results:
Adverse effects:
- No serious events occurred during the studies. The most commonly reported adverse effects were transitory dissociation, psychotic symptoms, confusion, mild increase in blood pressure, headache or anxiety. These adverse effects usually declined in the 80 min following ketamine's administration.
- The positive psychotic symptoms were evaluated with the Brief Psychiatric Rating Scale (BPRS) in the six studies (Berman et al., 2000; Zarate et al., 2006, 2012; Diazgranados et al., 2010; Sos et al., 2013; Lapidus et al., 2014). At baseline, no significant difference was found between ketamine and placebo (n=6 studies; test for overall effect: SMD=0.13, 95% CI: 0.14 to 0.40, p=0.35; test for heterogeneity: $\chi 2=0.62$, df=5, p=0.99, I 2=0%). At 30–40 min, BPRS scores were higher with ketamine in comparison with placebo (n¼6 studies; test for overall effect: SMD=1.08, 95% CI: 0.62 to 1.55, p=0.00001; test for heterogeneity: $\chi 2=11.27$, df=5, p=0.05, I 2=56%), but no more difference was observed at 80 min (n=4 studies; test for overall effect: SMD=0.06, 95% CI: 0.37 to 0.49, p=0.78; test for heterogeneity: $\chi 2=3.97$, df=3, p=0.26, I 2=25%).

Effects:
- Overall The standardized mean differences (SMD) were calculated at: baseline (n=6 studies; test for overall effect: SMD=0.06, 95% CI: 0.22 to 0.33, p=0.67; test for heterogeneity: $\chi 2=3.12$, df=5, p=0.05, I 2=0%). Day 1 (n=6 studies; test for overall effect: SMD= 1, 95% CI: 1.3 to 0.71, p=0.00001; test for heterogeneity: $\chi 2=4.3$, df=5, po0.51, I 2=0%). Day 2 (n=5 studies; test for overall effect: SMD= 1.03, 95= CI: 1.45 to 0.6,

p=0.00001; test for heterogeneity: $\chi 2$=5.98, df=4, p=0.2, I 2=33%). Day 3–4 (n=6 studies; test for overall effect: SMD= 0.77, 95% CI: 1.1 to 0.44, p=0.00001; test for heterogeneity: $\chi 2$=6.43, df=5, p=0.27, I 2=22%). Day 7 (n=5 studies; test for overall effect: SMD= 0.36, 95% CI: 0.65 to 0.08, p=0.01; test for heterogeneity: $\chi 2$=1.43, df=4, p=0.84, I 2=0%). Day 14 (n=2 studies; test for overall effect: SMD= 0.38, 95%CI: 0.87 to 0.11, p=0.13; test for heterogeneity: $\chi 2$=0.01, df=1, p=0.93, I 2=0%), showing a significant antidepressive action of ketamine from day 1 to day 7 in comparison with placebo.
- Finally, the mean percentages of improvement, weighted for sample size, from baseline depression scores were calculated for both ketamine and placebo groups and showed a major efficacy in ketamine group at day 1 (41.17% vs 6.06%), at day 2 (41.24% vs .94%), at day 3– 4 (34.24% vs 7.03%), at day 7 (20.04% vs 7.18%) and at day 14 (15.38% vs 5.87%).
- In order to make sure that the route of administration did not affect our results, analyses were repeated by excluding the intranasal data and no marked difference was observed neither at day 1 (n=5 studies; test for overall effect: SMD=1.04, 95% CI: 1.37 to 0.71, p=0.00001; test for heterogeneity: $\chi 2$=4.11, df=4, p=0.39, I 2=3%), day 2 (n=4 studies; test for overall effect: SMD= 1.24, 95% CI: 1.64 to 0.83, p=0.00001; test for heterogeneity: $\chi 2$=2.11, df=3, p=0.55, I 2=0%), day 3–4 (n=5 studies; test for overall effect: SMD= 0.87, 95% CI: 1.19 to 0.55, p=0.00001; test for heterogeneity: $\chi 2$=3.56, df=4, p=0.47, I 2=0%), or at day 7 (n=4 studies; test for overall effect: SMD=0.42, 95% CI: 0.74 to 0.11, p=0.009; test for heterogeneity: $\chi 2$=0.71, df=3, p=0.87, I 2=0%).
- In order to assess whether ketamine's efficacy may differ in bipolar or unipolar disorders, analyses were repeated by including studies with patients suffering from bipolar depression and studies with patients suffering from unipolar depression. In the study by Berman et al. (2000), 1 patient with bipolar disorder and 8 patients with recurrent depressive disorder were included; therefore, the clinical sample was considered as patients with unipolar depression. The efficacy of ketamine from day 1 to day 7 was not markedly affected when including only patients with unipolar disorder. However, SMDs when including only bipolar disorder excluded 0 at day 1, day 2, day 3–4 but the statistical significance was lost for all other measures, i.e. days 7 and day 14.
- Finally, the mean percentages of improvement, weighted for sample size, from baseline depression scores were calculated in the ketamine group for both unipolar and bipolar depression. Unipolar group demonstrated a greater ketamine's efficacy as compared with the bipolar group at day 1 (41.25% vs 40.99%), at day 2 (41.74% vs 40.58%), at day 3–4 (35.57% vs 31.42%), and at day 7 (22.06% vs 16.18%).
- Leave-one-out sensitivity analyses showed no marked difference after

the exclusion of each single study, showing that the overall results were not driven by one study for day 1, day 2, day 3–4, and day 14. However, when excluding the data from Sos et al. (2013) or from Zarate et al. (2006) the significance of SMD at day 7 was lost.
- Meta-regression models were used to explore whether some clinical variables (age, sex, alcohol abuse, substance abuse, anxiety disorder, lifetime antidepressant medication, and duration of current episode and illness) may contribute to significant SMDs or heterogeneity. No significant relationship was found (all p>40.05).

Discussion:

- This meta-analysis, based on the primary data obtained from authors of seminal studies, showed that ketamine was effective, as compared with placebo, in treatment-resistant major depressive episode and that this efficacy was significant since the first day and persisted during one week.
- Furthermore, the present results suggested that ketamine may be particularly useful in unipolar disorder, whereas the maintenance of its efficacy in bipolar depression failed to reach significance after 4 days.
- Finally, demographic and clinical characteristics on the included samples did not explain the time course of ketamine's efficacy.
- Ketamine was also relatively safe and possible induced-positive symptoms tend to disappear in the minutes following its administration. No serious side effect was found in the different included studies. The tolerability of ketamine's infusion was generally good and the majority of reported side effects were transitory. In the present meta-analysis, ketamine-induced psychotic symptoms were found significantly increased 40 min after ketamine administration, but the difference with placebo disappeared 80 min after ketamine administration. Accordingly, possible manic switch seemed to have a similar pattern. Indeed, some authors had reported an increase in manic scores at 40 min but no difference was reported at 80 min (Zarate et al., 2006, Zarate et al, 2012; Diazgranados et al., 2010). Unfortunately, these data were described in very few studies and, therefore, they were not entered in the present metaanalysis.
- These observations suggested that both psychotic or manic symptoms possibly induced by ketamine were transient and should spontaneously be controlled in the first 2 h following drug administration.
- Furthermore, the present results argue that the route of administration may not affect the antidepressive effect of ketamine. Indeed, antidepressive effects from nasal administration (Lapidus et al., 2014) did not differ from those following intravenous administration (Berman et al., 2000; Zarate et al., 2006, 2012; Diazgranados et al., 2010; Sos et al., 2013). This observation was in accordance with studies having reported

antidepressive effects after oral (Lara et al., 2014; Irwin et al., 2013) or intramuscular (Chilukuri et al., 2014) administration of ketamine.
- The main limitation of the meta-analysis was the limited number of trials and data included in the analyses. Poor available data may be responsible of poor statistical power, especially for meta-regression analyses.

Discussion:
By using seminal data of randomized and controlled trials obtained directly from authors, the present meta-analysis provided a high level of evidence that ketamine is relatively safe and contributes to a rapid antidepressive action that persist to one week with only a single dose treatment. The results highlight some perspectives, especially regarding the possible differential action in bipolar or unipolar depression.

Han et al. (2016). Efficacy of ketamine in the rapid treatment of major depressive disorder: a meta-analysis of randomized, double-blind, placebo-controlled studies.

Han et al (2016) made a meta-analysis of the clinical studies examining ketamine as a possible treatment for major depression disorder. They searched the major databases for studies utilising the following inclusion criteria: i) randomized, double-blind, placebo-controlled studies comparing ketamine and placebo (active or not); ii) MDD patients aged >18 years; iii) provided informed consent; and iv) mood assessed by Hamilton Depression Rating Scale (HDRS), Montgomery–Åsberg Depression Rating Scale (MADRS), or Clinical Global Impression (CGI). Meanwhile, studies were excluded based on the following criteria: i) no control group; ii) patients with "narrow" or secondary depression diagnoses (eg, postpartum depression and vascular depression); iii) case reports and reviews; and iv) duplicate studies.

Nine studies met the aforementioned inclusion/exclusion criteria and were used to perform meta-analysis (Singh et al, 2016; Hu et al, 2016; Berman et al, 2000;Murrough et al, 2013; Zarate et al, 2006; Ghasemi et al, 2014; Lapidus et al, 2014; Hu et al, 2014; Sos et al, 2013).
Totally, the nine studies contained 368 adult patients with Major Depression Disorder. Part of included patients had various degrees of TRD.
In the intervention group, patients from eight studies received 0.5 mg/kg ketamine through intravenous infusions ((Singh et al, 2016; Hu et al, 2016; Berman et al, 2000;Murrough et al, 2013; Zarate et al, 2006; Ghasemi et al, 2014; Lapidus et al, 2014; Hu et al, 2014), and patients from one study received 0.54 mg/kg ketamine(Sos et al, 2013). Two studies used active

placebo (electroconvulsive therapy and midazolam)(Murrough et al, 2013 and Ghasemi et al 2014).

Response rate was chosen as a primary outcome, being the most consistently reported estimates of acute treatment efficacy. Remission rate was also analyzed, as it was considered more clinically relevant by the authors, than response rate. They defined response as at least a 50% reduction in the absolute HDRS or MADRS score from baseline, or significant improvement in the CGI, at the conclusion of therapy. When trials reported results from all three rating scales, HDRS was preferentially selected. Three treatment time points were chosen (24 and 72 h, and day 7) to assess the rapid antidepressive effect of ketamine.

Results:
Adverse effects:
- The infusion of ketamine was well tolerated. There were no serious adverse effects reported in the ketamine group.

Effects:
- Response rate at 24h time point was available for eight RCTs. Overall, 84 of 161 (52.2%) and 11 of 140 patients (7.8%) receiving ketamine and placebo, respectively, were classified as responders. The pooled OR was 10.09 (95% CI: 4.96–20.52, z=6.38, P,0.00001), indicating a significantly higher efficacy of ketamine than placebo in achieving response 1 day after the treatment. Heterogeneity was very low (I^2 =0%, P=0.57). Egger's test showed that the outcome was not significantly influenced by publication bias.
- Remission rate at this time point was available for six RCTs. Overall, 26 of 126 (20.6%) and 3 of 105 patients (2.8%) receiving ketamine and placebo, respectively, met the remission criteria. The pooled OR was 5.25 (95% CI: 1.82–15.17, z=3.06, P=0.002), indicating a significantly higher efficacy of ketamine than placebo on achieving remission 1 day after the treatment. Heterogeneity was very low (I^2 =0%, P=0.94).
- Response rate at 72h time point was available for nine RCTs. Overall, 94 of 196 (47.9%) and 23 of 172 patients (13.4%) receiving ketamine and placebo, respectively, were classified as responders. The pooled OR was 7.42 (95% CI: 3.97–13.88 z=6.27, P,0.00001), indicating a significantly higher efficacy of ketamine than placebo on achieving response 3 days after the treatment. Heterogeneity was very low (I^2 =0%, P=0.90). Egger's test showed that the outcome was not significantly influenced by publication bias.
- Remission rate at this time point was available for six RCTs. Overall, 30 of 126 (23.8%) and 5 of 105 patients (4.7%) receiving ketamine and

placebo, respectively, met the remission criteria. The pooled OR was 4.04 (95% CI: 1.66–9.85, z=3.07, P=0.002), indicating a significantly higher efficacy of ketamine than placebo on achieving remission 3 days after the treatment. Heterogeneity was very low (I 2 =0%, P=0.88).
- Response rate at 7 days time point was available for nine RCTs. Overall, 78 of 196 (39.8%) and 23 of 172 patients (13.4%) receiving ketamine and placebo, respectively, were classified as responders. The pooled OR was 5.66 (95% CI: 2.92–10.97, z=5.13, P,0.00001), indicating a significantly higher efficacy of ketamine than placebo in achieving response 7 days after the treatment. Heterogeneity was very low (I 2 =0%, P=0.90). Egger's test showed that the outcome was not significantly influenced by publication bias.
- Remission rate at this time point was available for six RCTs. Overall, 33 of 126 (26.2%) and 5 of 105 patients (4.7%) receiving ketamine and placebo, respectively, met the remission criteria. The pooled OR was 4.60 (95% CI: 1.88–11.26, z=3.34, P=0.0008), indicating a significantly higher efficacy of ketamine than placebo in achieving remission 7 days after the treatment. Heterogeneity was very low (I 2 =0%, P=0.96).
- Among the included studies, there were four crossover studies. The authors conducted a subgroup analysis according to the type of included studies. The pooled analysis of the four crossover studies showed that the effect sizes on response rate were 16.21, 7.19, and 5.13 at 24 and 72 h, and day 7, respectively; the effect sizes on remission rate were 5.78, 5.55, and 7.74 at 24 and 72 h, and day 7, respectively.
- The pooled analysis of the other five studies showed that the effect sizes on response rate were 9.36, 7.59, and 5.96 at 24 and 72 h, and day 7, respectively; the effect sizes on remission rate were 5.00, 3.50, and 3.87 at 24 and 72 h, and day 7, respectively. These results were similar to the results from the meta-analysis of nine included studies

Discussion:
- In this meta-analysis of nine randomized, double-blind, placebo-controlled studies of intravenous ketamine for MDD patients, included more and better quality studies then the one by Romeo et al (2015).
- In the pooling analysis of these included studies, ketamine infusion was found to be significantly superior to placebo (active or not) in the acute treatment phase. The significantly higher response and remission rates started as early as day 1, and lasted until days 3 and 7. The effect sizes on response rate were 10.09, 7.42, and 5.66 at 24 and 72 h, and day 7, respectively. The effect sizes on remission rate were 5.25, 4.04, and 4.60 at 24 and 72 h, and day 7, respectively.
- These data indicated the usefulness of ketamine in the acute treatment of

patients with MDD.
- The infusion of ketamine was well tolerated.
- Additionally, as more than one-half of patients included in the meta-analysis had TRD, the study indicated that ketamine might be a good choice in the acute treatment phase for TRD patients.
- In the study, almost all relevant randomised, double-blind, placebo-controlled studies were thought to be included. However, there might be some studies missing because they were published in journals that were not indexed by international databases.
- Murrough et al (2015) and Salehi et al (2015) could not provide complete data. However, those two studies reported that ketamine was associated with a higher response rate. Therefore, the missing data of these two studies would not significantly affect the conclusion of this review.
- Limitations of the study included that the number of included patients with MDD was relatively small. Second, the comparative efficacy of ketamine and placebo was assessed only in studies with treatment durations of 1–7 days. Thus, mid- and long-term antidepressant effects of ketamine could not be examined here. Third, the authors were not able to assess in their review whether repeated ketamine infusion could cause ketamine tolerance or not, and also the psychotomimetic side effects were not assessed. Finally, the dose of ketamine administered in eight of nine studies was 0.5 mg/kg; however, the best dose of ketamine was not studied here.

Conclusion:
In conclusion, by pooling analysis of nine randomized, double-blind, placebo-controlled studies, the authors found that ketamine was effective in the rapid treatment of MDD with a response rate of 39.8%–52.2% and a remission rate of 20.6%–26.2%. The meta-analysis provided powerful evidence that the effectiveness of ketamine was significantly better than placebo. While these results are very highly encouraging, several questions still need to be investigated in future largescale clinical studies about the mid- and long-term antidepressant effects, best dose, and ketamine tolerance.

Ketamine for the treatment of bipolar depression

Previous research:
Albericha et al (2017) conducted a systematic review of the clinical literature concerning ketamine for the treatment of bipolar depression. They identified at the time 10 relevant papers: one clinical randomised controlled trial (Zarate et al, 2012), 5 cohort studies (Papolos et al, 2013; Luckenbaugh et al, 2012; Rybakowski et al, 2013; Permoda-Osip et al, 2013 and

Kantrowitz et al, 2015) and 4 case-series (Atigari and Healy, 2013; Cusin et al, 2012; Best, 2014 and Lara et al, 2013). Albericha et al (2017) concluded that ketamine has been shown to be swiftly effective in reducing depressive symptoms and attempted suicides in depressed subjects with bipolar depression, although this effect has not been shown to last over time. The duration of the antidepressive effect varies from 3 to 14 days, depending on the scale used to measure symptoms. Based on the results obtained, they thought ketamine might be recommendable as an adjuvant treatment for patients taking antidepressive treatment or mood stabilisers with an incomplete response, for those who need to have a swift response or in resistant patients.

In addition to the literature examined by Albericha et al (2017), one more RCT have been conducted on the treatment of Bipolar Depression with Ketamine, which is Diazgranados et al (2010). We will start the examination of the literature with this study:

Diazgranados et al (2010). A Randomized Add-on Trial of an N-methyl-D-aspartate Antagonist in Treatment-Resistant Bipolar Depression.

Diazgranados et al (2010) recruited 18 individuals with BPD-I or II, without psychotic features, and currently experiencing a major depressive episode of at least 4 weeks duration as diagnosed by the Structured Clinical Interview for Axis I DSM-IV Disorders, for a double-blind, randomized, crossover, placebo-controlled study to assess the efficacy and safety of a single intravenous infusion of the ketamine, combined with lithium or valproate therapy for the treatment of BPD I or II depression.

Participants were required to have a MADRS score of ≥ 20 at screening and at the start of each ketamine/placebo infusion. Patients were also required to have previously failed at least 1 adequate antidepressant trial, and to have failed a prospective open trial of a mood stabilizer while at the NIMH (lithium or valproate for at least 4 weeks at therapeutic levels). All participants were in good physical health as determined by medical history, physical examination, blood labs, electrocardiogram (ECG), chest x-ray, urinalysis, and toxicology. No comorbid substance abuse or dependence for at least 3 months prior to enrolling in the study was allowed.
Exclusion criteria included: any serious unstable medical condition; previous treatment with ketamine; or concomitant treatment with psychotropic medications other than lithium or valproate in the 2 weeks before randomization (5 weeks for fluoxetine). Female participants could not be pregnant or nursing.

After non-response to open treatment with lithium or valproate, participants received intravenous infusions of ketamine hydrochloride (0.5 mg/kg) and saline solution 2 weeks apart using a randomized, double-blind, crossover design. Infusions were administered via an infusion pump over 40 minutes by an blinded anesthesiologist
They received no other psychotropic medications (including benzodiazepines) or structured psychotherapy.

Participants were rated 60 minutes before the infusion, and at 40, 80, 110, and 230 minutes post-infusion. They were also rated on Days 1, 2, 3, 7, 10, and 14 post-infusion. The MADRS was the primary outcome measure. Secondary outcome measures included: the 17-item Hamilton Depression Rating Scale (HDRS), the Beck Depression Inventory (BDI), the Visual Analogue Scale (VAS), the Hamilton Anxiety Rating Scale (HAM-A), the Brief Psychiatric Rating Scale (BPRS), the Clinician Administered Dissociative Scale (CADSS), and the Young Mania Rating Scale (YMRS).

In total, 13 of 18 (72%) subjects completed both phases. Three patients dropped out in the first randomized phase of the study: 1 patient 1 day after infusion owing to worsening mood/suicidal ideation (this subject had a history of suicide attempts and suicidal ideation on and off prior to study entry), 1 patient 3 days after infusion owing to low mood, and another 10 days after infusion owing to hypomania. In the second phase, 1 patient dropped out after 8 days owing to high anxiety, and another dropped out after 10 days owing to low mood. Four of the 5 dropouts were taking valproate for mood stabilization. The patient who dropped out owing to hypomania was receiving placebo, and the other dropouts occurred during the ketamine phase. Thirteen of 17 (76%) subjects completed the ketamine phase and 15 of 16 (94%) subjects completed the placebo phase. Nine of 10 (90%) patients using lithium as a mood stabilizer completed the study; in contrast, 4 of 8 (50%) patients using valproate completed the study.

Results:
Adverse Effects:
-The treatment were well tolerated and nauseous adverse-effects were observed.

Effects:
- Patients receiving ketamine first had a nonsignificant decrease in MADRS scores from the first baseline rating (mean MADRS score, 31.2 [SD, 4.4]) to the second-phase baseline rating (mean, 29.4 [SD, 8.1]; $F_{14}=0.91$, $P=.36$). Patients receiving placebo first also had a

nonsignificant decrease in MADRS scores from the first- (mean, 33.9 [SD, 4.8]) to the second-phase baseline rating (mean, 32.9 [SD, 3.8]; F14=0.78, P=.39).
- An additional analysis was conducted to understand the potential for carryover effects. The primary analysis was run using only the first-phase data, so the drug factor was a betweensubjects measure. In this case, the drug × time interaction approached significance (F10,148=1.71, P=.08). The drug main effect was not significant (F1,16=1.92, P=.19), but the time effect was significant (F10,148=2.93, P=.002). Given the small sample size, effect sizes were calculated to determine whether they differed between the first phase and the full study. Results indicated that effect sizes were similar to the full study. For instance, the effect at 40 minutes was 0.63 (95% CI, −0.04 to 1.30) and the effect at day 1 was 0.66 (95% CI, −0.01 to 1.33); these values compare with 0.52 and 0.67, respectively, in the full analysis.
- No patients responded or remitted while taking placebo through the first 3 days; 1 patient (6%) receiving placebo had response and remission at days 7 and 10. Nine of 16 (56%) patients receiving ketamine responded, and 2 of 16 (13%) remitted at 40 minutes; 7 of 16 (44%) responded and 5 of 16 (31%) patients receiving ketamine remitted after 1 day.
- When only completers were included in the analysis, the McNemar test showed a significantly higher response rate from 40 minutes through day 3 with ketamine, but only the result at 230 minutes remained significant after applying the Hochberg-adjusted Bonferroni procedure to adjust for multiple comparisons. None of the remission rates were significantly different. Twelve of 17 (71%) patients responded to ketamine and 1 of 16 (6%) responded to placebo at some point during the trial. The median time to initial response was 40 minutes. After responding, losing response was defined as reaching less than 25% improvement from baseline. Under those conditions, the response to ketamine lasted an average of 6.8 days (standard error, 1.4 days); 4 patients responded for 1 week, and 3 additional patients had a response lasting 2 weeks or more.
- To confirm the change in depressive symptoms as assessed by the MADRS, similar statistical models were used for the secondary measures. For the Hamilton Scale for Depression, a significant interaction was observed between drug and time (F10,251=2.75, P=.003). When receiving ketamine, patients had fewer depressive symptoms from 40 minutes to 3 days and at 14 days postinfusion. Similar results were obtained for the Beck Depression Inventory (F10,205=3.76, P<.001), in which differences were present for the same times. With the visual analog scale, depressive symptoms were lower with ketamine from 40 minutes to 3 days postinfusion (F10,187=3.92, P<.001).
- Anxiety symptoms, as assessed by both the Hamilton Anxiety Rating

Scale and the visual analog scale, decreased significantly. A linear mixed model using the Hamilton Anxiety Rating Scale showed significantly less anxiety for subjects receiving ketamine compared with placebo ($F_{7,147}=2.10$, $P=.047$) at the first postinfusion observation and at 230 minutes through day 3. Drug differences were significant at day 10 but not at days 7 or 14. Similar findings were obtained with the visual analog scale, which showed significantly fewer symptoms in subjects receiving ketamine ($F_{10,254}=3.02$, $P=.001$) from 40 minutes through day 2.

- The linear mixed model with manic symptoms, as assessed by the Young Mania Rating Scale, showed a significant interaction between time and drug ($F_{10,220}=2.50$, $P=.007$) (Figure 4). Patients receiving ketamine had significantly higher scores at 40 minutes, but significantly lower scores at days 2 and 14. The difference at 40 minutes came from a nonsignificant decrease in Young Mania Rating Scale scores on placebo and a slight, nonsignificant increase when receiving ketamine. Compared with baseline, there was no significant change in manic symptoms in patients receiving placebo, but Young Mania Rating Scale scores significantly declined with ketamine from 80 minutes through day 2 postinfusion. One patient who was concomitantly receiving lithium reached a Young Mania Rating Scale score of 15 at 40 minutes while taking ketamine, but the symptoms were no longer higher than baseline by 80 minutes. Of the patients receiving placebo and valproate, one patient reached a score of 13 on day 7 and a score of 21 on day 10.

- The statistical model for Brief Psychiatric Rating Scale positive symptoms showed a significant drug×time interaction ($F_{10,248}=4.45$, $P<.001$). Ketamine and placebo differed only at 40 minutes postinfusion, and this difference was due to a small, nonsignificant decrease with placebo and an even smaller increase with ketamine. On the Clinician Administered Dissociative Scale, the significant interaction ($F_{10,263}=16.52$, $P<.001$) pointed to a ketamine/placebo difference at 40 minutes only where patients had a large increase on ketamine.

- An analysis of individual MADRS items showed that 8 of 10 symptoms changed significantly, even after correction for multiple comparisons. Reduced sleep and suicidal thoughts were not significant, and reduced appetite scores were significantly increased. All other symptoms decreased significantly.

- All responders to ketamine had an initial response within the first hours after infusion. An additional linear mixed model was performed after adding the type of mood stabilizer (lithium or valproate) as a factor in the model, but no significant effects were observed (mood stabilizer, $F_{1,15}=0.21$, $P=.65$; mood stabilizer×time, $F_{10,207}=0.35$, $P=.97$; mood stabilizer×drug, $F_{1,140}=0.65$, $P=.42$; mood stabilizer×time×drug, $F_{10,232}=0.85$, $P=.58$).

- No serious adverse events occurred during the study. Adverse events occurring during the infusion in 10% or more of subjects receiving ketamine or placebo included feeling woozy or loopy, feeling lethargic or drowsy, cognitive impairment, fear or anxiety, nausea, dizziness, odd sensations, blurred vision, and headache. Adverse events associated only with ketamine (≥10% of subjects) included dissociation; feeling strange, weird, or bizarre; dry mouth; tachycardia; and increased blood pressure.
- Two participants who experienced increased blood pressure and tachycardia returned to normal within minutes after the infusion. No adverse event was significantly different from placebo at 80 minutes or thereafter. No significant changes occurred in electrocardiography, respiratory, or laboratory values during the study.

Discussion:
- This double-blind, placebo-controlled, proof-of-concept study found that a single intravenous infusion of ketamine in patients with treatment-resistant bipolar depression resulted in a robust and rapid (within minutes) antidepressant response. This was the first study detailing the rapid antidepressant effects of a single ketamine infusion in patients with treatment-resistant bipolar depression.
- Depression scores improved significantly more in patients receiving ketamine than in those receiving placebo, and this improvement occurred as early as 40 minutes postinfusion. This difference was statistically significant for 4 different efficacy scales: MADRS, Hamilton Scale for Depression, self-rated Beck Depression Inventory, and visual analog scale depression, as well as the Hamilton Anxiety Rating Scale and visual analog scale anxiety scales.
- These findings are particularly noteworthy because a substantial proportion of study participants had been prescribed complex polypharmacy regimens in the past with substantial treatment failures. The mean number of past antidepressant trials was 7, and more than 55% of participants failed to respond to electroconvulsive therapy.
- Limitations of the present study includes small group size, participants being a refractory subgroup of patients with treatment-resistant bipolar depression who were relatively late in their course of illness, why the results may not be generalizable to patients with BPD who have different illness and course characteristics (eg, rapid cycling course and current substance use disorders). Another key issue is the possibility that the response seen in this study resulted from the patients' use of lithium or valproate rather than ketamine. This seems unlikely because the mean duration of therapeutic levels of mood stabilizers before receiving the first infusion was, on average, 7 weeks. In addition, most patients included in the study had previously failed to respond to trials of either

or both of these medicines.
- Next, the study findings could be explained by the notion that subjects cycled out of their major depressive episode. This is also unlikely given that only one subject included in the study met rapid cycling criteria. Furthermore, the use of the placebo phase should protect against findings due to random switching.
- It is interesting to note that although none of the subjects taking placebo met the stringent 50% response criteria in the first week, they had an improvement of 16% at 40 minutes, 14% at 230 minutes, and 10% at day 3. In addition, 31% of patients had at least a 20% improvement at 230 minutes, and 1 had a 40% improvement on day 3. This implies that some clinical improvement occurred with placebo. Furthermore, at least 10% of patients receiving placebo experienced adverse events similar to those occurring with an active drug. While the clinical improvement and adverse events experienced by subjects receiving placebo does not mean that they could not discern placebo from the active drug, it does imply that they experienced changes consistent with having received an active drug.

Conclusion:

Taken together, the present results support the hypothesis that targeting the NMDA receptor complex brings about a rapid antidepressant effect in patients with bipolar depression. Future studies should examine strategies for long-term maintenance of ketamine's rapid antidepressant response.

Zarate et al (2012). Replication of Ketamine's Antidepressant Efficacy in Bipolar Depression: A Randomized Controlled Add-on Trial.

Methods:

Zarate et al (2012) recruited 15 individuals with BPD-I or II, without psychotic features, and currently experiencing a major depressive episode of at least 4 weeks duration as diagnosed by the Structured Clinical Interview for Axis I DSM-IV Disorders, for a double-blind, randomized, crossover, placebo-controlled study to assess the efficacy and safety of a single intravenous infusion of the ketamine, combined with lithium or valproate therapy for the treatment of BPD I or II depression.

Participants were required to have a MADRS score of ≥ 20 at screening and at the start of each ketamine/placebo infusion. Patients were also required to have previously failed at least 1 adequate antidepressant trial, and to have failed a prospective open trial of a mood stabilizer while at the NIMH (lithium or valproate for at least 4 weeks at therapeutic levels). All participants were in good physical health as determined by medical history,

physical examination, blood labs, electrocardiogram (ECG), chest x-ray, urinalysis, and toxicology. No comorbid substance abuse or dependence for at least 3 months prior to enrolling in the study was allowed.
Exclusion criteria included: any serious unstable medical condition; previous treatment with ketamine; or concomitant treatment with psychotropic medications other than lithium or valproate in the 2 weeks before randomization (5 weeks for fluoxetine). Female participants could not be pregnant or nursing.

After non-response to open treatment with lithium or valproate, participants received intravenous infusions of ketamine hydrochloride (0.5 mg/kg) and saline solution 2 weeks apart using a randomized, double-blind, crossover design. Infusions were administered via an infusion pump over 40 minutes by an blinded anesthesiologist
They received no other psychotropic medications (including benzodiazepines) or structured psychotherapy.

Participants were rated 60 minutes before the infusion, and at 40, 80, 110, and 230 minutes post-infusion. They were also rated on Days 1, 2, 3, 7, 10, and 14 post-infusion. The MADRS was the primary outcome measure. Secondary outcome measures included: the 17-item Hamilton Depression Rating Scale (HDRS), the Beck Depression Inventory (BDI), the Visual Analogue Scale (VAS), the Hamilton Anxiety Rating Scale (HAM-A), the Brief Psychiatric Rating Scale (BPRS), the Clinician Administered Dissociative Scale (CADSS), and the Young Mania Rating Scale (YMRS).

In total, 11 of 15 (73%) subjects completed both phases. All 4 patients who dropped out of the study did so in the first phase; at the time, 3 had received ketamine and 1 had received placebo. Two of the dropouts who received ketamine responded briefly and then began to lose improvement, one after 7 days and the other after 3 days. The other 2 dropouts did not reach response criteria and left the study after 3 days. Fourteen (93%) patients received the ketamine infusion and 12 (80%) received the placebo infusion. Eleven of 14 (79%) completed the ketamine phase, and 11 of 12 (92%) completed the placebo phase. Nine of 11 (82%) patients receiving lithium completed the full study; one dropped out during the ketamine phase, and one dropped out during the placebo phase. Two of the 4 (50%) patients receiving valproate completed the study; both dropped out during the ketamine phase.

Results:
Adverse effects:

- No serious adverse events occurred during the study.
- Adverse events occurring during the infusion in 10% or more of the subjects receiving ketamine or placebo included feeling woozy or loopy, feeling lethargic or drowsy, cognitive impairment, fear or anxiety, nausea, dizziness, odd sensations, blurred vision, and headache. No adverse event was significantly different from placebo at 80 minutes or thereafter.
- Headaches, drowsiness or sedation, early morning awakening, and difficulty falling asleep were reported in ≥10% of the sample in both the ketamine and placebo phases. Dry mouth, dizziness or faintness, difficulty falling asleep, and flatulence were reported for ketamine only; irritability and muscle, bone, or joint pain were reported for placebo only.

Effects:
- With the ITT sample, the linear mixed model with the MADRS showed a significant drug by time interaction ($F_{10,187}=5.94$, $p<.001$). Post-hoc tests indicated significantly fewer depressive symptoms in patients who received ketamine versus those who received placebo from 40 minutes to 3 days post-infusion.
- After correction for multiple comparisons, no significant difference between the drugs was observed at baseline, or at Days 7, 10, or 14 ($p=.83$, $p=.34$, $p=.93$, and $p=.19$, respectively). The effects were moderate to large at 40 minutes ($d=0.89$, 95% C.I.=0.61–1.16) through 230 minutes ($d=0.85$, 95% C.I.=0.57–1.14), and moderate to large at Day 1 ($d=0.70$, 95% C.I.=0.42–0.98) and Day 2 ($d=0.65$, 95% C.I.=0.37–0.93). The biggest effect size was observed at 40 minutes post-infusion.
- When only those who completed the study were examined, the drug by time interaction was significant ($F_{10,145}=4.95$, $p<.001$). Differences between the drugs were observed from 40 minutes to Day 3. The effect at Day 1 was similar to that observed with the full sample ($d=0.68$, 95% C.I.=0.38–0.98).
- A linear mixed model compared baseline MADRS scores for each drug and drug order. No significant effects were noted for either drug ($p=.65$) or order of drug administration (order: $p=.43$; order×drug: $p=.10$). No significant difference was noted in baseline MADRS and the first and second infusions, regardless of whether patients received ketamine first or placebo first. To examine whether carryover may have affected the results, a linear mixed model was run using only the first phase of the study, and a significant drug by time interaction was noted ($F_{10,66}=5.46$, $p<.001$).
- The median time to ketamine response was 40 minutes. The median

time to relapse (25% improvement from baseline following response for one day) was 2 days. The mean time to relapse was 4.5 (SE=1.3) days. Two patients maintained response for at least 1 week, a third patient responded for at least 10 days, and a fourth patient responded until the final rating on Day 14.
- Using 50% change in MADRS as the response criteria, 64% of patients receiving ketamine responded at 40 minutes, 50% responded at 230 minutes, and 43% responded at Day 1. Remission was defined as a MADRS score ≤10. Under those criteria, 7% of patients receiving ketamine experienced remission at 40 minutes, 36% met remission criteria at 230 minutes, and 29% met remission criteria at Day 1. Altogether, 79% of subjects responded to ketamine at some point during the study; 0% responded to placebo.
- Compared to baseline, patients receiving placebo improved an average of 5% at 40 minutes, 9% at 230 minutes, and 1% at Day 1. In contrast, patients receiving ketamine improved an average of 50% at 40 minutes, 45% at 230 minutes, and 41% at Day 1. The type of mood stabilizer that patients received concomitantly did not affect response.
- On the BDI, patients who received ketamine had lower suicidal ideation scores from 40 minutes to Day 2 and at Day 10.

Discussion:
- This double-blind, placebo-controlled, proof-of-concept study replicated previous finding that a single intravenous infusion of ketamine or any intervention (i.e., pharmacological, somatic device, or therapy), resulted in a robust and rapid (within 1 hour) antidepressant response in patients with bipolar depression. This difference was statistically significant on the suicide item of 3 different efficacy scales: MADRS, HDRS, and self-rated BDI. Onset occurred within 40 minutes and remained significant for 3 days.
- In addition, anxiety symptoms, which are a well-recognized risk factor for suicide, also improved significantly and rapidly following ketamine administration.
- Depressive and anxiety symptom scores improved significantly more in patients who received ketamine than in those who received placebo, and this improvement was observed as early as 40 minutes post-infusion. This difference was statistically significant across different efficacy scales—the MADRS, HDRS, self-rated BDI, and VAS-Depression—as well as the HAM-A and VAS-Anxiety scales. The fact that symptoms improved so rapidly is particularly striking given that most participants had a course of illness marked by frequent hospitalizations, multiple adequate medication trials, suicide attempts, comorbid anxiety disorders, unemployment, and considerable disability.

- Ketamine exerted rapid antisuicidal effects compared to placebo in these patients. This were the first controlled report detailing such rapid antisuicidal effects (within 1 hour) associated with a single infusion of ketamine in patients with bipolar depression.
- Limitations to the study exist. The sample size was small. In addition, these patients had a long course of illness marked by multiple past medication trials and treatment with ECT. Thus, the results may not be generalizable to BPD patients with different illness and course characteristics.

Conclusion:

Taken together, these findings support the hypothesis that targeting the NMDA receptor complex brings about rapid antidepressant and antisuicidal effects in patients with bipolar depression. However, because the antidepressant effects of ketamine were not long-lasting for most patients, it will be important to develop alternate strategies to sustain ketamine's rapid antidepressant effects

Edited by Dr. Oliver Rumle Hovmand

SOURCES

Classical psychedelics:
- Ables MF and Eng EW (1967) Group treatment of chronic alcoholism with LSD-25. In: Highlights of the twelfth annual conference in cooperative studies in psychiatry. Perry Point, MD: Veterans Administration Central Neuropsychiatric Research Laboratory.
- Ables MF, Eng EW and Curtin ME (1970) Group treatment of chronic alcoholism with LSD-25: study II. Newsletter for research Jensen SE (1962) A treatment program for alcoholics in a mental hospital. Q J Stud Alcohol 23: 315–320.
- Abraham HD, Aldridge AM. Adverse consequences of lysergic acid diethylamide. Addiction. 1993;88:1327–1334.
- Abramson H, editor. (Ed) (1967). The use of LSD in psychotherapy and alcoholism. New York: Bobbs-Merrill
- Abramson HA, editor. The Use of LSD in Psychotherapy and Alcoholism. New York: Bobbs-Merrill; 1963.
- Abramson HA, editor. The Use of LSD in Psychotherapy. New York: Josiah Macy Jr. Foundation Publications; 1960.
- Abuzzahab FS, Anderson BJ. A review of LSD treatment in alcoholism. Int Pharmacopsychiat. 1971;6:223–235.
- Adolfi F, Couto B, Richter F et al. Convergence of interoception, emotion, and social cognition: a twofold fMRI meta-analysis and lesion approach. Cortex 88, 124–142 (2017).
- Akash KG, Balarama KS and Paulose CS (2008) Enhanced 5-Ht(2a) receptor status in the hypothalamus and corpus striatum of ethanoltreated rats. Cell Mol Neurobiol 28: 1017–1025.
- Allen M, Dietz M, Blair KS et al. Cognitive-affective neural plasticity following active-controlled mindfulness intervention. J. Neurosci. 32(44), 15601–15610 (2012).
- American Psychiatric Association. DSM-IV-TR: Diagnostic and Statistical Manual of Mental Disorders, Fourth Edition, Text Revision. Washington, DC: American Psychiatric Association; 2000.
- Anchisi D, Zanon M. A Bayesian perspective on sensory and cognitive integration in pain perception and placebo analgesia. PLoS ONE 10(2), e0117270 (2015).
- Arminjon, M. (2011). The four postulates of freudian unconscious neurocognitive convergences. Front. Psychol. 2:125.
- Atasoy, S., Roseman, L., Kaelen, M., Kringelbach, M. L., Deco, G., and CarhartHarris, R. L. (2017b). Connectome-harmonic decomposition of human brain activity reveals dynamical repertoire re-organization under LSD. 7:17661. doi: 10.1038/s41598-017-17546-0
- Baggott MJ, Erowid E, Erowid F, Robertson LC. Chronic visual changes in hallucinogen users: a web-based questionnaire. Poster presented at the 2006 meeting of the College on Problems of Drug Dependence; Scottsdale, AZ. 2006.
- Baggott, M. J. (2015). Psychedelics and creativity: a review of the quantitative literature. PeerJ. PrePrints 3:e1468. doi: 10.7287/peerj.preprints.1202v1
- Baliki MN, Baria AT, Apkarian AV. The cortical rhythms of chronic back pain. J. Neurosci. 31(39), 13981–13990 (2011).
- Baliki MN, Geha PY, Apkarian AV, Chialvo DR. Beyond feeling: chronic pain hurts the brain, disrupting the default-mode network dynamics. J. Neurosci. 28(6), 1398–1403 (2008).
- Baliki MN, Mansour AR, Baria AT, Apkarian AV. Functional reorganization of the default mode network across chronic pain conditions. PLoS ONE 9(9), e106133 (2014).
- Barrett, F. S., and Griffiths, R. R. (2017). Classic hallucinogens and mystical experiences: phenomenology and neural correlates. Curr Top Behav Neurosci. 2018;36:393-430.
- Barrett, F. S., Johnson, M. W., and Griffiths, R. R. (2017a). Neuroticism is associated with challenging experiences with psilocybin mushrooms. Pers. Individ. Dif. 117, 155–160.
- Barrett, F. S., Preller, K. H., Herdener, M., Janata, P., and Vollenweider, F. X. (2017b). Serotonin 2A receptor signaling underlies LSD-induced alteration of the neural response to dynamic changes in music. Cereb. Cortex doi: 10.1093/cercor/bhx257 [Epub ahead of print].
- Baumeister, R. F., and Exline, J. J. (2002). Mystical self loss: a challenge for psychological theory. Int. J. Psychol. Relig. 12, 15–20.
- Belser, A. B., Agin-Liebes, G., Swift, T. C., Terrana, S., Devenot, N., Friedman, H. L., et al. (2017). Patient experiences of psilocybin-assisted psychotherapy: an interpretative phenomenological analysis. J. Humanist. Psychol. 57, 354–388
- Bender L, Siva Sankar DV. Chromosome damage not found in leukocytes of children treated with LSD-25. Science. 1968;159:749.
- Beringer, K. (1927b). Der Meskalinrausch (Mescaline Intoxication). Berlin: Springer.
- Blewett DB, Chwelos N. Handbook for the Therapeutic Use of Lysergic Acid Diethylamide-25: Individual and Group Procedures. 1959. [Accessed September 16, 2018]. http://www.erowid.org/psychoactives/guides/handbook_lsd25.shtml.
- Bonny, H. L., and Pahnke, W. N. (1972). The use of music in psychedelic (LSD) psychotherapy. J. Music Ther. 9, 64–87.
- Bonson KR, Buckholtz JW, Murphy DL. Chronic administration of serotonergic antidepressants attenuates the subjective effects of LSD in humans. Neuropsychopharmacology. 1996;14:425–436.
- Bonson KR, Murphy DL. Alterations in responses to LSD in humans associated with chronic administration of tricyclic antidepressants, monoamine oxidase inhibitors or lithium. Behav Brain Res. 1996;73:229–233.
- Boulougouris V, Glennon JC, Robbins TW. Dissociable effects of selective 5-HT2A and 5-HT2C receptor antagonists on serial spatial reversal learning in rats. Neuropsychopharmacology 2008; 33: 2007–19. Harvey JA. Role of the serotonin 5-HT(2A) receptor in learning. Learn Mem 2003; 10: 355–62.
- Bouso JC, Gonzalez D, Fondevila S, et al. Personality, psychopathology, life attitudes and neuropsychological performance among ritual users of Ayahuasca: a longitudinal study. PLoS One 2012; 7: e42421.
- Bouso, J. C., Fábregas, J. M., Antonijoan, R. M., Rodríguez-Fornells, A., and Riba, J. (2013). Acute effects of ayahuasca on neuropsychological performance: differences in executive function between experienced and occasional users. Psychopharmacology 230, 415–424.
- Bowen WT, Soskin RA and Chotlos JW (1970) Lysergic acid diethylamide as a variable in the hospital treatment of alcoholism: a follow-up study. J Nerv Ment Dis 150: 111–118.
- Brandrup E, Vanggaard T. (1977) LSD treatment in a severe case of compulsive neurosis. Acta Psychiatr Scand 55:127–141.
- Brewer JA, Garrison KA. The posterior cingulate cortex as a plausible mechanistic target of meditation: findings from

neuroimaging. Ann. NY Acad. Sci. 1307, 19–27 (2014).
- Brogaard, B. (2013). Serotonergic hyperactivity as a potential factor in developmental, acquired and drug-induced synesthesia. Front. Hum. Neurosci. 7:657. doi: 10.3389/fnhum.2013.00657
- Buchanan RW, Carpenter WT. Concept of Schizophrenia. In: Sadock RJ, Sadock VA, editors. Kaplan and Sadock's Comprehensive Textbook of Psychiatry. 8th ed. Volume 1. Philadelphia: Lippincott, William, Wilkins; 2005. pp. 1329–1345.
- Buchborn T, Schroder H, Hollt V, Grecksch G. Repeated lysergic acid diethylamide in an animal model of depression: normalisation of learning behaviour and hippocampal serotonin 5-HT2 signalling. J Psychopharmacol 2014; 28: 545–52.
- Buckholtz NS, Zhou DF, Freedman DX, et al. (1990) Lysergic acid diethylamide (LSD) administration selectively downregulates serotonin2 receptors in rat brain. Neuropsychopharmacology 3: 137–148.
- Buckner RL, Andrews-Hanna JR, Schacter DL. The brain's default network: anatomy, function, and relevance to disease. Ann. NY Acad. Sci. 1124, 1–38 (2008).
- Callaway JC, Grob CS. Ayahuasca preparations and serotonin reuptake inhibitors: a potential combination for severe adverse interactions. J Psychoactive Drugs. 1998;30:367–369.
- Carhart-Harris RL, Erritzoe D, Williams T, et al. Neural correlates of the psychedelic state as determined by fMRI studies with psilocybin. Proc Natl Acad Sci USA 2012; 109: 2138–43.
- Carhart-Harris RL, Kaelen M, Bolstridge M, et al. The paradoxical psychological effects of lysergic acid diethylamide (LSD). Psychol Med 2016; 46: 1379–90.
- Carhart-Harris, Bolstridge, Day, Rucker, Watts, Erritzoe, Kaelen, Giribaldi, Bloomfield, Pilling, Rickard, Forbes, Feilding, Taylo, Curran and Nutt. Psilocybin with psychological support for treatment-resistant depression: six-month follow-up. Psychopharmacology (Berl). 2018 Feb;235(2):399-408.
- Carhart-Harris, Bolstridge, Rucker, Day, Erritzoe, Kaelen, Bloomfield, Rickard, Forbes, Fielding, Taylor, Pilling, Curran and Nutt. Psilocybin with psychological support for treatment-resistant depression: an open-label feasibility study. Lancet Psychiatry 2016; 3: 619–27
- Carhart-Harris, R. L., and Nutt, D. J. (2017). Serotonin and brain function: a tale of two receptors. J. Psychopharmacol. 31, 1091–1120
- Carhart-Harris, R. L., Erritzoe, D., Haijen, E., Kaelen, M., and Watts, R. (2017b). Psychedelics and connectedness. Psychopharmacology 235, 547–550
- Carhart-Harris, R. L., Kaelen, M., Whalley, M. G., Bolstridge, M., Feilding, A., and Nutt, D. J. (2015). LSD enhances suggestibility in healthy volunteers. Psychopharmacology 232, 785–794. doi: 10.1007/s00213-014-3714-z
- Carhart-Harris, R. L., Muthukumaraswamy, S., Roseman, L., Kaelen, M., Droog, W., Murphy, K., et al. (2016c). Neural correlates of the LSD experience revealed by multimodal neuroimaging. Proc. Natl. Acad. Sci. U.S.A. 113, 4853–4858.
- Carter OL, Burr DC, Pettigrew JD, Wallis GM, Hasler F, Vollenweider FX. Using psilocybin to investigate the relationship between attention, working memory, and the serotonin 1A and 2A receptors. J Cogn Neurosci. 2005;17:1497–1508.
- Carter OL, Pettigrew JD, Burr DC, Alais D, Hasler F, Vollenweider FX. Psilocybin impairs high-level but not low-level motion perception. Neuroreport. 2004;15:1947–1951.
- Carter OL, Pettigrew JD, Hasler F, Wallis GM, Liu GB, Hell D, Vollenweider FX. Modulating the rate and rhythmicity of perceptual rivalry alternations with the mixed 5-HT2A and 5-HT1A agonist psilocybin. Neuropsychopharmacology. 2005;30:1154–1162. [PubMed]
- Carter, O. L., Burr, D. C., Pettigrew, J. D., Wallis, G. M., Hasler, F., and Vollenweider, F. X. (2005). Using psilocybin to investigate the relationship between attention, working memory, and the serotonin 1A and 2A receptors. J. Cogn. Neurosci. 17, 1497–1508.
- Carter, O. L., Hasler, F., Pettigrew, J. D., Wallis, G. M., Liu, G. B., and Vollenweider, F. X. (2007). Psilocybin links binocular rivalry switch rate to attention and subjective arousal levels in humans. Psychopharmacology 195, 415–424.
- Carter, O. L., Pettigrew, J. D., Burr, D. C., Alais, D., Hasler, F., and Vollenweider, F. X. (2004). Psilocybin impairs high-level but not low-level motion perception. Neuroreport 15, 1947–1951.
- Charney DS, Mihic SJ, Harris RA. Hypnotics and sedatives. In: Brunton LL, Lazo JS, Parker KL, editors. Goodman & Gilman's The Pharmacological Basis of Therapeutics. 11th edition. New York: McGraw-Hill; 2006. pp. 401–427.
- Chwelos N, Blewett DB, Smith CM, Hoffer A. Use of d-lysergic acid diethylamide in the treatment of alcoholism. Quart J Stud Alcohol. 1959;20:577–590.
- Cohen MM, Hirschhorn K, Frosch WA. In vivo in vitro chromosomal damage induced by LSD-25. New Engl J Med. 1967;277:1043–1049.
- Cohen MM, Marinello MJ, Back N. Chromosomal damage in human leukocytes induced by lysergic acid diethylamide. Science. 1967;155:1417–1419. [PubMed]
- Cohen S, Ditman KS. Complications associated with lysergic acid diethylamid (LSD-25) JAMA. 1962;181:161–162.
- Cohen S. LSD and the anguish of dying. Harper's Magazine. 1965;231:69–78.
- Cohen S. Lysergic acid diethylamide: side effects and complications. Journal of Nervous and Mental Disease. 1960;130:30–40.
- Condrau G (1949) Klinische Erfahrungen an Geisteskranken Mit Lysergsaure diathylamid. Acta Psychiatrica Scandinavica 24: 9–32. Rucker et al (2016). Psychedelics in the treatment of unipolar mood disorders: a systematic review. J Psychopharmacol. 2016 Dec;30(12):1220-1229.
- Craig AD. How do you feel-now? The anterior insula and human awareness. Nat. Rev. Neurosci. 10(1), 59–70 (2009).
- Craig AD. Significance of the insula for the evolution of human awareness of feelings from the body. Ann. NY Acad. Sci. 1225, 72–82 (2011)
- Crochet R, Sandison R, Walk A, editors. Hallucinogenic Drugs and Their Psychotherapeutic Use. Springfield, IL: Thomas; 1963.
- Cunningham KA and Anastasio NC (2014) Serotonin at the nexus of impulsivity and cue reactivity in cocaine addiction. Neuropharmacology 76 Pt B: 460–478
- Denson R and Sydiaha D (1970) A controlled study of LSD treatment in alcoholism and neurosis. Br J Psychiatry 116: 443–445.
- Di Lernia D, Serino S, Cipresso P, Riva G. Ghosts in the machine. Interoceptive modeling for chronic pain treatment. Front. Neurosci. 10, 314 (2016).
- Di Lernia D, Serino S, Riva G. Pain in the body. Altered interoception in chronic pain conditions: a systematic review. Neurosci. Biobehav. Rev. 71, 328–341 (2016).
- Díaz, J. L. (2010). Sacred Plants and Visionary Consciousness. Available at: http://link.springer.com/article/10.1007/s11097-010-9157-z
- Dishotsky NI, Loughman WD, Mogar RE, Lipscomb WR. LSD and genetic damage. Is LSD chromosome damaging, carcinogenic, mutagenic, or teratogenic? Science. 1971;172:431–440.

- Ditman KS, Moss T, Forgy E, et al. (1970) Characteristics of alcoholics volunteering for lysergide treatment. Q J Stud Alcohol 31: 414–422
- Dittrich A. Psychological aspects of altered states of consciousness of the LSD type: measurement of their basic dimensions and prediction of individual differences. In: Pletscher A, Ladewig D, editors. Fifty years of LSD Concurrent status and perspectives of hallucinogens. New York: Parthenon; 1993. pp. 101–118.
- Dittrich, A., Lamparter, D., and Maurer, M. (2010). 5D-ASC: Questionnaire for the Assessment of Altered States of Consciousness. A Short Introduction. Zurich: PSIN PLUS.
- Doblin R (1991) Pahnke's 'Good Friday Experiment': a long-term followup and methodological critique. J Transpersonal Psychol 23(1): 1–28
- Dodick DW, Rozen TD, Goadsby PJ, Silberstein SD. Cluster headache. Cephalalgia 2000;20:787–803.
- Dolder, P. C., Schmid, Y., Müller, F., Borgwardt, S., and Liechti, M. E. (2016). LSD acutely impairs fear recognition and enhances emotional empathy and sociality. Neuropsychopharmacology 41, 2638–2646
- Dos Santos RG, Osorio FL, Crippa JAS, Hallak JEC. Classical hallucinogens and neuroimaging: a systematic review of human studies: hallucinogens and neuroimaging. Neurosci. Biobehav. Rev. 71, 715–728 (2016).
- Duschek S, Montoro CI, Reyes Del Paso GA. Diminished interoceptive awareness in fibromyalgia syndrome. Behav. Med. 43(2), 100–107 (2017).
- Eisner BG and Cohen S (1958) Psychotherapy with lysergic acid diethylamide. J Nervous and Mental Dis 127: 528–539.
- Eisner, B. G., and Cohen, S. (1958). Psychotherapy with lysergic acid diethylamide. J. Nerv. Ment. Dis. 127, 528–539.
- Ekbom K. Some remarks on the terminology of cluster headache. Cephalalgia 1988;8:59–60.
- Family, N., Vinson, D., Vigliocco, G., Kaelen, M., Bolstridge, M., Nutt, D. J., et al. (2016). Semantic activation in LSD: evidence from picture naming. Lang. Cogn. Neurosci. 31, 1320-1327.
- Fanciullacci M, Bene ED, Franchi G, Sicuteri F. Brief report: phantom limp pain: sub-hallucinogenic treatment with lysergic acid diethylamide (LSD-25). Headache 17(3), 118–119 (1977).
- Fantegrossi WE, Woods JH, Winger G. Transient reinforcing effects of phenylisopropylamine and indolealkylamine hallucinogens in rhesus monkeys. Behav Pharmacol. 2004;15:149–157.
- Farb NA, Segal ZV, Anderson AK. Mindfulness meditation training alters cortical representations of interoceptive attention. Soc. Cogn. Affect. Neurosci. 8(1), 15–26 (2013).
- Fiorella D, Helsley S, Rabin RA, Winter JC. Potentiation of LSD-induced stimulus control by fluoxetine in the rat. Life Sci. 1996;59:PL283–PL287.
- First MB, Spitzer RL, Gibbon M, Williams JBW. Structured clinical interview for DSM-IV-TR Axis 1 Disorders Research Version Patient Edition (SCID-I/P) Biometrics Research. New York: New York State Psychiatric Institute; 2001.
- Forcehimes AA (2004) De profundis: Spiritual transformations in Alcoholics Anonymous. J Clin Psychol 60: 503–517.
- Forman, R. K. C. (ed.) (1998). The Innate Capacity: Mysticism Psychology, and Philosophy. New York, NY: Oxford University Press
- Frecska E, Luna LE. The adverse effects of hallucinogens from intramural perspective. Neuropsychopharmacol Hung. 2006;8:189–200.
- Frecska E, Luna LE. The adverse effects of hallucinogens from intramural perspective. Neuropsychopharmacol Hung. 2006;8:189–200.
- Frecska, E., White, K. D., and Luna, L. E. (2004). Effects of ayahuasca on binocular rivalry with dichoptic stimulus alternation. Psychopharmacology 173, 79–87
- Frokjaer VG, Mortensen EL, Nielsen FA, et al. (2008) Frontolimbic serotonin 2a receptor binding in healthy subjects is associated with personality risk factors for affective disorder. Biol Psychiatry 63: 569–576.
- Funderburk FR, Griffiths RR, McLeod DR, Bigelow GE, Mackenzie A, Liebson IA, Nemeth-Coslett R. Relative abuse liability of lorazepam and diazepam: an evaluation in 'recreational' drug users. Drug Alcohol Depend. 1988;22:215–222.
- Gable RS. Comparison of acute lethal toxicity of commonly abused psychoactive substances. Addiction. 2004;99:686–696.
- Gable RS. Toward a comparative overview of dependence potential and acute toxicity of psychoactive substances used nonmedically. Am J Drug Alcohol Abuse. 1993;19:263–281.
- Garcia-Romeu A, Griffiths RR, Johnson MW. (2014) Psilocybin-occasioned mystical experiences in the treatment of tobacco addiction. Curr Drug Abuse Rev 7:157–164.

- Gasser P, Holstein D, Michel Y, Doblin R, Yazar-Klosinski B, Passie T, Brenneisen R. (2014) Safety and efficacy of lysergic acid diethylamide-assisted psychotherapy for anxiety associated with life-threatening diseases. J Nerv Ment Dis 202:513–520.

- Gasser P, Kirchner K, Passie T. (2015) LSD-assisted psychotherapy for anxiety associated with a life-threatening disease: a qualitative study of acute and sustained subjective effects. J Psychopharmacol 29:57–68.
- Gaynes BN. Identifying difficult-to-treat depression: differential diagnosis, subtypes, and comorbidities. J Clin Psychiatry 2009; 70 (suppl 6): 10–15.
- George AK, Paul J, Kaimal SB, et al. (2010) Decreased cerebral cortex and liver 5-HT2a receptor gene expression and enhanced ALDH activity in ethanol-treated rats and hepatocyte cultures. Neurol Res 32: 510–518
- Ghitza UE, Zhai H, Wu P, et al. (2010) Role of BDNF and GDNF in drug reward and relapse: A review. Neurosci Biobehav Rev 35: 157–171.
- Glennon RA, Titeler M, McKenney JD. Evidence for 5-HT2 involvement in the mechanism of action of hallucinogenic agents. Life Sci. 1984;35:2505–2511.
- Gonzales VO Centro Espirita Beneficiente União do Vegetal 546 US. US Supreme Court. 2006. no 04-1084, decided 21 February 2006.
- González-Maeso J, Weisstaub NV, Zhou M, Chan P, Ivic L, Ang R, Lira A, Bradley-Moore M, Ge Y, Zhou Q, Sealfon SC, Gingrich JA. Hallucinogens recruit specific cortical 5-HT(2A) receptor-mediated signaling pathways to affect behavior. Neuron. 2007;53:439–452.
- Gouzoulis-Mayfrank E, Heekeren K, Neukirch A, Stoll M, Stock C, Daumann J, Obradovic M, Kovar KA. Inhibition of return in the human 5HT2A agonist and NMDA antagonist model of psychosis. Neuropsychopharmacology. 2006;31:431–441.
- Gouzoulis-Mayfrank E, Heekeren K, Neukirch A, Stoll M, Stock C, Obradovic M, Kovar KA. Psychological effects of (S)-ketamine and N,N-dimethyltryptamine (DMT): a double-blind, cross-over study in healthy volunteers. Pharmacopsychiatry. 2005;38:301–311.
- Gouzoulis-Mayfrank E, Heekeren K, Thelen B, Lindenblatt H, Kovar KA, Sass H, Geyer MA. Effects of the hallucinogen psilocybin on habituation and prepulse inhibition of the startle reflex in humans. Behav Pharmacol. 1998;9:561–566

- Gouzoulis-Mayfrank E, Thelen B, Habermeyer E, Kunert HJ, Kovar KA, Lindenblatt H, Hermle L, Spitzer M, Sass H. Psychopathological, neuroendocrine and autonomic effects of 3,4-methylenedioxyethylamphetamine (MDE), psilocybin and d-methamphetamine in healthy volunteers Results of an experimental double-blind placebo-controlled study. Psychopharmacology (Berl) 1999;142:41–50.
- Gouzoulis-Mayfrank E, Thelen B, Maier S, Heekeren K, Kovar KA, Sass H, Spitzer M. Effects of the hallucinogen psilocybin on covert orienting of visual attention in humans. Neuropsychobiology. 2002;45:205–212.
- Greenblatt DJ, Shader RI. Clinical pharmacokinetics of the benzodiazepines. In: Smith DE, Wesson DR, editors. The Benzodiazepines: Current Standards for Medical Practice. Lancaster, PA: MTP Press; 1985. pp. 43–58.
- Gresch PJ, Smith RL, Barrett RJ, et al. (2005) Behavioral tolerance to lysergic acid diethylamide is associated with reduced serotonin2a receptor signaling in rat cortex. Neuropsychopharmacology 30: 1693–1702.
- Griffiths R, Richards W, Johnson M, et al. (2008) Mystical-type experiences occasioned by psilocybin mediate the attribution of personal meaning and spiritual significance 14 months later. J Psychopharmacol 22: 621–632.
- Griffiths RR, Bigelow GE, Henningfield JE. Similarities in animal and human drug-taking behavior. Advances in Substance Abuse. 1980;1:1–90.
- Griffiths RR, Johnson MW, Richards WA, et al. (2011) Psilocybin occasioned mystical-type experiences: immediate and persisting doserelated effects. Psychopharmacology (Berl) 218(4): 649–665.
- Griffiths RR, Richards WA, Johnson MW, et al. (2008) Mystical-type experiences occasioned by psilocybin mediate the attribution of personal meaning and spiritual significance 14 months later. J Psychopharmacol 22(6): 621–632.
- Griffiths RR, Richards WA, McCann U, et al. (2006) Psilocybin can occasion mystical-type experiences having substantial and sustained personal meaning and spiritual significance. Psychopharmacology (Berl) 187(3): 268–283; discussion 284–292.
- Griffiths RR, Richards WA, McCann U, Jesse R. Psilocybin can occasion mystical-type experiences having substantial and sustained personal meaning and spiritual significance. Psychopharmacology. 2006;187:268–283.
- Griffiths, R. R., Johnson, M. W., Carducci, M. A., Umbricht, A., Richards, W. A., Richards, B. D., et al. (2016). Psilocybin produces substantial and sustained decreases in depression and anxiety in patients with life-threatening cancer: a randomized double-blind trial. J. Psychopharmacol. 30, 1181–1197.
- Griffiths, R. R., Johnson, M. W., Richards, W. A., Richards, B. D., McCann, U., and Jesse, R. (2011). Psilocybin occasioned mystical-type experiences: immediate and persisting dose-related effects. Psychopharmacology 218, 649–665
- Griffiths, R., Richards, W., Johnson, M., McCann, U., and Jesse, R. (2008). Mystical type experiences occasioned by psilocybin mediate the attribution of personal meaning and spiritual significance 14 months later. J. Psychopharmacol. 22, 621–632.
- Grinspoon L, Bakalar JB. Psychedelic Drugs Reconsidered. New York: Basic Books; 1979.
- Grivaz P, Blanke O, Serino A. Common and distinct brain regions processing multisensory bodily signals for peripersonal space and body ownership. Neuroimage 147, 602–618 (2017).
- Grob CS, Danforth AL, Chopra GS, Hagerty M, McKay CR, Halberstadt AL, Greer GR. (2011) Pilot study of psilocybin treatment for anxiety in patients with advanced-stage cancer. Arch Gen Psychiatry 68:71–78.
- Grob CS, Greer GR, Mangini M. Hallucinogens at the turn of the century: an introduction. J Psychoactive Drugs. 1998;30:315–319.
- Grob CS, McKenna DJ, Callaway JC, Brito GS, Neves ES, Oberlaender G, Saide OL, Labigalini E, Tacla C, Miranda CT, Strassman RJ, Boone KB. Human psychopharmacology of hoasca, a plant hallucinogen used in ritual context in Brazil. J Nerv Ment Dis. 1996;184:86–94.
- Grob CS. Psilocybin research with advanced-stage cancer patients. Multidisciplinary Association for Psychedelic Studies (MAPS) Bulletin. 2005;15:8.
- Grof S (1975) Realms of the Human Unconscious. New York, NY: Viking.
- Grof S (1980) LSD Psychotherapy. Pomona, CA: Hunter House.
- Grof S (2008) LSD Psychotherapy. 4 edn. Ben Lomond, CA: Multidisciplinary Association for Psychedelic Studies.
- Grof S, Goodman LE, Richards WA, Kurland AA. LSD-assisted psychotherapy in patients with terminal cancer. Int. Pharmacopsychiatry 8(3), 129–144 (1973).
- Grof S, Halifax J. The Human Encounter with Death. New York: EP Dutton; 1977.
- Grof S. LSD Psychotherapy. Pomona, CA: Hunter House; 1980.
- Grof S. Perinatal roots of wars, totalitarianism, and revolutions: observations from LSD research. J Psychohist. 1977;4:269–308.
- Grof, S. (1976). Realms of the Human Unconscious: Observations from LSD Research. New York, NY: E.P. Dutton
- Grof, S. (1980). LSD Psychotherapy. Pomona, CA: Hunter House.
- Gutstein HB, Akil H. Opioid analgesics. In: Brunton LL, Lazo JS, Parker KL, editors. Goodman & Gilman's The Pharmacological Basis of Therapeutics. 11th ed. New York: McGraw-Hill; 2006. pp. 547–590.
- Halberstadt AL, Geyer MA. Multiple receptors contribute to the behavioral effects of indoleamine hallucinogens. Neuropharmacology 2011; 61: 364–81.
- Halpern JH, Pope HG. Do hallucinogens cause residual neuropsychological toxicity? Drug Alcohol Depend. 1999;53:247–256.
- Halpern JH, Pope HG. Hallucinogen persisting perception disorder: what do we know after 50 years? Drug Alcohol Depend. 2003;69:109–119.
- Halpern JH, Sherwood AR, Hudson JI, Yurgelun-Todd D, Pope HG. Psychological and cognitive effects of long-term peyote use among Native Americans. Biol Psychiatry. 2005;58:624–631.
- Halpern JH. The use of hallucinogens in the treatment of addiction. Addiction Research. 1996;4:177–189.
- Hanes KR. (1996) Serotonin, psilocybin, and body dysmorphic disorder: a case report. J Clin Psychopharmacol 16:188–189.
- Harner MJ. Jivaro Souls. American Anthropologist. 1962;64:258–272.
- Harner MJ. The sound of rushing water. Natural History Magazine. 1968;77:28–33. 60–61.
- Hartogsohn, I. (2016). Set and setting, psychedelics and the placebo response: an extra-pharmacological perspective on psychopharmacology. J. Psychopharmacol. 30, 1259–1267
- Hashmi JA, Baliki MN, Huang L et al. Shape shifting pain: chronification of back pain shifts brain representation from nociceptive to emotional circuits. Brain 136, 2751–2768 (2013).
- Hasler F, Bourquin D, Brenneisen R, Bär T, Vollenweider FX. Determination of psilocin and 4-hydroxyindole-3-acetic acid in plasma by HPLC-ECD and pharmacokinetic profiles of oral and intravenous psilocybin in man. Pharm Acta Helv. 1997;72:175–184. [PubMed]
- Hasler F, Bourquin D, Brenneisen R, Vollenweider FX. Renal excretion profiles of psilocin following oral administration of psilocybin: a controlled study in man. J Pharm Biomed Anal. 2002;30:331–339.
- Hasler F, Grimberg U, Benz MA, Huber T, Vollenweider FX. Acute psychological and physiological effects of psilocybin in

healthy humans: a double-blind, placebo-controlled dose-effect study. Psychopharmacology. 2004;172:145–156.
- Headache Classification Subcommittee of the International Headache Society. The International Classification of Headache Disorders. Cephalalgia 2004;24 (suppl 1):44–48.
- Heimann, H. (1963). Observations on Disturbed Time Perception in Model Psychosis. Available at: http://europepmc.org/abstract/med/14112701
- Hendricks PS, Thorne CB, Clark CB, Coombs DW, Johnson MW. Classic psychedelic use is associated with reduced psychological distress and suicidality in the United States adult population. J Psychopharmacol 2015; 29: 280–88.
- Hidalgo WT. Estudio comparativo psicofisiologico de la mescalina, dietilamida del acido D-lisérgico y psilocybina. Acta Med Venez. 1960;8:56–62.
- Hintzen, A., and Passie, T. (2010). The Pharmacology of LSD: A Critical Review. Oxford: Oxford University Press
- Hoch PH, Pennes HH, Cattell JP. Psychoses produced by administration of drugs. Res Publ Assoc Res Nerv Ment Dis. 1953;32:287–296.
- Hoffer A (1967) A program for treatment of alcoholism: LSD, malvaria, and nicotinic acid. In: Abramson HA (ed) The Use of LSD in Psychotherapy and Alcoholism. Indianapolis: Bobbs-Merrill. pp. 343–406.
- Hoffer A, Callbeck MJ. Drug-induced schizophrenia. J Ment Sci. 1960;106:138–159.
- Hofmann A, Heim R, Brack A, et al. (1959) Psilocybin und Psilocin, zwei psychotrope Wirkstoffe aus mexikanischen Rauschpilzen. Helvetica Chimica Acta 42: 1557–1572.
- Hollister LE, Hartman AM. Mescaline, lysergic acid diethylamide and psilocybin: comparison of clinical syndromes, effects on color perception and biochemical measures. Comprehens Psychiat. 1962;3:235–241.
- Hollister LE, Shelton J and Krieger G (1969) A controlled comparison of lysergic acid diethylamide (LSD) and dextroamphetmine in alcoholics. Am J Psychiatry 125: 1352–1357.
- Hollister LE. Clinical, biochemical and psychologic effects of psilocybin. Arch Int Pharmacodyn Ther. 1961;130:42–52.
- Hood, R. W. (2001). Review: cleansing the doors of perception: the religious significance of entheogenic plants and chemicals. Int. J. Psychol. Relig. 11, 285–286
- Huxley, A. (1945). The Perennial Philosophy. London: Harper Publications.
- Iovieno N, Tedschini E, Ameral VE, et al. (2011) Antidepressants for major depressive disorder in patients with co-morbid axis-III disorder: a meta-analyses of patient characteristics and placebo response rates in randomized controlled trials. Int Clin Psychopharmacol 26: 69–74.
- Irwin S, Egozcue J. Chromosomal abnormalities in leukocytes from LSD-25 user. Science. 1967;157:313–314.
- Isbell H. Comparison of the reactions induced by psilocybin and LSD-25 in man. Psychopharmacologia. 1959;1:29–38.

- Jackson DD. (1962) LSD and the New Beginning. J Nerv Ment Dis 135:435–439. [PubMed]
- James W (1902) The Varieties of Religious Experience. Cambridge, MA: Harvard University Press.
- James, W. (1902). The Varieties of Religious Experience: A Study in Human Nature. New York, NY: Longmans, Green and Co. doi: 10.1037/10004-000
- Jensen KB, Regenbogen C, Ohse MC, Frasnelli J, Freiherr J, Lundstrom JN. Brain activations during pain: a neuroimaging meta-analysis of patients with pain and healthy controls. Pain 157(6), 1279–1286 (2016).
- Jensen SE (1963) Treatment of chronic alcoholism with lysergic acid diethylamide. Can Psychiatr Assoc J 8: 182–188.
- Johnson BA (2008) Update on neuropharmacological treatments for alcoholism: Scientific basis and clinical findings. Biochem Pharmacol 75: 34–56.
- Johnson BA, Jasinski DR, Galloway GP, et al. (1996) Ritanserin in the treatment of alcohol dependence – a multi-center clinical trial. Ritanserin Study Group. Psychopharmacology (Berl) 128: 206–215
- Johnson FG (1969) LSD in the treatment of alcoholism. Am J Psychiatry 126: 481–487.
- Johnson M, Richards W, Griffiths R (2008) Human hallucinogen research: guidelines for safety. J Psychopharmacol 22:603–620
- Jones KA, Srivastava DP, Allen JA, et al. (2009) Rapid modulation of spine morphology by the 5-HT2A serotonin receptor through kalirin-7 signaling. Proc Natl Acad Sci U S A 106: 19575–19580.
- Kaelen, M., Barrett, F. S., Roseman, L., Lorenz, R., Family, N., Bolstridge, M., et al. (2015). LSD enhances the emotional response to music. Psychopharmacology 232, 3607–3614
- Kaelen, M., Giribaldi, B., Raine, J., Evans, L., Timmerman, C., Rodriguez, N., et al. (2018). The hidden therapist: evidence for a central role of music in psychedelic therapy. Psychopharmacology 235, 505–519.
- Kaelen, M., Roseman, L., Kahan, J., Santos-Ribeiro, A., Orban, C., Lorenz, R., et al. (2016). LSD modulates music-induced imagery via changes in parahippocampal connectivity. Eur. Neuropsychopharmacol 26, 1099–1109
- Kast E. (1966) LSD and the dying patient. Chic Med Sch Q 26:80–87.
- Kast E. Attenuation of anticipation: a therapeutic use of lysergic acid diethylamide. Psychiatr. Quarterly 41(4), 646–657 (1967).
- Kast EC, Collins VJ. (1964) Lysergic acid diethylamide as an analgesic agent. Anesth Analg 43:285–291.

- Kast EC. (1970) A concept of death, in Psychedelics: The Uses and Implications of Hallucinogenic Drugs (Aaronson B, Osmond H, editors. eds) pp 366–381, Anchor Books, Garden City, NY.
- Keeler MH, Reifler CB. Suicide during an LSD reaction. Am J Psychiatry. 1967;123:884–885.
- Klüver, H. (1926). Mescal visions and eidetic vision. Am. J. Psychol. 37, 502–515
- Klüver, H. (1928). Mescal: The "Divine" Plant and Its Psychological Effects. London: Kegan Paul, Trench, Trubner & Co.
- Kometer, M., and Vollenweider, F. X. (2016). Serotonergic hallucinogen-induced visual perceptual alterations. Curr. Top. Behav. Neurosci. doi: 10.1007/7854_2016_461 [Epub ahead of print].
- Kometer, M., and Vollenweider, F. X. (2016). Serotonergic hallucinogen-induced visual perceptual alterations. Curr. Top. Behav. Neurosci. doi: 10.1007/7854_2016_461 [Epub ahead of print].
- Kometer, M., Cahn, B. R., Andel, D., Carter, O. L., and Vollenweider, F. X. (2011). The 5-HT2A/1A agonist psilocybin disrupts modal object completion associated with visual hallucinations. Biol. Psychiatry 69, 399–406
- Kometer, M., Schmidt, A., Bachmann, R., Studerus, E., Seifritz, E., and Vollenweider, F. X. (2012). Psilocybin biases facial recognition, goal-directed behavior, and mood state toward positive relative to negative emotions through different serotonergic subreceptors. Biol. Psychiatry 72, 898–906.
- Kraehenmann, R., Pokorny, D., Aicher, H., Preller, K. H., Pokorny, T., Bosch, O. G., et al. (2017a). LSD increases primary process thinking via serotonin 2A receptor activation. Front. Pharmacol. 8:814
- Kraehenmann, R., Pokorny, D., Vollenweider, L., Preller, K. H., Pokorny, T., Seifritz, E., et al. (2017b). Dreamlike effects of LSD on waking imagery in humans depend on serotonin 2A receptor activation. Psychopharmacology 234, 2031–2046.

- Krampe H and Ehrenreich H (2010) Supervised disulfiram as adjunct to psychotherapy in alcoholism treatment. Curr Pharm Des 16: 2076–2090.
- Krebs TS, Johansen PØ. Psychedelics and mental health: a population study. PLoS One 2013; 8: e63972.
- Kuramochi H, Takahashi R. Psychopathology of LSD intoxication; Study of experimental psychosis induced by LSD-25: description of LSD symptoms in normal oriental subjects. Arch Gen Psychiatry. 1964;11:151–161.
- Kurland A, Savage C, Pahnke WN, Grof S, Olsson JE. LSD in the treatment of alcoholics. Pharmakopsychiatr Neuropsychopharmakol. 1971;4:83–94.
- Kurland AA, Grof S, Pahnke WN, Goodman LE. Psychedelic drug assisted psychotherapy. In: Goldberg IK, Malitz S, Kutscher AH, editors. Patients With Terminal Cancer Psychotheramacological Agents for the Terminally Ill and Bereaved. New York: Columbia University Press; 1973. pp. 86–133.
- Kurland AA, Pahnke WN, Unger S, Savage C, Goodman E. Psychedelic psychotherapy (LSD) in the treatment of the patient with a malignancy. In: Cerletti A, Bove FJ, editors. The Present Status of Psychotropic Drugs: Pharmacological and Clinical Aspects. Amsterdam, Holland: Excerpta Medica; 1969. pp. 432–434.
- Kurland AA, Savage C, Pahnke WN, Grof S and Olsson JE (1971) LSD in the treatment of alcoholism. In: Vinar O, Votava Z, Bradley PB (eds) Advances in neuropsychopharmacology: proceedings of the 7th congress of the collegium internationale neuro-psychopharmacologicum. Amsterdam: North-Holland, 361–372.
- Kurland AA, Unger S, Shaffer JW, et al. (1967) Psychedelic therapy utilizing LSD in the treatment of the alcoholic patient: A preliminary report. Am J Psychiatry 123: 1202–1209.

- Kurland AA. LSD in the supportive care of the terminally ill cancer patient. J Psychoactive Drugs. 1985;17:279–290.
- Kuypers, K. P. C., Riba, J., de la Fuente Revenga, M., Barker, S., Theunissen, E. L., and Ramaekers, J. G. (2016). Ayahuasca enhances creative divergent thinking while decreasing conventional convergent thinking. Psychopharmacology 233, 3395–3403.
- Laoutidis ZG and Mathiak K (2013) Antidepressants in the treatment of depression/depressive symptoms in cancer patients. A systematic review and meta-analysis. BMC Psychiatry 13: 140.
- Leary T, Litwin GH, Metzner R. Reactions to psilocybin administered in a supportive environment. J Nerv Ment Dis. 1963;137:561–573.
- Leary T, Metzner R, Alpert R. The Psychedelic Experience: A Manual Based on the Tibetan Book of the Dead. New York: Citadel Press; 1964.
- Leary T. The religious experience: Its production and interpretation. Psychedelic Rev. 1964;1:324–346.
- Leary, G. D. (1963). Lysergic acid diethylamide (LSD-25) and ego functions. Arch. Gen. Psychiatry 8, 461–474
- Leary, T., Litwin, G. H., and Metzner, R. (1963). Reactions to psilocybin administered in a supportive environment. J. Nerv. Ment. Dis. 137, 561–573
- Leary, T., Metzner, R., and Alpert, R. (1964). The Psychedelic Experience: A Manual Based on the Tibetan Book of the Dead. New York, NY: University Books.
- Lebedev, A. V., Kaelen, M., Lövdén, M., Nilsson, J., Feilding, A., Nutt, D. J., et al. (2016). LSD-Induced Entropic Brain Activity Predicts Subsequent Personality Change. Hum Brain Mapp. 2016 Sep;37(9):3203-13.
- Lee MA, Shlain B. Acid dreams: The Complete Social History of LSD: The CIA, the Sixties, and Beyond, Revised Edition. New York: Grove Press; 1992.
- Leonard HL, Rapoport JL. (1987) Relief of obsessive-compulsive symptoms by LSD and psilocin. Am J Psychiatry 144:1239–1240.
- Lerner AG, Gelkopf M, Skladman I, Oyffe I, Finkel B, Sigal M, Weizman A. Flashback and hallucinogen persisting perception disorder: clinical aspects and pharmacological treatment approach. Isr J Psychiatry Relat Sci. 2002;39:92–99.
- Letheby, C., and Gerrans, P. (2017). Self unbound: ego dissolution in psychedelic experience. Neurosci. Conscious. Neurosci Conscious. 2017 Jun 30;2017
- Leuner H (1967) Present state of psycholytic therapy and its possibilities. In: Abramson HA (ed) The Use of LSD in Psychotherapy and Alcoholism. Indianapolis: Bobbs-Merrill, pp. 101–116
- Leuner H (1981) Halluzinogene. Bern: Huber.
- Leuner H. Die Experimentelle Psychose. Berlin: Springer; 1962.
- Liechti, M. E., Dolder, P. C., and Schmid, Y. (2017). Alterations of consciousness and mystical-type experiences after acute LSD in humans. Psychopharmacology 234, 1499–1510.
- Liechti, M. E., Dolder, P. C., and Schmid, Y. (2017). Alterations of consciousness and mystical-type experiences after acute LSD in humans. Psychopharmacology 234, 1499–1510.
- Long SY. Does LSD induce chromosomal damage and malformations? a review of the literature. Teratology. 1972;6:75–90.
- Lowy B. New records of mushroom stones from Guatemala. Mycologia. 1971;63:983–993.
- Ludwig A, Levine J, Stark L, Lazar R. A clinical study of LSD treatment in alcoholism. Am J Psychiatry. 1969;126:59–69.
- Ludwig AM, Levine J and Stark LH (1970) LSD and alcoholism: a clinical study of treatment efficacy. Springfield, IL: Charles C Thomas.
- Ludwig AM, Levine J, Stark L and Lazar R (1969) A clinical study of LSD treatment in alcoholism. Am J Psychiatry 126: 59–69. Pahnke WN, Kurland AA, Unger S, Savage C and Grof S (1970) The experimental use of psychedelic (LSD) psychotherapy. JAMA 212: 1856–1863.
- Luke, D. P., and Terhune, D. B. (2013). The induction of synaesthesia with chemical agents: a systematic review. Front. Psychol. 4:753. doi: 10.3389/fpsyg.2013.00753
- MacLean, K. A., Johnson, M. W., and Griffiths, R. R. (2011). Mystical experiences occasioned by the hallucinogen psilocybin lead to increases in the personality domain of openness. J. Psychopharmacol. 25, 1453–1461
- Maclean, K. A., Leoutsakos, J.-M. S., Johnson, M. W., and Griffiths, R. R. (2012). Factor analysis of the mystical experience questionnaire: a study of experiences occasioned by the hallucinogen psilocybin. J. Sci. Study Relig. 51, 721–737
- Majic, T., Schmidt, T. T., and Gallinat, J. (2015). Peak experiences and the afterglow phenomenon: when and how do therapeutic effects of hallucinogens depend on psychedelic experiences? J. Psychopharmacol. 29, 241–253
- Malitz S, Esecover H, Wilkens B, Hoch H. Some observations on psilocybin: a new hallucinogen in volunteer subjects. Compr Psychiatry. 1960;1:8–17.
- Mangini M. Treatment of alcoholism using psychedelic drugs: a review of the program of research. J Psychoactive Drugs. 1998;30:381–418.
- Masters R and Houston J (2000) The Varieties of Psychedelic Experience: The Classic Guide to the Effects of LSD on the Human Psyche. Rochester, Vermont: Park Street Press

- Masters REL, Houston J. The Varieties of Psychedelic Experience. New York: Holt, Rinehart, & Winston; 1966.
- Masters, R. E. L., and Houston, J. (1966). The Varieties of Psychedelic Experience. New York, NY: Holt, Rinehart and Winston.
- Maxwell JA (2009) Designing a qualitative study. In: Bickman L and Rog DJ (eds) Handbook of Applied Social Research Methods. Los Angeles, CA: Sage, pp. 214–253
- McCabe OL. Psychedelic drug crises: toxicity and therapeutics. Journal of Psychedelic Drugs. 1977;9:107–121.
- McGlothlin W, Cohen S, McGlothlin MS. (1967). Long lasting effects of LSD on normals. Arch Gen Psychiatry. 17: 521–532
- McGlothlin WH, Arnold DO. LSD revisited A ten-year follow-up of medical LSD use. Arch Gen Psychiatry. 1971;24:35–49.
- Metzner R, Litwin G, Weil G. The relation of expectation and mood to psilocybin reactions: a questionnaire study. Psychedelic Review. 1965;5:3–39.
- Metzner R. Forward. In: Adamson S, editor. Through the Gateway of the Heart: Accounts of Experiences with MDMA and other Empathogenic Substances. San Francisco: Four Trees Press; 1985.
- Metzner R. Introduction: visionary mushrooms of the Americas. In: Metzner R, Darling DC, editors. Teonanácatl: Sacred Mushroom of Visions. El Verano, CA: Four Trees Press; 2004. pp. 1–48.
- Miller WR and C'de Baca J (2001) Quantum Change : When Epiphanies and Sudden Insights Transform Ordinary Lives. New York: Guilford Press
- Millière, R. (2017). Looking for the self: phenomenology, neurophysiology and philosophical significance of drug-induced ego dissolution. Front. Hum. Neurosci. 11:245.
- Miner EJ, Isbell H, Wolbach AB. Cross tolerance between mescaline and LSD-25 with a comparison of the mescaline and LSD reactions. Psychopharmacologia. 1962;3:1–14.
- Mogar RE, Aldrich RW. The use of psychedelic agents with autistic schizophrenic children. Psychedelic Review. 1969;10:5–13.
- Moreno FA, Delgado PL. (1997) Hallucinogen-induced relief of obsessions and compulsions. Am J Psychiatry 154:1037–1038.
- Moreno, Wiegand, Taitano and Delgado. Safety, tolerability, and efficacy of psilocybin in 9 patients with obsessive-compulsive disorder. J Clin Psychiatry. 2006 Nov;67(11):1735-40.
- Mouraux A, Diukova A, Lee MC, Wise RG, Iannetti GD. A multisensory investigation of the functional significance of the "pain matrix". Neuroimage 54(3), 2237–2249 (2011).
- Natale, M., Kowitt, M., Dahlberg, C. C., and Jaffe, J. (1978b). Effect of psychototmimetics (LSD and dextroamphetamine) on the use of figurative language during psychoanalysis. J. Consult. Clin. Psychol. 46, 1579–1580
- National Institute on Drug Abuse. LSD, NIDA Infofacts. Rockville, MD: National Institute on Drug Abuse; 2006.
- National Institute on Drug Abuse. National Institute on Drug Abuse, Research Report Series. 2001. Hallucinogens and dissociative drugs. NIH Publication No 01-4209.
- Nicholas MK, Ashton-James C. Embodied pain: grasping a thorny problem? Pain 158(6), 993–994 (2017).
- Nichols DE (2014) The Heffter Research Institute: Past and hopeful future. J Psychoactive Drugs 46: 20–26.
- Nichols DE, Hoffman AJ, Oberlender RA, Jacob P, 3rd, Shulgin AT. Derivatives of 1-(1,3-benzodioxol-5-yl)-2-butanamine: representatives of a novel therapeutic class. J Med Chem. 1986;29:2009–2015.
- Nichols DE. Hallucinogens. Pharmacol Ther. 2004;101:131–181.
- Nour, M. M., Evans, L., Nutt, D., and Carhart-Harris, R. L. (2016). Ego-dissolution and psychedelics: validation of the Ego-Dissolution Inventory (EDI). Front. Hum. Neurosci. 10:269.
- Novak SJ. LSD before Leary: Sidney Cohen's critique of 1950s psychedelic drug research. Isis. 1997;88:87–110.
- O'Brien CP. Drug addiction and drug abuse. In: Brunton LL, Lazo JS, Parker KL, editors. Goodman & Gilman's The Pharmacological Basis of Therapeutics. 11th ed. New York: McGraw-Hill; 2006. pp. 607–627.
- Osmond H, Albahary R, Cheek F and Sarett M (1967) Some problems in the use of LSD 25 in the treatment of alcoholism. In: Abramson HA (ed) The use of LSD in psychotherapy and alcoholism. Indianapolis, IN: Bobbs-Merrill, 434–457.
- Osorio Fde L, Sanches RF, Macedo LR, et al. Antidepressant effects of a single dose of ayahuasca in patients with recurrent depression: a preliminary report. Rev Bras Psiquiatr 2015; 37: 13–20.
- Ostuzzi G, Matcham F, Dauchy S, et al. (2015) Antidepressants for the treatment of depression in people with cancer. Cochrane Database Syst Rev 6: CD011006.
- Ott J. Pharmacotheon: Entheogenic Drugs, their Plant Sources and History. Kennewick, WA: Natural Products Co; 1996.
- Pahnke W (1963) Drugs and mysticism: An analysis of the relationship between psychedelic drugs and the mystical consciousness. Ph.D. Thesis, Harvard University
- Pahnke W. Thesis presented to the President and Fellows of Harvard University for the PhD in Religion and Society. 1963. Drugs and mysticism: An analysis of the relationship between psychedelic drugs and the mystical consciousness.
- Pahnke WN, Kurland AA, Goodman LE, Richards WA. (1969) LSD-assisted psychotherapy with terminal cancer patients. Curr Psychiatr Ther 9:144–152.
- Pahnke WN, Kurland AA, Goodman LE, Richards WA. LSD-assisted psychotherapy with terminal cancer patients. Curr. Psychiatr. Ther. 9, 144–152 (1969).
- Pahnke WN, Kurland AA, Unger S, Savage C, Grof S. (1970a) The experimental use of psychedelic (LSD) psychotherapy. JAMA 212:1856–1863.
- Pahnke WN, Kurland AA, Unger S, Savage C, Wolff MC, Goodman LE. (1970b) Psychedelic therapy (utilizing LSD) with cancer patients. J Psychedelic Drugs 3:63–75.
- Pahnke WN. Psychedelic drugs and mystical experience. Int Psychiatry Clin. 1969;5:149–162.
- Pahnke WN. The psychedelic mystical experience in the human encounter with death. Harv Theol Rev. 1969;62(1):1-21.
- Passie T, Seifert J, Schneider U, Emrich HM. The pharmacology of psilocybin. Addict Biol. 2002;7:357–364.
- Patel JK, Pinals DA, Breier A. Schizophrenia and other psychoses. In: Tasman A, Kay J, Lieberman JA, editors. Psychiatry. Second Edition. Volume 2. New Jersey: John Wiley & Sons, Ltd; 2003. pp. 1131–1206.
- Pokorny, T., Preller, K. H., Kometer, M., Dziobek, I., and Vollenweider, F. X. (2017). Effect of psilocybin on empathy and moral decisionmaking. Int. J. Neuropsychopharmacol. 20, 747–757.
- Poling A, Bryceland J. Voluntary drug self-administration by nonhumans: a review. J Psychedelic Drugs. 1979;11:185–190.
- Preller, K. H., and Vollenweider, F. X. (2016). Phenomenology, structure, and dynamic of psychedelic states. Curr. Top. Behav. Neurosci.doi: 10.1007/7854_2016_459
- Puchalski CM (2012) Spirituality in the cancer trajectory. Ann Oncol 23 (Suppl 3): 49–55.
- Rapaport, D. (1950). On the psycho-analytic theory of thinking. Int. J. Psycho Anal. 31, 161–170

- Reitman J, Vasilakis A. The lost freshman. Rolling Stone Magazine. 2004;944:62–66.
- Reynolds PC, Jindrich EJ. A mescaline associated fatality. J Anal Toxicol. 1985;9:183–184.
- Rhead JC. The use of psychedelic drugs in the treatment of severely disturbed children: a review. J Psychedelic Drugs. 1977;9:93–101.
- Riba J, Rodriguez-Fornells A, Urbano G, Morte A, Antonijoan R, Montero M, Callaway JC, Barbanoj MJ. Subjective effects and tolerability of the South American psychoactive beverage Ayahuasca in healthy volunteers. Psychopharmacology. 2001;154:85–95.
- Richards WA, Grof S, Goodman LE, Kurland AA. LSD-Assisted psychotherapy and the human encounter with death. Journal of Transpersonal Psychology. 1972;4:121–150.
- Richards WA, Rhead JC, Dileo FB, et al. (1977) The peak experience variable in DPT-assisted psychotherapy with cancer patients. J Psychoactive Drugs 9: 1–10.
- Richards WA, Rhead JC, Grof S, Goodman LE, Di Leo F, Rush L. DPT as an adjunct in brief psychotherapy with cancer patients. Omega. 1979;10:9–26.
- Richards WA. Entheogens in the study of mystical and archetypal experiences: Research in the Social Scientific Study of Religion. Brill. 2003;13:143–155.
- Richards WA. Entheogens in the study of religious experiences: current status. J Religion Health. 2005;44:377–389.
- Richards WA. Psychedelic Drug-assisted psychotherapy with persons suffering from terminal cancer. Journal of Altered States of Consciousness. 1980;5:309–319.
- Rinkel M, Atwell CR, DiMascio A, Brown J. Experimental Psychiatry V Psilocybine: A New Psychotogenic Drug. N Engl J Med. 1960;262:295–299.
- Rosell DR, Thompson JL, Slifstein M, et al. (2010) Increased serotonin 2a receptor availability in the orbitofrontal cortex of physically aggressive personality disordered patients. Biol Psychiatry 67: 1154–1162.
- Roseman, L., Sereno, M. I., Leech, R., and Kaelen, M. (2016). LSD alters eyes-closed functional connectivity within the early visual cortex in a retinotopic fashion. Hum. Brain Mapp. 37, 3031–3040.
- Rösner S, Hackl-Herrwerth A, Leucht S, et al. (2010a) Acamprosate for alcohol dependence. Cochrane Database Syst Rev 9: CD004332.
- Rösner S, Hackl-Herrwerth A, Leucht S, et al. (2010b) Opioid antagonists for alcohol dependence. Cochrane Database Syst Rev 12: CD001867
- Ross, Bossis, Guss, Agin-Liebes, Malone, Cohen, Mennenga, Belser, Kalliontzi, Babb, Su, Corby and Schmidt. Rapid and sustained symptom reduction following psilocybin treatment for anxiety and depression in patients with life-threatening cancer: a randomized controlled trial. J Psychopharmacol. 2016 Dec; 30(12): 1165–1180.
- Ross, S., Bossis, A., Guss, J., Agin-Liebes, G., Malone, T., Cohen, B., et al. (2016). Rapid and sustained symptom reduction following psilocybin treatment for anxiety and depression in patients with life-threatening cancer: a randomized controlled trial. J. Psychopharmacol. 30, 1165–1180.
- Ruck CA, Bigwood J, Staples D, Ott J, Wasson RG. Entheogens. J Psychedelic Drugs. 1979;11:145–146.
- Rümmele W, Gnirss F. Untersuchungen mit Psilocybin, ein psychotropen Substanz aus Psilocybe Mexicana, Schweizerische, Archive für Neurologie. Neurochirurgie und Psychiatrie. 1961;87:365–385.
- Savage C, McCabe OL, Kurland A, et al. (1973) LSD-assisted psychotherapy in the treatment of severe chronic neurosis. J Altered States Consciousness 1: 31–47.
- Savage C, McCabe OL. Residential psychedelic (LSD) therapy for the narcotic addict: a controlled study. Arch Gen Psychiatry. 1973;28:808–814.
- Savage, C. (1955). Variations in ego feeling induced by D-lysergic acid diethyl amide (LSD-25). Psychoanal. Rev. 42, 1–16.
- Schmid, Y., Enzler, F., Gasser, P., Grouzmann, E., Preller, K. H., Vollenweider, F. X., et al. (2015). Acute effects of lysergic acid diethylamide in healthy subjects. Biol. Psychiatry 78, 544–553.
- Schultes RE, Hoffman A, Rätsch C. Plants of the Gods: Their Sacred, Healing, and Hallucinogenic Powers. Revised Edition. Rochester, VT: Healing Arts Press; 2001.
- Schultes RE. Hallucinogens of plant origin. Science. 1969;163:245–254
- Scott NW, Fayers PM, Aaronson NK, Bottomley A, de Graeff A, Groenvold M, Gundy C, Koller M, Petersen M, Sprangers MAG. (2008). EORTC QLQ-C30 Reference Values. Brussels, Belgium: EORTC Quality of Life Group.
- Sessa, B. (2008). Is it time to revisit the role of psychedelic drugs in enhancing human creativity? J. Psychopharmacol. 22, 821–827
- Sewell et al (2006). Response of cluster headache to psilocybin and LSD. Neurology. 2006 Jun 27;66(12):1920-2.
- Shanon, B. (2002). The Antipodes of the Mind: Charting the Phenomenology of the Ayahuasca Experience. New York, NY: Oxford University Press.
- Shanon, B. (2002). The Antipodes of the Mind: Charting the Phenomenology of the Ayahuasca Experience. New York, NY: Oxford University Press.
- Shelton RC, Sanders-Bush E, Manier DH, Schwartz SH (2009) Elevated 5-HT2a receptors in postmortem prefrontal cortex in major depression is associated with reduced activity of protein kinase A. Neuroscience 158: 1406–1415.
- Sherwood JN, Stolaroff MJ and Harman WW (1962) The psychedelic experience – a new concept in psychotherapy. J Neuropsychiatr 4: 69–80.
- Shulgin AT, Shulgin A. Pihkal: A Chemical Love Story. Berkeley, CA: Transform Press; 1991.
- Shulgin AT, Shulgin A. Tihkal: The Continuation. Berkeley, CA: Transform Press; 1997.
- Siegel, R. K., and Jarvik, M. E. (1975). "Drug-induced hallucinations in animals and man," in Hallucinations: Behavior, Experience, and Theory, eds R. K. Siegel and L. J. West (New York, NY: John Wiley & Sons), 81–161.
- Siegel, R. K., and Jarvik, M. E. (1975). "Drug-induced hallucinations in animals and man," in Hallucinations: Behavior, Experience, and Theory
- Sigafoos J, Green VA, Edrisinha C, Lancioni GE. (2007) Flashback to the 1960s: LSD in the treatment of autism. Dev Neurorehabil 10:75–81.
- Sinke, C., Halpern, J. H., Zedler, M., Neufeld, J., Emrich, H. M., and Passie, T. (2012). Genuine and drug-induced synesthesia: a comparison. Conscious. Cogn. 21, 1419–1434.
- Smart RG, Storm T, Baker EF and Solursh L (1966) A controlled study of lysergide in the treatment of alcoholism. 1. The effects on drinking behavior. Q J Stud Alcohol 27: 469–482.
- Smart RG, Storm T, Baker EF and Solursh L (1967) Lysergic acid diethylamide (LSD) in the treatment of alcoholism; an investigation of its effects on drinking behavior, personality structure, and social functioning. Toronto: Published for the Alcoholism and Drug Addiction Research Foundation of Ontario: University of Toronto Press
- Smart RG, Storm T, Baker EFW, Solursh L. A controlled study of lysergid in the treatment of alcoholism: The effects on

drinking behavior. Quart J Stud Alcohol. 1966;27:469–485.
- Snyder SH. Psychotogenic drugs as models for schizophrenia. Neuropsychopharmcology. 1988;1:197–199.
- Soloff PH, Price JC, Meltzer CC, et al. (2007) 5HT2a receptor binding is increased in borderline personality disorder. Biol Psychiatry 62: 580–587. Anisman H, Du L, Palkovits M, et al. (2008) Serotonin receptor subtype and P11 mRNA expression in stress-relevant brain regions of suicide and control subjects. J Psychiatry Neurosci 33: 131–141.
- Spielberger CS, Gorsuch RL, Lushene RE. (1970). Manual for the State Trait Anxiety Inventory. Palo Alto, CA: Consulting Psychologists Press
- Spitzer, M., Thimm, M., Hermle, L., Holzmann, P., Kovar, K. A., Heimann, H., et al. (1996). Increased activation of indirect semantic associations under psilocybin. Biol. Psychiatry 39, 1055–1057.
- Stace, W. T. (1960). Mysticism and Philosophy. New York, NY: MacMillan.
- Stockings GT. A clinical study of the mescaline psychosis, with special reference to the mechanism of the genesis of schizophrenia and other psychotic states. J Mental Sciences. 1940;86:29–47.
- Stolaroff MJ. The Secret Chief Revealed: Conversations with Leo Zeff, Pioneer in the Underground Psychedelic Therapy Movement. Sarasota, FL: Multidisciplinary Association for Psychedelic Studies (MAPS); 2004.
- Stolz J, Marsden C, Middlemiss D. Effect of chronic antidepressant treatment and subsequent withdrawal on [3H]-5-hydroxytryptamine and [3H]-spiperone binding in rat frontal cortex and serotonin receptor mediated behaviour. Psychopharmacology. 1983;80:150–155.
- Strassman RJ, Qualls CR. Dose-response study of N,N-dimethyltryptamine in humans: neuroendocrine, autonomic, and cardiovascular effects. Arch Gen Psychiatry. 1994;51:85–97.
- Strassman RJ. Adverse reactions to psychedelic drugs: a review of the literature. The Journal of Nervous and Mental Disease. 1984;172:577–595.
- Strassman RJ. DMT: The Spirit Molecule. Rochester, VT: Park Street Press; 2001.
- Strassman RJ. Human hallucinogen interactions with drugs affecting serotonergic neurotransmission. Neuropsychopharmacology. 1992;7:241–243.
- Strassman RJ. Human hallucinogenic drug research in the United States: a present-day case history and review of the process. J Psychoactive Drugs. 1991;23:29–38.
- Strassman, R. J. (1984). Adverse reactions to psychedelic drugs. A review of the literature. J. Nerv. Ment. Dis. 172, 577–595.
- Strassman, R. J., Qualls, C. R., Uhlenhuth, E. H., and Kellner, R. (1994). Dose response study of N,N-dimethyltryptamine in humans. II. Subjective effects and preliminary results of a new rating scale. Arch. Gen. Psychiatry 51, 98–108.
- Studerus, E., Gamma, A., Kometer, M., and Vollenweider, F. X. (2012). Prediction of psilocybin response in healthy volunteers. PLoS One 7:e30800
- Studerus, E., Kometer, M., Hasler, F., and Vollenweider, F. X. (2011). Acute, subacute and long-term subjective effects of psilocybin in healthy humans: a pooled analysis of experimental studies. J. Psychopharmacol. 25, 1434–1452.
- Tabor A, Keogh E, Eccleston C. Embodied pain-negotiating the boundaries of possible action. Pain 158(6), 1007–1011 (2017).
- Terhune, D. B., Luke, D. P., Kaelen, M., Bolstridge, M., Feilding, A., Nutt, D., et al. (2016). A placebo-controlled investigation of synaesthesia-like experiences under LSD. Neuropsychologia 88, 28–34
- Thompson PM, Cruz DA, Olukotun DY, et al. (2012) Serotonin receptor, Sert mRNA and correlations with symptoms in males with alcohol dependence and suicide. Acta Psychiatr Scand 126: 165–174.
- Tjio JH, Pahnke WN, Kurland AA. LSD and chromosomes, A controlled experiment. JAMA. 1969;210:849–856.
- Tomsovic M and Edwards RV (1970) Lysergide treatment of schizophrenic and nonschizophrenic alcoholics: a controlled evaluation. Q J Stud Alcohol 31: 932–949.
- Tsuchioka M, Takebayashi M, Hisaoka K, et al. (2008) Serotonin (5-HT) induces glial cell line-derived neurotrophic factor (GDNF) mRNA expression via the transactivation of fibroblast growth factor receptor 2 (FGFR2) in rat C6 glioma cells. J Neurochem 106: 244–257.
- Umbricht D, Vollenweider FX, Schmid L, Grubel C, Skrabo A, Huber T, Koller R. Effects of the 5-HT2A agonist psilocybin on mismatch negativity generation and AX-continuous performance task: implications for the neuropharmacology of cognitive deficits in schizophrenia. Neuropsychopharmacology. 2003;28:170–181.
- Underwood MD, Mann JJ, Huang YY, et al. (2008) Family history of alcoholism is associated with lower 5-HT2A receptor binding in the prefrontal cortex. Alcohol Clin Exp Res 32: 593–599
- Ungerleider JT, Frank IM. Management of acute panic reactions and drug flashbacks resulting from LSD ingestion. In: Bourne P, editor. Acute Drug Emergencies. New York: Academic Press; 1976. pp. 133–138.
- Vaidya VA, Marek GJ, Aghajanian GK, et al. (1997) 5-HT2A receptormediated regulation of brain-derived neurotrophic factor mRNA in the hippocampus and the neocortex. J Neurosci 17: 2785–2795
- Van Dusen W, Wilson W, Miners W and Hook H (1967) Treatment of alcoholism with lysergide. Q J Stud Alcohol 28: 295–304.
- van Vliet JA, Bahra A, Martin V, et al. Intranasal sumatriptan in cluster headache: randomized placebo-controlled double-blind study. Neurology 2003;60:630–633.
- Vollenweider FX and Kometer M (2010) The neurobiology of psychedelic drugs: Implications for the treatment of mood disorders. Nat Rev Neurosci 11: 642–651.
- Vollenweider FX, Csomor PA, Knappe B, Geyer MA, Quednow BB. The effects of preferential 5-HT2A agonist psilocybin on prepulse inhibition of startle in healthy human volunteers depend on interstimulus interval. Neuropsychopharmacology. 2007 Feb 14;
- Vollenweider FX, Geyer MA. A systems model of altered consciousness: integrating natural and drug-induced psychoses. Brain Res Bull. 2001;56:495–507.
- Vollenweider FX, Leenders KL, Scharfetter C, Maguire P, Stadelmann O, Angst J. Positron emission tomography and fluorodeoxyglucose studies of metabolic hyperfrontality and psychopathology in the psilocybin model of psychosis. Neuropsychopharmacology. 1997;16:357–372.
- Vollenweider FX, Vollenweider-Scherpenhuyzen MF, Babler A, et al. (1998) Psilocybin induces schizophrenia-like psychosis in humans via a serotonin-2 agonist action. Neuroreport 9: 3897–3902
- Vollenweider FX, Vontobel P, Hell D, Leenders KL. 5-HT modulation of dopamine release in basal ganglia in psilocybin-induced psychosis in man – a PET study with [11C]raclopride. Neuropsychopharmacology. 1999;20:424–433.
- Vollenweider, F. X., Csomor, P. A., Knappe, B., Geyer, M. A., and Quednow, B. B. (2007). The effects of the preferential 5-HT2A agonist psilocybin on prepulse inhibition of startle in healthy human volunteers depend on interstimulus interval. Neuropsychopharmacology 32, 1876–1887.
- Wackermann, J., Wittmann, M., Hasler, F., and Vollenweider, F. X. (2008). Effects of varied doses of psilocybin on time interval reproduction in human subjects. Neurosci. Lett. 435, 51–55.

- Waldman, A. (2017). A Really Good Day: How Microdosing Made a Mega Difference in My Mood, My Marriage, and My Life. New York, NY: Knopf Doubleday Publishing Group
- Ward, J. (2013). Synesthesia. Annu. Rev. Psychol. 64, 49–75
- Watts, R., Day, C., Krzanowski, J., and Carhart-Harris, R. (2017). Patients' accounts of increased "Connectedness" and "Acceptance" after psilocybin for treatment resistant depression. J. Humanist. Psychol. 57:002216781770958. doi: 10.1177/0022167817709585
- Weil A. The Natural Mind: A Revolutionary Approach to the Drug Problem. Revised Edition. Boston, MA: Houghton Mifflin Co; 2004.
- Weiss RS (1995) Learning from Strangers: The Art and Method of Qualitative Interview Studies. New York, NY: Free Press.
- Whelan and Johnson. Lysergic acid diethylamide and psilocybin for the management of patients with persistent pain: a potential role? Pain Manag. (2018) 8(3), 217–229.
- Wiesbeck GA, Weijers HG, Chick J, et al. (1999) Ritanserin in relapse prevention in abstinent alcoholics: Results from a placebo-controlled double-blind international multicenter trial. Ritanserin in Alcoholism Work Group. Alcohol Clin Exp Res 23: 230–235.
- Winkelman, M. J. (2017). The mechanisms of psychedelic visionary experiences: hypotheses from evolutionary psychology. Front Neurosci. 2017 Sep 28;11:539.
- Wittmann M, Carter O, Hasler F, Cahn BR, Grimberg U, Spring P, Hell D, Flohr H, Vollenweider FX. Effects of psilocybin on time perception and temporal control of behaviour in humans. J Psychopharmacol. 2007;21:50–64.
- Wittmann, M., Carter, O., Hasler, F., Cahn, B. R., Grimberg, U., Spring, P., et al. (2007). Effects of psilocybin on time perception and temporal control of behaviour in humans. J. Psychopharmacol. 21, 50–64
- Wolbach AB, Isbell H, Miner EJ. Cross tolerance between mescaline and LSD-25 with a comparison of the mescaline and LSD reactions. Psychopharmacologia. 1962;3:1–14.
- Wolbach AB, Miner EJ, Isbell H. Comparison of psilocin with psilocybin, mescaline and LSD-25. Psychopharmacologia. 1962;3:219–223.
- Wong, S. (2017). Leading the high life. New Sci. 234, 22–23.
- Zeidan F, Vago DR. Mindfulness meditation-based pain relief: a mechanistic account. Ann. NY Acad. Sci. 1373(1), 114–127 (2016).

Ayahuasca and DMT

- Airaksinen, M.M.; Lecklin, A.; Saano, V.; Tuomisto, L.; Gynther, J. Tremorigenic effect and inhibition of tryptamine and serotonin receptor binding by beta-carbolines. *Pharmacol Toxicol.*, 1987, 60(1), 5-8.
- Araujo, A.M; Carvalho, F.; Bastos, Mdl.; *et al.* The hallucinogenic world of tryptamines; an updated review. *Arch Toxicol*, 2015, 89, 1151-1173.
- Arrevalo, G. Interview with Guillermo Arrevalo, a Shipibo urban shaman, by Roger Rumrrill. Interview by Roger Rumrrill. *Psychoactive Drugs*, 2005, 37(2), 203-207.
- Barbosa PC, Cazorla IM, Giglio JS, Strassman R. A six-month prospective evaluation of personality traits, psychiatric symptoms and quality of life in ayahuasca-naïve subjects. J Psychoactive Drugs. 2009;41(3):205-12. DOI: 10.1080/02791072. 2009.10400530. PMID: 19999673.
- Barbosa, P., Mizumoto, S., Bogenschutz, M. and Strassman, R. (2012) Health status of ayahuasca users. Drug Test Anal 4: 601–609.
- Barbosa, P.C.R.; Cazorla, I.M.; Giglio, J.S.; Strassman, R. A six- month prospective evaluation of personality traits, psychiatric symptoms and quality of life in ayahuasca-naive subjects. *Psy- choactive Drugs*, 2009, 41(3), 205-212.
- Barbosa, P.C.R.; Giglio, J.S.; Dalgalarrondo, P. (2005). Altered states of consciousness and short-term psychological after-effects induced by the first time ritual use of ayahuasca in an urban context in brazil. *Psychoactive Drugs*, 2005, 37(2), 193-201.
- Bewernick BH, Hurlemann R, Matusch A, et al. Nucleus accumbens deep brain stimulation decreases ratings of depression and anxiety in treatment-resistant depression. Biol Psychiatry. 2010;67:110–116.
- Beyer, S.V. *Singing to the plants: A guide to Mestizo shamanism in the upper Amazon* . Albuquerque: University of New Mexico Press, 2009.
- Blainey, M.G. Forbidden therapies: Santo Daime, ayahuasca, and the prohibition of entheogens in Western society. *J Relig Health*, 2015, 54, 287-302.
- Bouayed, J.; Rammal, H.; Soulimani, R. Oxidative stress and anxi- ety: Relationship and cellular pathways. *Oxidative Med & Cell Longevity*, 2009, 2(2), 63-67.
- Bouso, J., González, D., Fondevila, S., Cutchet, M., Fernández, X., Ribeiro Barbosa, P. et al. (2012) Personality, psychopathology, life attitudes and neuropsychological performance among ritual users of ayahuasca: a longitudinal study. PLoS One 7: e42421.
- Bouso, J., Palhano-Fontes, F., Rodríguez-Fornells, A., Ribeiro, S., Sanches, R., Crippa, J. et al. (2015) Long-term use of psychedelic drugs is associated with differences in brain structure and personality in humans. Eur Neuropsychopharmacol 25: 483–492.
- Bouso, J.C.; Fabregas, J.M.; Antonijoan, R.M.; Rodriguez-Fornells, A.; Riba, J. Acute effects of ayahuasca on neuropsychological per- formance: Differences in executive function between experienced and occasional users. *Psychopharmacology*, 2013, 230(3), 415-424.
- Bresnick, T.; Levin, R. Phenomenal qualities of ayahuasca inges- tion and its relation to fringe consciousness and personality. *Con- sciousness Studies*, 2006, 13(9), 5-24.

Edited by Dr. Oliver Rumle Hovmand

- Brierley DI, Davidson C. Developments in harmine pharmacology—implications for ayahuasca use and drug-dependence treatment. Prog Neuropsychopharmacol Biol Psychiatry. 2012; 39(2):263-72. DOI: 10.1016/j.pnpbp.2012.06.001. PubMed PMID: 22691716.
- Bullis, R.K. The "vine of the soul" vs. the controlled substances act: Implications of the Hoasca case. *Psychoactive Drugs*, 2008, 40(2), 193-199.
- Cakic, V.; Potkonyak, J.; Marshall, A. (2010). N,N- Dimethyltryptamine (DMT): Subjective effects and patterns of use among Australian recreational users. *Drug and Alcohol Depend*, 2010, 111(1-2), 30-37.
- Callaway JC, Grob CS. Ayahuasca preparations and serotonin reuptake inhibitors: a potential combination for severe adverse interactions. J Psychoactive Drugs. 1998;30(4):367-9. DOI: 10. 1080/02791072.1998.10399712. PubMed PMID: 9924842.
- Callaway JC. Fast and slow metabolizers of Hoasca. J Psychoactive Drugs. 2005;37(2):157-61. DOI: 10.1080/02791072. 2005.10399797. PubMed PMID: 16149329.
- Callaway, J.C. Various alkaloid profiles in decoctions of B*aniste- riopsis caapi*. *J Psychoactive Drugs*, 2005, 37(2), 151-155.
- Callaway, J.C.; Airaksinen, M.M.; McKenna, D.J.; Brito, G.S.; Grob, C.S. Platelet serotonin uptake sites increased in drinkers of ayahuasca.. *Psychopharmacology*, 1994, 116(3), 385-387.
- Callaway, J.C.; McKenna, D.J.; Grob, C.S.; Brito, G.S.; Raymon, L.P.; Poland, R. E., Mash, D. C. Pharmacokinetics of hoasca alka- loids in healthy humans. *Ethnopharmacol.*, 1999, 65(3), 243-256.
- Callaway, J.C.; McKenna, D.J.; Grob, C.S.; *et al.* Pharmacokinetics of Hoasca alkaloids in healthy humans. *J Ethnopharmacol*, 1999, 65, 243-256.
- Carbonaro, T.M.; Eshleman, A.J.; Forster, M.J.; *et al.* The role of 5-HT2A, 5-HT 2C and mGlu2 receptors in the behavioural effects of tryptamine hallucinogens N,N-dimethyltryptamine and N,N- diisopropyltryptamine in rats and mice. *Psychopharmacology (Berl)*, 2015, 232, 275-284.
- Carbonaro, T.M.; Gatch, M.B. Neuropharmacology of N,N- dimethyltryptamine. *Brain Res Bull*, 2016, 126, 74-88.
- Cardenas, A.V .; Gomez, A.P . Urban use of yaje (ayahuasca) in Colombia. *Adicciones*, 2004, 16, 323
- Cole, J.M.; Pieper, W.A. the effects of N,N-dimenthyltryptamine on operant behaviour in squirrel monkeys. *Psychopharmacologia*, 1973, 16, 107-112.
- Da Silveira, D., Grob, C., de Rios, M., Lopez, E., Alonso, L., Tacla, C. et al. (2005) Ayahuasca in adolescence: a preliminary psychiatric assessment. J Psychoactive Drugs 37: 129–133.
- De Araujo, D., Ribeiro, S., Cecchi, G., Carvalho, F., Sanchez, T., Pinto, J. et al. (2012) Seeing with the eyes shut: neural basis of enhanced imagery following ayahuasca ingestion. Hum Brain Mapp 33: 2550–2560.
- de Rios, M. Ayahuasca: The health vine. *Social Psychiatry*, Win 1971, 17(4), 256-269.7.
- Demarchelier, C.; Gurni, A.; Ciccia, G.; *et al.* Ritual and medicinal plants of the Ese'ejas of the Amazonian rainforest (Madre de Dios, Peru). *J Ethnopharmacol.*, 1996, 52, 45-51.
- Doering-Silveira E, Grob CS, de Rios MD, Lopez E, Alonso LK, Tacla C, et al. Report on psychoactive drug use among adolescents using ayahuasca within a religious context. J Psychoactive Drugs. 2005;37(2):141-4. DOI: 10.1080/02791072. 2005.10399794. PubMed PMID: 16149326.
- Doering-Silveira, E., Grob, C.S., de Rios, M.D., *et al.* Report on psychoactive drug use among adolescents using ayahuasca within a religious context. J. Psychoactive Drugs, 2005, 37, 141-144.
- dos Santos RG, Grasa E, Valle M, Ballester MR, Bouso JC, Nomdede ́u JF, et al. Pharmacology of ayahuasca administered in two repeated doses. Psychopharmacology (Berl). 2012;219:1039- 53.
- dos Santos RG, Landeira-Fernandez J, Strassman RJ, Motta V, Cruz AP. Effects of ayahuasca on psychometric measures of anxiety, panic-like and hopelessness in Santo Daime members. J Ethnopharmacol. 2007;112:507-13.
- dos Santos RG, Valle M, Bouso JC, Nomdede ́u JF, Rodrı ́guezEspinosa J, McIlhenny EH, et al. Autonomic, neuroendocrine and immunological effects of ayahuasca: a comparative study with d-amphetamine. J Clin Psychopharmacol. 2011;31:717- 26.
- dos Santos RG, Valle M, Bouso JC, Nomdede ́u JF, Rodrı ́guezEspinosa J, McIlhenny EH, et al. Autonomic, neuroendocrine and immunological effects of ayahuasca: a comparative study with d-amphetamine. J Clin Psychopharmacol. 2011;31(6):717- 26. DOI: 10.1097/JCP.0b013e31823607f6. PubMed PMID: 22005052.
- dos Santos RG. A critical evaluation of reports associating ayahuasca with life-threatening adverse reactions. J Psychoactive Drugs. 2013;45(2):179-88. DOI: 10.1080/02791072.2013. 785846. PubMed PMID: 23909005.
- dos Santos, R. (2013) Safety and side effects of ayahuasca in humans – an overview focusing on developmental toxicology. J Psychoactive Drugs 45: 68–78.
- dos Santos, R., Grasa, E., Valle, M., Ballester, M., Bouso, J., Nomdedéu, J. et al. (2012) Pharmacology of ayahuasca administered in two repeated doses. Psychopharmacology 219: 1039–1053.
- dos Santos, R., Valle, M., Bouso, J., Nomdedéu, J., Rodríguez-Espinosa, J., McIlhenny, E. et al. (2011) Autonomic, neuroendocrine and immunological effects of ayahuasca. A comparative study with d-amphetamine. J Clinical Psychopharmacol 31: 717–726.

- dos Santos, R.G.; Grasa, E.; Valle, M.; Ballester, M.R.; Bouso, J.C.; Nomdedeu, J.F.; Riba, J. Pharmacology of ayahuasca administered in two repeated doses. *Psychopharmacology*, 2012, 219(4), 1039-1053.
- dos Santos, R.G.; Osorio, F.L.; Crippa, J.A.S.; *et al*. Antidepressive and anxiolytic effects of ayahuasca: a systematic literature review of animal and human studies. *Rev Bras Psiquiatr.*, 2016, 38, 65-72.
- Drevets WC, Savitz J, Trimble M. The subgenual anterior cingulate cortex in mood disorders. CNS Spectr. 2008;13:663–681.
- Fabregas JM, Gonza´lez D, Fondevila S, Cutchet M, Ferna´ndez X, Barbosa PCR, et al. Assessment of addiction severity among ritual users of ayahuasca. Drug Alcohol Depend. 2010;111(3):257- 61. DOI: 10.1016/j.drugalcdep.2010.03.024. PubMed PMID: 20554400.
- Fábregas, J., González, D., Fondevila, S., Cutchet, M., Fernández, X., Barbosa, P. et al. (2010) Assessment of addiction severity among ritual users of ayahuasca. Drug Alcohol Depend 111: 257–261.
- Fantagrossi, W.E.; Woods, J.H.; Winger, G. Transient reinforcing effects of phenylisopropylamine and indolealkylamine hallucinogens in rhesus monkeys. *Behav Pharmacol.*, 2004, 15, 149-157.
- Farzin, D.; Mansouri, N. Antidepressant-like effect of harmane and other beta-carbolines in the mouse forced swim test. *Eur Neuropsy- chopharmacol.* 2006, 16(5), 324-328.
- Fiedler, L.; Jungaberle, H.; Verres, R. Motives for the consumption of psychoactive substances demonstrated in the example of the use of ayahuasca in the Santo Daime community. *Zeitschr Fur Medizin Psychol.*, 2011, 20, 137-144.
- Finn, D.P.; Marti, O.; Harbuz, M.; S, Valles, A.; Belda, X.; Mar- quez, C.; Hudson, A.L. Behavioral, neuroendocrine and neuro- chemical effects of the imidazoline I2 receptor selective ligand BU224 in naive rats and rats exposed to the stress of the forced swim test. *Psychopharmacology*, 2003, 167(2), 195-202.
- Fitzgerald PB, Laird AR, Maller J, et al. A meta-analytic study of changes in brain activation in depression. Hum Brain Mapp. 2008;29:683–695.
- Fontanilla, D.; Johannessen, M.; Hajipour, A.R.; Cozzi, N.V.; Jackson, M.B.; Ruoho, A.E. The hallucinogen N,N-dimethyltryptamine (DMT) is an endogenous sigma-1 receptor regulator. *Science*, 2009, 323(5916), 934-937.
- Fortunato, J.J.; Reus, G.Z.; Kirsch, T.;R.; Stringari, R.B.; Fries, G.R.; Kapczinski, F.; Quevedo, J. Chronic administration of harmine elicits antidepressant-like effects and increases BDNF lev- els in rat hippocampus. *J Neural Transm*, 2010a, 117(10), 1131-1137.
- Fortunato, J.J.; Reus, G.Z.; Kirsch, T.R.; Stringari, R.B.; Fries, G.R.; Kapczinski, F.; Quevedo, J. Effects of beta-carboline harmine on behavioral and physiological parameters observed in the chronic mild stress model: Further evidence of antidepressant properties. *Brain Res Bull*, 2010b, 81(4-5), 491-496.
- Fortunato, J.J.; Reus, G.Z.; Kirsch, T.R.; Stringari, R.B.; Stertz, L.; Kapczinski, F.; Quevedo, J. Acute harmine administration induces antidepressive-like effects and increases BDNF levels in the rat hippocampus. *Progr in Neuro-Psychopharmacol Biol Psychiatry*, 2009, 33(8), 1425-1430.
- Fotiou, E. From medicine men to day trippers: Shamanic tourism in Iquitos, Peru. *Dissertation Abstracts Int Section A: Humanities and Social Sci*, 2011, 72(1-A), 256.
- Freedland, C.S.; Mansbach, R.S. Behavioral profile of constituents in ayahuasca, an Amazonian psychoactive plant mixture. *Drug and Alcohol Depend.*,1999, 54(3), 183-194.
- Frison, G.; Favretto, D.; Zancanaro, F.; Fazzin, G.; Ferrara, S.D. A case of beta-carboline alkaloid intoxication following ingestion of *Peganum harmala* seed extract. *Forensic Sci Int*, 2008, 179(2-3), e37-43.
- Gable RS. Risk assessment of ritual use of oral dimethyltryptamine (DMT) and harmala alkaloids. Addiction. 2007;102(1):24-34. DOI: 10.1111/j.1360-0443.2006.01652.x. PubMed PMID: 17207120
- Gable, R. S. Risk assessment of ritual use of oral N,N- dimethyltryptamine (DMT) and harmala alkaloids. *Addiction*, 2007, 102(1), 24-34. In: Winkelman, M.J.; Roberts, T.B. (eds.): Psychedelic Medicine (Vol 2): New Evidence for Hallucinogenic Substances as T reatments.
- Garcia-Sevilla, J.A.; Escriba, P.V.; Guimon, J. Imidazoline recep- tors and human brain disorders. *Annals New York Acad Sci*, 1999, 881, 392-409.
- Gaujac, A.; Navickiene, S.; Collins, M.I.; Brandt, S.D.; de An- drade, J.; B. Analytical techniques for the determination of tryp- tamines and carbolines in plant matrices and in psychoactive bev- erages consumed during religious ceremonies and neo-shamanic urban practices. *Drug Testing & Analysis*, 2012, 4(7-8), 636-648.
- Gillin, J.C.; Cannon, E.; Magyar, R.; *et al*. Failure of N,N- dimethyltryptamine to evoke tolerance in cats. *Biol Psychiatry*, 1973, 7, 213-220.
- Grob, C.S.; McKenna, D.J.; Callaway, J.C.; Brito, G.S.; Neves, E.S.; Oberlaender, G.; Boone, K.B. Human psychopharmacology of hoasca, a plant hallucinogen used in ritual context in Brazil. *Nervous & Mental Dis*, 1996, 184(2), 86-94.
- Groisman, A.; de Rios, M.D. Ayahuasca, the U.S. Supreme Court, and the UDV-U.S. government case: Culture, religion, and implica- tions of a legal dispute. In: Winkelman, M.J.; Roberts, T.B. (eds.): Psychedelic Medicine: New Evidence for Hallucinogenic Sub- stances as Treatments. 2007, pp. 251-269. Praeger Publishers, Westport, CT.
- Halaris, A.; Piletz, J.E. Relevance of imidazoline receptors and agmatine to psychiatry: A decade of progress. *A N Y Acad Sci*, 2003, 1009, 1-20.

- Halpern JH, Sherwood AR, Passie T, Blackwell KC, Ruttenber AJ. Evidence of health and safety in American members of a religion who use a hallucinogenic sacrament. Med Sci Monit. 2008;14(8): SR15-22. PubMed PMID: 18668010.
- Hamilla, Hallaka, Dursuna and Bakera. Ayahuasca: Psychological and Physiologic Effects, Pharmacology and Potential Uses in Addiction and Mental Illness. *Current Neuropharmacology*, 2018, 16, 1-19
- Herraiz, T.; Gonzalez, D.; Ancin-Azpilicueta, C.; Aran, V.J.; Guillen, H. Beta-carboline alkaloids in *Peganum harmala* and inhi- bition of human monoamine oxidase (MAO). *Food & Chem Toxi- col*, 2010, 48(3), 839-845.
- Holman, C. Surfing for a shaman: Analyzing an ayahuasca website. *Annals Tourism Res*, 2011, 38(1), 90-109.
- Kavenska, V.; Simonova, H. Ayahuasca tourism: participants in shamanic rituals and their personality styles, motivation, benefits and risks. *J Psychoactive Drugs*, 2015 Nov-Dec;47(5):351-9.
- Keiser, M. J.; Setola, V.; Irwin, J.J.; Laggner, C.; Abbas, A.I.; Hufeisen, S.J.; Roth, B.L. Predicting new molecular targets for known drugs. *Nature*, 2009, 462(7270), 175-181.
- Kjellgren, A.; Eriksson, A.; Norlander, T. Experiences of encounters with ayahuasca-"the vine of the soul." *Psychoactive Drugs*, 2009, 41(4), 309-315.
- Kovacic, B.; Domino, E.F. Tolerance and limited cross-tolerance to the effects of N, N-dimethyltryptamine (DMT) and lysergic acid diethylamide-25 (LSD) on food-rewarded bar pressing in the rat. *J Pharmacol Exp Ther.*, 1976, 197, 495-502.
- Labate, B.C. Consumption of ayahuasca by children and pregnant women: Medical controversies and religious perspectives. *Psy- choactive Drugs*, 2011, 43(1), 27-35.
- Lanaro R, Calemi DB, Togni LR, Costa JL, Yonamine M, Cazenave Sde O, et al. Ritualistic use of Ayahuasca versus street use of similar substances seized by the police: a key factor involved in the potential for intoxications and overdose? J Psychoactive Drugs. 2015;47(2):132-9. DOI: 10.1080/02791072.2015.1013202. PubMed PMID: 25950593.
- Langer, S.Z.; Lee, C.R.; Segonzac, A.; *et al.* Possible endocrine role of the pineal gland for 6-methoxytetrahydro-beta-carboline, a putative endogenous neuromodulator of the [3H]imipramine recog- nition site. *Eur J Pharmcol*, 1984, 102(2), 379-380.
- Lemlij, M. Primitive group treatment. *Psychiatria Clinica*, 1978, 11(1), 10-14.
- Liester, M.B.; Prickett, J.I. Hypotheses regarding the mechanisms of ayahuasca in the treatment of addictions. *J Psychoactive Drugs*, 2012, 44(3), 200-208.
- Loizaga-Velder A, Verres R. Therapeutic effects of ritual ayahuasca use in the treatment of substance dependence— qualitative results. J Psychoactive Drugs. 2014;46(1):63-72. DOI: 10.1080/02791072.2013.873157. PubMed PMID: 24830187.
- Louis, E.D.; Zheng, W.; Jurewicz, E.C.; Watner, D.; Chen, J.; Factor-Litvak, P.; Parides, M. Elevation of blood beta-carboline al- kaloids in essential tremor. *Neurology*, 2002, 59(12), 1940-1944.
- Mabit, J. Ayahuasca in the treatment of addictions. In: Winkelman, M.J.; Roberts, T.B. (eds.): Psychedelic Medicine (Vol 2): New Evidence for Hallucinogenic Substances as Treatments. 2007, pp. 87-105. Praeger Publishersm Westport, CT.
- Malcolm BJ, Lee KC. Ayahuasca: An ancient sacrament for treatment of contemporary psychiatric illness? Ment Health Clin [Internet]. 2017;7(1):39-45. DOI: 10.9740/mhc.2017.01.039.
- McKenna D, Riba J. New World tryptamine hallucinogens and the neuroscience of ayahuasca. Curr Top Behav Neurosci. 2015; in press.
- McKenna, D.J. The healing vine: Ayahuasca as medicine in the 21st century. In: Winkelman, M.J.; Roberts, T.B. (eds.): Psyche- delic Medicine: New Evidence for Hallucinogenic Substances as Treatments (Vol 1). 2007, pp. 21-44. Praeger Publishers.
- Merkl A, Schneider GH, Schönecker T, et al. Antidepressant effects after short-term and chronic stimulation of the subgenual cingulate gyrus in treatment-resistant depression. Exp Neurol. 2013;249:160–168.
- Metzner, R. Hallucinogenic drugs and plants in psychotherapy and shamanism. *J Psychoactive Drugs*, 1998, 30(4), 234-242.
- Moreno RA, Moreno DH. Hamilton (HAM-D) & Montgomery & Asberg (MADRS) depression rating scales. Rev Psiquiatr Clín. 1998;25:262–272
- Morgenstern, J.; Langenbucher, J.; Labouvie, E.W. The generalizability of the dependence syndrome across substances: An ex- amination of some properties of the proposed DSM-IV dependence criteria. *Addiction*, 1994, 89(9), 1105-1113.
- Osório Fde L, Sanches RF, Macedo LR, Santos RG, Maia-deOliveira JP, Wichert-Ana L, et al. Antidepressant effects of a single dose of ayahuasca in patients with recurrent depression: a preliminary report. Rev Bras Psiquiatr. 2015;37(1):13-20. DOI: 10. 1590/1516-4446-2014-1496. PubMed PMID: 25806551.
- Osório, F.d. L.; de Macedo, L.R.H.; de Sousa, J.P.M.; Pinto, J.; Quevedo. J.; Crippa, J.A.d.S.; Hallak, J.C.E. The therapeutic potential of harmine and ayahuasca in depression: Evidence from exploratory animal and human studies In R. G. dos Santos (Ed.), *The ethnopharmacology of ayahuasca*, 2011, (pp. 75-85). Kerala, India: Transworld Research Network.
- Osório, Sanches, Macedo, dos Santos, Maia-de-Oliveira, Wichert-Ana, de Araujo, Riba, Crippa, and Hallak. Antidepressant effects of a single dose of ayahuasca in patients with recurrent depression: a preliminary report (2014). Revista Brasileira de Psiquiatria. 2015;37:13–20
- Ott, J. Pharmahuasca: Human pharmacology of oral DMT plus harmine. *Psychoactive Drugs*, 1999, 31(2), 171-177.
- Palhano-Fontes, F., Andrade, K., Tofoli, L., Santos, A., Crippa, J., Hallak, J. et al. (2015) The psychedelic state induced by ayahuasca modulates the activity and connectivity of the default mode network. PLoS One 10: e0118143.

- Paterson, L.M.; Robinson, E.S.; Nutt, D.J.; Hudson, A.L. In vivo estimation of imidazoline(2) binding site turnover. *Annals N Y Acad Sci.* 2003, 1009, 367-370.
- Piletz, J.E.; Zhu, H.; Ordway, G.; Stockmeier, C.; Dilly, G.; Reis, D.; Halaris, A. Imidazoline receptor proteins are decreased in the hippocampus of individuals with major depression. *Biol Psychia- try,* 2000, 48(9), 910-919.
- Pizzagalli DA, Holmes AJ, Dillon DG, et al. Reduced caudate and nucleus accumbens response to rewards in unmedicated individuals with major depressive disorder. Am J Psychiatry. 2009;166:702–710.
- Plucinska J. A British tourist has been killed at a Peruvian ayahuasca ceremony. Time [Internet]. 2015 Dec [cited 2016 May 3]. Available from: http://time.com/4154455/peru-ayahuascamurder-amazon-hallucinogen
- Reus, G.Z.; Stringari, R.B.; de Souza, B.; Petronilho, F.; Dal- Pizzol, F.; Hallak, J.E.; Quevedo, J. Harmine and imipramine promote antioxidant activities in prefrontal cortex and hippocampus. *Oxidative Med & Cell Longevity,* 2010, 3(5), 325-331.
- Rhodium Archive. 2009. A Hypothesis of the Mechanisms Under- lying Visual Distortions Caused by Psychedelic Drugs. Available at http://www.erowid.org/archive/rhodium/pharmacology/ visual dis- tortions.html).
- Riba J, Barbanoj MJ. Bringing ayahuasca to the clinical research laboratory. J Psychoactive Drugs. 2005;37:219-30.
- Riba J, Rodrı́guez-Fornells A, Barbanoj MJ. Effects of ayahuasca on sensory and sensorimotor gating in humans as measured by P50 suppression and prepulse inhibition of the startle reflex, respectively. Psychopharmacology (Berl). 2002;165(1):18-28. DOI: 10.1007/s00213-002-1237-5. PubMed PMID: 12474114
- Riba J, Rodrı́guez-Fornells A, Urbano G, Morte A, Antonijoan R, Montero M, et al. Subjective effects and tolerability of the South American psychoactive beverage ayahuasca in healthy volunteers. Psychopharmacology (Berl). 2001;154:85-95.
- Riba J, Romero S, Grasa E, Mena E, Carrio´ I, Barbanoj MJ. Increased frontal and paralimbic activation following ayahuasca, the pan-Amazonian inebriant. Psychopharmacology (Berl). 2006;186: 93-8.
- Riba J, Valle M, Urbano G, et al. Human pharmacology of ayahuasca: subjective and cardiovascular effects, monoamine metabolite excretion, and pharmacokinetics. J Pharmacol Exp Ther. 2003;306:73–83.
- Riba J, Valle M, Urbano G, Yritia M, Morte A, Barbanoj MJ. Human pharmacology of ayahuasca: subjective and cardiovascular effects, monoamine metabolite excretion, and pharmacokinetics. J Pharmacol Exp Ther. 2003;306:73-83.
- Riba, J., Rodríguez-Fornells, A., Urbano, G., Morte, A., Antonijoan, R., Montero, M. et al. (2001). Subjective effects and tolerability of the South American psychoactive beverage ayahuasca in healthy volunteers. Psychopharmacology 154: 85–95.
- Riba, J., Romero, S., Grasa, E., Mena, E., Carrió, I. and Barbanoj, M. (2006) Increased frontal and paralimbic activation following ayahuasca, the pan-Amazonian inebriant. Psychopharmacology 186: 93–98.
- Riba, J., Valle, M., Urbano, G., Yritia, M., Morte, A. and Barbanoj, M. (2003) Human pharmacology of ayahuasca: subjective and cardiovascular effects, monoamine metabolite excretion and pharmacokinetics. J Pharmacol Exp Ther 306: 73–83.
- Riba, J.; McIlhenny, E.H.; Valle, M.; Bouso, J.C.; Barker, S.A. Metabolism and disposition of N,N-dimethyltryptamine and harmala alkaloids after oral administration of ayahuasca. *Drug Testing & Analysis,* 2012, 4(7-8), 610-616.
- Riba, J.; RodriguezFornells, A.; Urbano, G.; Morte, A.; Antoni- joan, R.; Montero, M.; Barbanoj, M.J. Subjective effects and toler- ability of the South American psychoactive beverage ayahuasca in healthy volunteers. *Psychopharmacology,* 2001, 154(1), 85-95.
- Riba, J.; Valle, M.; Urbano, G.; Yritia, M.; Morte, A.; Barbanoj, M.J. Human pharmacology of ayahuasca: Subjective and cardio- vascular effects, monoamine metabolite excretion, and pharma- cokinetics. *J Pharmacol ExpTherapeutics,* 2003, 306(1), 73-83.
- Saavedra, J.M.; Axelrod, J. Psychotomimetic N-methylated tryp- tamines: Formation in brain *in vivo* and *in vitro. Science,* 1972, 175(4028), 1365-1366.
- Samoylenko, V.; Rahman, M.M.; Tekwani, B.L.; Tripathi, L.M.; Wang, Y.H.; Khan, S.I.; Muhammad, I. *Banisteriopsis caapi,* a unique combination of MAO inhibitory and antioxidative constitu- ents for the activities relevant to neurodegenerative disorders and Parkinson's disease. *J Ethnopharmacology,* 2010, 127(2), 357-367.
- Sanches, Osório, dos Santos, Macedo, Maia-de-Oliveira, Wichert-Ana, de Araujo, Riba, Crippa and Hallak. Antidepressant Effects of a Single Dose of Ayahuasca in Patients With Recurrent Depression - A SPECT Study. J Clin Psychopharmacol. 2016 Feb;36(1):77-81.
- Schenberg, E.E. Ayahuasca and cancer treatment. *SAGE Open Medicine,* 2013, 1.
- Shanon, B. Altered temporality. *Consciousness Studies,* 2001, 8(1), 35-58.
- Shanon, B. The antipodes of the mind: charting the phenomenology of the ayahuasca experience, 2007, Oxford University Press, Ox- ford, UK.
- Stahl, S.M. Stahl's essential psychopharmacology: Neuroscientific basic and practical applications. 2008, Cambridge, NY: Cam- bridge University Press.
- Strassman, R. Subjective effects of DMT and the development of the hallucinogen rating scale. *Newsletter Multidisciplinary Assoc for Psychedelic Studies,* 1992, 3(2).
- Strassman, R.J.; Qualls, C.R. Dose-response study of N,N- dimethyltryptamine in humans. I. neuroendocrine, autonomic, and cardiovascular effects. *Arch Gen Psychiatry,* 1994, 51(2), 85-97.
- Szmulewicz AG, Valerio MP, Smith JM. Switch to mania after ayahuasca consumption in a man with bipolar disorder: a case report. Int J Bipolar Disord. 2015;3:4. DOI: 10.1186/s40345-014- 0020-y. PubMed PMID: 25713771.

- Thomas G, Lucas P, Capler NR, Tupper KW, Martin G. Ayahuascaassisted therapy for addiction: results from a preliminary observational study in Canada. Curr Drug Abuse Rev. 2013;6(1): 30-42. DOI: 10.2174/15733998113099990003. PubMed PMID: 23627784.
- Tupper KW, Labate BC. Ayahuasca, psychedelic studies and health sciences: the politics of knowledge and inquiry into an Amazonian plant brew. Curr Drug Abuse Rev. 2014;7:71–80.
- Tupper, K.W. *Ayahuasca, entheogenic education & public policy. 2011,* (Ph.D, Simon Fraser University, Vancouver, British Columbia, Canada).
- Tupper, K.W.; Labate, B.C. Plants, psychoactive substances and the international narcotics control board: the control of nature and the nature of control. *Human Rights and Drugs.,* 2012, 2, 17-28.
- Urani, A.; Roman, F.J.; Phan, V.L.; Su, T.P.; Maurice, T. The antidepressant-like effect induced by sigma(1)-receptor agonists and neuroactive steroids in mice submitted to the forced swimming test. *Pharmacol ExpTherap,* 2001, 298(3), 1269-1279.
- Volpi-Abadie J, Kaye AM, Kaye AD. Serotonin syndrome. Ochsner J. 2013;13(4):533-40. PubMed PMID: 24358002.
- Wang, J.; Mack, A.L.; Coop, A.; Matsumoto, R.R. Novel sigma (sigma) receptor agonists produce antidepressant-like effects in mice. *Eur Neuropsychopharmacol,* 2007, 17(11), 708-716.
- Wiltshire PE, Hawksworth DL, Edwards KJ. Light microscopy can reveal the consumption of a mixture of psychotropic plant and fungal material in suspicious death. J Forensic Leg Med. 2015;34: 73-80. DOI: 10.1016/j.jflm.2015.05.010. PubMed PMID: 26165663.
- Winkelman M. Psychedelics as medicines for substance abuse rehabilitation: evaluating treatments with LSD, peyote, ibogaine and ayahuasca. Curr Drug Abuse Rev. 2014;7(2):101-16. DOI: 10. 2174/1874473708666150107120011. PubMed PMID: 25563446.
- Winkelman, M. Drug tourism or spiritual healing? Ayahuasca seekers in Amazonia. *Psychoactive Drugs,* 2005, 37(2), 209-218.

MDMA
- Adamson S, Metzner R. The nature of the MDMA experience and its role in healing, psychotherapy and spiritual practice. Revision 1988;10:59–72.
- Adolphs R, Gosselin F, Buchanan T, Tranel D, Schyns P, Damasio A (2005) A mechanism for impaired fear recognition after amygdala damage. Nature 433:68–72
- American Psychiatric Association (2013) The diagnostic and statistical manual of mental disorders, 5th edn. American Psychiatric Association, Washington, DC
- Baggott M, Jerome L, Stuart R. 3,4-Methylenedioxymethamphetamine (MDMA). A review of the English-language scientific and medical literature. Published on-line: http:// www. maps. org/research/mdma/protocol/litreview. html, 2001
- Baggott MJ, Coyle JR, Siegrist JD, et al. (2016) Effects of 3,4-methylenedioxymethamphetamine on socioemotional feelings, authenticity, and autobiographical disclosure in healthy volunteers in a controlled setting. J Psychopharmacol 30: 378–387.z
- Baggott MJ, Kirkpatrick MG, Bedi G, et al. (2015) Intimate insight: MDMA changes how people talk about significant others. J Psychopharmacol 29: 669–677.
- Bartz JA, Hollander E. The neuroscience of affiliation: forging links between basic and clinical research on neuropeptides and social behavi
- Bastiaansen J et al (2011) Diagnosing autism spectrum disorders in adults: the use of Autism Diagnostic Observation Schedule (ADOS) module 4. J Autism Dev Disord 41:1256–1266
- Baumann MH, Wang X, Rothman RB. 3,4-Methylenedioxymethamphetamine (MDMA) neurotoxicity in rats: a reappraisal of past and present findings. Psychopharmacology (Berl) 2007;189(4):407–24. http://dx.doi.org/10.1007/s00213-006-0322-6.
- Beck AT, Steer RA, Ball R, Ranieri W (1996) Comparison of Beck Depression Inventories-IA and -II in psychiatric outpatients. J Pers Assess 67:588–597
- Bedi G, Hyman D and de Wit H (2010) Is ecstasy an "empathogen"? Effects of +/-3,4-methylenedioxymethamphetamine on prosocial feelings and identification of emotional states in others. Biol Psychiatry 68: 1134–1140.
- Bejerot S, Eriksson JM, Mortberg E (2014) Social anxiety in adult autism spectrum disorder. Psychiatry Res 220:705–707. https://doi.org/10. 1016/j.psychres.2014.08.030
- Bershad AK, Weafer JJ, Kirkpatrick MG, Wardle MC, Miller MA, de Wit H (2016) Oxytocin receptor gene variation predicts subjective responses to MDMA. Soc Neurosci 11:592–599. https://doi.org/10. 1080/17470919.2016.1143026
- Bouso, Doblin, Farré, Alcázar and Gómez-Jarabo. MDMA-Assisted Psychotherapy Using Low Doses in a Small Sample of Women with Chronic Posttraumatic Stress Disorder. Journal of Psychoactive Drugs Volume 40 (3), September 2008.
- Bouso, J.C. & Gómez-Jarabo, G. 2003. Investigación terapéutica con MDMA. Medicina Clínica 121 (8): 318.
- Camí J, Farré M, Mas M, Roset PN, Poudevida S, Mas A, et al. Human pharmacology of 3, 4- methylenedioxymeth-amphetamine ("Ecstasy"): psychomotor performance and subjective effects. J Clin Psychopharmacol 2000;20(4):455–66. http://dx.doi.org/10. 1007/s00213-006-0410-7.
- Carhart-Harris RL, Bolstridge M, Day CMJ, et al. (2018) Psilocybin with psychological support for treatment-resistant depression: Six-month follow-up. Psychopharmacology (Berl) 235: 399–408.
- Carhart-Harris RL, Murphy K, Leech R, et al. The effects of acutely administered 3,4-methylenedioxymethamphetamine on spontaneous brain function in healthy volunteers measured with arterial spin labeling and blood oxygen level-dependent resting state functional connectivity. Biol Psychiatry 2015; 78: 554–62.
- Carhart-Harris RL, Wall MB, Erritzoe D, et al. (2014) The effect of acutely administered MDMA on subjective and BOLD-fMRI responses to favourite and worst autobiographical memories. Int J Neuropsychopharmacol 17: 527–540.
- Caudevilla, F. 2003. Éxtasis: Una revisión de la literatura sobre la MDMA. Medicina Clínica 120 (13): 505-15.
- Caudevilla, F. 2006. MDMA (éxtasis). Madrid: Amargord.
- Check E. Psychedelic drugs: the ups and downs of Ecstasy. Nature 2004;429(6988): 126–8. http://dx.doi.org/10.1038/429126a.
- Cisler JM, Steele JS, Lenow JK, et al. Functional reorganization of neural networks during repeated exposure to the traumatic memory in posttraumatic stress disorder: an exploratory fMRI study. J Psychiatr Res 2014; 48: 47–55.

Medical Psychedelics

- Coghlan S, Horder J, Inkster B, Mendez MA, Murphy DG, Nutt DJ (2012) GABA system dysfunction in autism and related disorders: from synapse to symptoms. Neurosci Biobehav Rev 36:2044–2055. https://doi.org/10.1016/j.neubiorev.2012.07.005
- Cohen S, Kamarck T, Mermelstein R (1983) A global measure of perceived stress. J Health Soc Behav 24:385–396
- Danforth A (2013) Courage, connection, clarity: a mixed-model, collective-case study of MDMA (ecstasy) experiences of autistic adults (doctoral dissertation). Retrieved from ProQuest Dissertations & Theses (PQDT) database. (UMI No. 3596826)
- Danforth AL, et al, MDMA-assisted therapy: A new treatment model for social anxiety in autistic adults, Prog NeuroPsychopharmacol Biol Psychiatry (2015), http://dx.doi.org/10.1016/j.pnpbp.2015.03.011
- Danforth AL, Struble CM, Yazar-Klosinski B, Grob CS (2016) MDMA-assisted therapy: a new treatment model for social anxiety in autistic adults. Prog Neuropsychopharmacol Biol Psychiatry 64:237–249. https://doi.org/10.1016/j.pnpbp.2015.03.011
- Danforth AL. Courage, connection, and clarity: a mixed-methods collective-case study of MDMA (Ecstasy) experiences of autistic adults (Doctoral dissertation); 2013 [Retrieved from ProQuest Dissertations and Theses. (UMI No. 3401141)]. Danforth A, Grob CS. Ecstasy. In: Fisher GL, Roget NA, editors. Encyclopedia of substance abuse prevention, treatment, and recovery, vol. 1. Sage; 2009. p. 352–4.
- Danforth, Grob, Struble, Feduccia, Walker, Jerome, Yazar-Klosinski and Emerson. Reduction in social anxiety after MDMA-assisted psychotherapy with autistic adults: a randomized, double-blind, placebo-controlled pilot study. Psychopharmacology (Berl). 2018; 235(11): 3137–3148.
- De La Garza II R, Fabrizio KR, Gupta A. Relevance of rodent models of intravenous MDMA self-administration to human MDMA consumption patterns. Psychopharmacology (Berl) 2007;189(4):425–34. http://dx.doi.org/10.1007/s00213-005-0255-5.
- de la Torre R, Farré M, Roset PN, Pizarro N, Abanades S, Segura M, Camí J. Human pharmacology of MDMA: pharmacokinetics, metabolism, and disposition. Therapeutic drug monitoring 2004;26(2):137–44.
- de la Torre R, Farré M, Roset PN, Pizarro N, Abanades S, Segura M, Segura J, Cami J (2004) Human pharmacology of MDMA: pharmacokinetics, metabolism, and disposition. Ther Drug Monit 26:137– 144
- Doblin, R.E. 2002. A clinical plan for MDMA (Ecstasy) in the treatment of posttraumatic stress disorder (PTSD): Partnering with the FDA. Journal of Psychoactive Drugs 34 (2): 185-94.
- Dolder PC, Muller F, Schmid Y, et al. (2018) Direct comparison of the acute subjective, emotional, autonomic, and endocrine effects of MDMA, methylphenidate, and modafinil in healthy subjects. Psychopharmacology (Berl) 235: 467–479
- Domes G, Heinrichs M, Gläscher J, Büchel C, Braus DF, Herpertz SC. Ot attenuates amygdala responses to emotional faces regardless of valence. Biol Psychiatry 2007a;62(10): 1187–90. http://dx.doi.org/10.1016/j.biopsych.2007.03.025.
- Domes G, Heinrichs M, Michel A, Berger C, Herpertz SC. Oxytocin improves "mind-reading" in humans. Biol Psychiatry 2007b;61(6):731–3. http://dx.doi.org/10.1016/j. biopsych.2006.07.01.
- Downing, J., The psychological and physiological effects of MDMA on normal volunteers. J Psychoactive Drugs, 1986. 18(4): p. 335-40.
- Dumont GJ et al (2009) Increased oxytocin concentrations and prosocial feelings in humans after ecstasy (3,4-methylenedioxymethamphetamine) administration. Social Neuroscience 4:359–366
- Dumont GJH, Verkes RJ. A review of acute effects of 3, 4- methylenedioxymethamphetamine in healthy volunteers. J Psychopharmacol 2006; 20(2):176–87. http://dx.doi.org/10.1177/0269881106063271.
- Farré M, De La Torre R, Mathúna BÓ, Roset PN, Peiro AM, Torrens M, et al. Repeated doses administration of MDMA in humans: pharmacological effects and pharmacokinetics. Psychopharmacology (Berl) 2004;173(3-4):364–75. http://dx.doi.org/10.1007/ s00213-004-1789-7.
- Feduccia AA, Mithoefe MC. MDMA-assisted psychotherapy for PTSD: are memory reconsolidation and fear extinction underlying mechanisms? Prog Neuropsychopharmacol Biol Psychiatry 2018; 84: 221–28.
- Fredman SJ, Monson CM, Adair KC. Implementing cognitive-behavioral conjoint therapy for PTSD with the newest generation of veterans and their partners. Cogn Behav Pract 2011; 18: 120–30.
- Gamma A, Buck A, Berthold T, Liechti ME, Vollenweider FX. 3,4-methylenedioxymethamphetamine (MDMA) modulates cortical and limbic brain activity as measured by [H(2)(15)O]-PET in healthy humans. Neuropsychopharmacology 2000; 23: 388–95.
- Greer GR, Tolbert R. A method of conducting therapeutic sessions with MDMA. J Psychoactive Drugs 1998;30(4):371–9. http://dx.doi.org/10.1080/02791072.1998. 10399713.
- Greer, G. and R. Tolbert, Subjective reports of the effects of MDMA in a clinical setting. J Psychoactive Drugs, 1986. 18(4): p. 319-27.
- Grinspoon L, Bakalar JB. Can drugs be used to enhance the psychotherapeutic process? Am J Psychother 1986;40(3):393–404.
- Grob CS, Poland RE, Chang L, Ernst T. Psychobiologic effects of 3,4- methylenedioxymethamphetamine in humans: methodological considerations and preliminary observations. Behav Brain Res 1996;73(1):103–7. http://dx.doi.org/10.1016/0166-4328(96)00078-2.
- Grob CS, Poland RE. MDMA. In: Lowinson JH, Ruiz P, Millman RB, Langrod JE, editors. Substance abuse: a comprehensive textbook. 4th ed. Philadelphia: Williams and Wilkins; 1995. p. 374–86.
- Grob CS. MDMA research: preliminary investigations with human subjects. Int J Drug Policy 1998;9(2):119–24. http://dx.doi.org/10.1016/S0955- 3959(98)00008-5. Grob CS. Deconstructing Ecstasy: the politics of MDMA research. Addict Res 2000;8(6): 549–88. http://dx.doi.org/10.3109/16066350008998989.
- Grob CS. The enigma of Ecstasy: implications for youth and society. Adolesc Psychiatry 2005;29:97–117.
- Guastella AJ, Einfeld SL, Gray KM, Rinehart NJ, Tonge BJ, Lambert TJ, et al. Intranasal oxytocin improves emotion recognition for youth with autism spectrum disorders. Biol Psychiatry 2010;67(7):692–4. http://dx.doi.org/10.1016/j.biopsych.2009.09.020.
- Hall AP, Henry JA. Acute toxic effects of 'Ecstasy'(MDMA) and related compounds: overview of pathophysiology and clinical management. Br J Anaesth 2006;96(6): 678–85. http://dx.doi.org/10.1093/bja/ael078.
- Harrington RD, Woodward JA, Hooton TM, Horn JR. Life-threatening interactions between HIV-1 protease inhibitors and the illicit drugs MDMA and γ-hydroxybutyrate. Arch Intern Med 1999;159(18):2221–4. http://dx.doi.org/10.1001/archinte.159.18.2221.
- Harris DS, Baggott M, Mendelson JH, Mendelson JE, Jones RT. Subjective and hormonal effects of 3,4-methylenedioxymethamphetamine (MDMA) in humans. Psychopharmacology (Berl) 2002;162(4):396–405. http://dx.doi.org/10.1007/s00213-002-1131-1
- Henry JA, Rella JG. Medical risks associated with MDMA use. In: Holland J, editor. Ecstasy, a complete guide. Rochester VT: Inner Traditions; 2001. p. 71–86.
- Huxster JK, Pirona A, Morgan MJ. The sub-acute effects of recreational Ecstasy (MDMA) use: a controlled study in humans. J Psychopharmacol 2006;20(2):281–90. http:// dx.doi.org/10.1177/0269881106060513.

- Hysek CM, Domes G, Liechti ME. MDMA enhances "mind reading" of positive emotions and impairs "mind reading" of negative emotions. Psychopharmacology (Berl) 2012;222(2):293–302. http://dx.doi.org/10.1007/s00213-012-2645-9.
- Hysek CM, Liechti ME (2012) Effects of MDMA alone and after pretreatment with reboxetine, duloxetine, clonidine, carvedilol, and doxazosin on pupillary light reflex. Psychopharmacology (Berl) 224:363–376. https://doi.org/10.1007/s00213-012-2761-6
- Hysek CM, Schmid Y, Simmler LD, et al. (2014) MDMA enhances emotional empathy and prosocial behavior. Soc Cogn Affect Neurosci 9: 1645–1652.
- Kamboj SK, Kilford EJ, Minchin S, et al. (2015) Recreational 3,4-methylenedioxy-N-methylamphetamine (MDMA) or 'ecstasy' and selffocused compassion: Preliminary steps in the development of a therapeutic psychopharmacology of contemplative practices. J Psychopharmacol 29: 961–970.
- Kamilar-Britt P, Bedi G (2015) The prosocial effects of 3,4- methylenedioxymethamphetamine (MDMA): controlled studies in humans and laboratory animals. Neurosci Biobehav Rev 57:433– 446.
- King B, Hollander E, Sikich L, McCracken J, Scahill L, Bregman J et al (2009) Lack of efficacy of citalopram in children with autism spectrum disorders and high levels of repetitive behavior. Arch Gen Psychiatry 66:583–590
- Kirkpatrick MG, Francis SM, Lee R, de Wit H, Jacob S (2014) Plasma oxytocin concentrations following MDMA or intranasal oxytocin in humans. Psychoneuroendocrinology 46:23–31. https://doi.org/10. 1016/j.psyneuen.2014.04.006
- Kirkpatrick MG, Lee R, Wardle MC, et al. (2014b) Effects of MDMA and intranasal oxytocin on social and emotional processing. Neuropsychopharmacology 39: 1654–1663.
- Kosfeld M, Heinrichs M, Zak PJ, Fischbacher U, Fehr E. Oxytocin increases trust in humans. Nature 2005;435(7042):673–6. http://dx.doi.org/10.1038/nature03701.
- Kuypers KP, Dolder PC, Ramaekers JG, Liechti ME (2017) Multifaceted empathy of healthy volunteers after single doses of MDMA: a pooled sample of placebo-controlled studies. J Psychopharmacol 31:589–598. https://doi.org/10.1177/0269881117699617
- Lamers CT, Ramaekers JG, Muntjewerff ND, Sikkema KL, Riedel WJ, Samyn N, et al. Dissociable effects of a single dose of Ecstasy (MDMA) on psychomotor skills and attentional performance. J Psychopharmacol 2003;17(4):379–87. http://dx.doi.org/10. 1177/0269881103174015.
- Lanius RA, Vermetten E, Loewenstein RJ, et al. (2010) Emotion modulation in PTSD: Clinical and neurobiological evidence for a dissociative subtype. Am J Psychiatry 167: 640–647.
- Lawn JC. Schedules of controlled substances; scheduling of 3,4- methylenedioxymethamphetamine (MDMA) into schedule I of the controlled substances act. Fed Regist 1986;51(198):36552–60.
- Lester SJ, Baggott M, Welm S, Schiller NB, Jones RT, Foster E, et al. Cardiovascular effects of 3, 4-methylenedioxymethamphetamine: a double-blind, placebo-controlled trial. Ann Intern Med 2000;133(12):969–73. http://dx.doi.org/10.7326/0003-4819-133- 12-200012190-00012.
- LeVay S. When science goes wrong: twelve tales from the dark side of discovery. New York, NY: Penguin Group; 2008. p. 78–98.
- Lieb R, Schuetz CG, Pfister H, von Sydow K, Wittchen HU. Mental disorders in Ecstasy users: a prospective-longitudinal investigation. Drug Alcohol Depend 2002;68(2): 195–207. http://dx.doi.org/10.1016/S0376-8716(02)00190-4.
- Liebowitz M, Gorman J, Fyer A, Klein D (1985) Social phobia: review of a neglected anxiety disorder. Arch Gen Psychiatry:42729–42739
- Liechti ME, Gamma A, Vollenweider FX. Gender differences in the subjective effects of MDMA. Psychopharmacology (Berl) 2001;154(2):161–8. http://dx.doi.org/10.1007/ s002130000648.
- Liechti ME, Kunz I, Kupferschmidt H. Acute medical problems due to Ecstasy use. Swiss Med Wkly 2005;135(43–44):652–7.
- Linehan M. Cognitive-behavioral treatment of borderline personality disorder. Guilford Press; 1993.
- Linehan MM (1993) Dialectical behavior therapy for treatment of borderline personality disorder: implications for the treatment of substance abuse. NIDA Res Monogr 137:201–201
- Mas M, Farré M, de la Torre R, Roset PN, Ortuño J, Segura J, et al. Cardiovascular and neuroendocrine effects and pharmacokinetics of 3,4-methylenedioxymethamphetamine in humans. J Pharmacol Exp Ther 1999;290(1):136–45.
- McCallie MS, Blum CM, Hood CJ (2006) Progressive muscle relaxation. J Hum Behav Soc Environ 13:51–66
- Milroy CM. "Ecstasy" associated deaths: what is a fatal concentration? Analysis of a case series. Forensic Sci Med Pathol 2011;7(3):248–52. http://dx.doi.org/10.1007/ s12024-010-9220-7.
- Mithoefer M (2016) A Manual for MDMA-Assisted Psychotherapy in the Treatment of Posttraumatic Stress Disorder. Version 8. http://www.maps.org/research/mdma/mdma-research-timeline/4887-a-manualfor-mdma-assisted-psychotherapy-in-the-treatment-of-ptsd
- Mithoefer MC, Wagner MT, Mithoefer AT, Jerome L, Martin SF, Yazar-Klosinski B, et al. Durability of improvement in post-traumatic stress disorder symptoms and absence of harmful effects or drug dependency after 3,4-methylenedioxymethamphetamine-assisted psychotherapy: a prospective long-term follow-up study. J Psychopharmacol 2013;27(1):28–39. http://dx. doi.org/10.1177/0269881112456611.
- Mithoefer, Mithoefer, Feduccia, Jerome, Wagner, Wymer, Holland, Hamilton, Yazar-Klosinski, Emerson and Doblin. 3,4-methylenedioxymethamphetamine (MDMA)-assisted psychotherapy for post-traumatic stress disorder in military veterans, firefighters, and police officers: a randomised, double-blind, dose-response, phase 2 clinical trial. Lancet Psychiatry. 2018 Jun;5(6):486-497.
- Mithoefer, Wagner, Mithoefer, Jerome and Doblin. The safety and efficacy of 3,4-methylenedioxymethamphetamineassisted psychotherapy in subjects with chronic, treatment-resistant posttraumatic stress disorder: the first randomized controlled pilot study. J Psychopharmacol. 2011 Apr; 25(4): 439–452.
- Mithoefer, Wagner, Mithoefer, Jerome, Martin, Yazar-Klosinski, Michel, Brewerton and Doblin. Durability of improvement in post-traumatic stress disorder symptoms and absence of harmful effects or drug dependency after 3,4-methylenedioxymethamphetamine-assisted psychotherapy: a prospective long-term follow-up study. J Psychopharmacol. 2013 Jan;27(1):28-39.
- Mithoefer. A Manual for MDMA-Assisted Psychotherapy in the Treatment of Posttraumatic Stress Disorder. MAPS 1115 Mission Street Santa Cruz, CA 95060.
- Nakamura K et al (2010) Brain serotonin and dopamine transporter bindings in adults with high-functioning autism. Arch Gen Psychiatry 67:59–68. https://doi.org/10.1001/archgenpsychiatry.2009.137
- Nutt DJ, King LA, Phillips LD. Drug harms in the UK: a multicriteria decision analysis. Lancet 2010;376(9752):1558–65. http://dx.doi.org/10.1016/S0140-6736(10)61462- 6.
- Oblak A, Gibbs T, Blatt G. Reduced GABA-A receptors and benzodiazepine binding sites in the posterior cingulate cortex and fusiform gyrus in autism. Brain Res 2012;1380: 218–28. http://dx.doi.org/10.1016/j.brainres.2010.09.021.

Medical Psychedelics

- Oehen, Traber, Widmer and Schnyder. A randomized, controlled pilot study of MDMA (±3,4-Methylenedioxymethamphetamine)- assisted psychotherapy for treatment of resistant, chronic Post-Traumatic Stress Disorder (PTSD). J Psychopharmacol. 2013 Jan;27(1):40-52.
- Ogden P, Minton K and Pain C (2006) Trauma and the Body: A Sensorimotor Approach to Psychotherapy (Norton Series on Interpersonal Neurobiology). New York: WW Norton & Company
- Ot'alora, Grigsby, Poulter, Van Derveer, Giron, Jerome, Feduccia, Hamilton, Yazar-Klosinski, Emerson, Mithoefer and Doblin. 3,4-Methylenedioxymethamphetamine-assisted psychotherapy for treatment of chronic posttraumatic stress disorder: A randomized phase 2 controlled trial. J Psychopharmacol. 2018 Oct 29:269881118806297
- Parrott AC, Lock J, Conner AC, Kissling C, Thome J. Dance clubbing on MDMA and during abstinence from Ecstasy/MDMA: prospective neuroendocrine and psychobiological changes. Neuropsychobiology 2008;57(4):165–80. http://dx.doi.org/10.1159/ 000147470
- Parrott AC. The psychotherapeutic potential of MDMA (3,4-methylene dioxymethamphetamine): an evidence-based review. Psychopharmacology (Berl) 2007;191(2):181–93. http://dx.doi.org/10.1007/s00213-007-0703-5.
- Passie T (2012) Healing with Entactogens: Therapist and Patient Perspectives on MDMA-assisted Group Psychotherapy. Santa Cruz, CA: Multidisciplinary Association for Psychedelic Studies.
- Pirona A, Morgan MJ. An investigation of the subacute effects of Ecstasy on neuropsychological performance, sleep and mood in regular Ecstasy users. J Psychopharmacol 2010. http://dx.doi.org/10.1177/0269881109102780
- Ricaurte GA, Yuan J, Hatzidimitriou G, Cord BJ, McCann UD. Severe dopaminergic neurotoxicity in primates after a common recreational dose regimen of MDMA ("Ecstasy"): retraction. Science 2003;301(5639):1479. http://dx.doi.org/10.1126/science.301. 5639.1479b.
- Riedlinger TJ, Riedlinger JE. Psychedelic and entactogenic drugs in the treatment of depression. J Psychoactive Drugs 1994;26(1):41–55. http://dx.doi.org/10.1080/ 02791072.1994.10472600.
- Rockville, MD: Substance Abuse and Mental Health Services Administration; 2014. Sumnall HR. The varieties of ecstatic experience: an exploration of the subjective experiences of Ecstasy. J Psychopharmacol 2006;20(5):670–82. http://dx.doi.org/10.1177/ 0269881106060764.
- Sanches RF, de Lima Osorio F, Dos Santos RG, et al. (2016) Antidepressant effects of a single dose of ayahuasca in patients with recurrent depression: A SPECT study. J Clin Psychopharmacol 36: 77–81.
- Schenk S. MDMA self-administration in laboratory animals: a summary of the literature and proposal for future research. Neuropsychobiology 2009;60(3-4):130–6. http:// dx.doi.org/10.1159/000253549.
- Simon NM, Worthington JJ, Doyle A, Hoge EA, Kinrys G, Fischmann D, Link N, Pollack MH (2004) An open-label study of levetiracetam for the treatment of social anxiety disorder. J Clin Psychiatry 65: 1219–1222
- Smilkstein MJ, Smolinske SC, Rumack BH. A case of MAO inhibitor/MDMA interaction: agony after Ecstasy. Clin Toxicol 1987;25(1–2):149–59. http://dx.doi.org/10.3109/ 15563658708992620
- Spek AA, van Ham NC, Nyklicek I (2013) Mindfulness-based therapy in adults with an autism spectrum disorder: a randomized controlled trial. Res Dev Disabil 34:246–253. https://doi.org/10.1016/j.ridd. 2012.08.009
- Spielberger C, Gorsuch R, Lushene R (1983) Manual for the state-trait anxiety inventory. Consulting Psychologists Press, Palo Alto
- Sripada RK, King AP, Garfinkel SN, et al. Altered resting-state amygdala functional connectivity in men with posttraumatic stress disorder. J Psychiatry Neurosci 2012; 37: 241–49.
- Stolaroff M. The secret chief revealed: conversations with a pioneer of the underground therapy movement. Sarasota FL: Multidisciplinary Association for Psychedelic Studies; 2004
- Substance Abuse Mental Health Services Administration. Results from the 2013 National Survey on Drug Use and Health: Summary of National Findings, NSDUH Series H-48, HHS Publication No. (SMA) 14–4863.
- Tancer ME, Johanson CE. The subjective effects of MDMA and mCPP in moderate MDMA users. Drug Alcohol Depend 2001;65(1):97–101. http://dx.doi.org/10.1016/S0376- 8716(01)00146-6.
- Uzunova G, Pallanti S, Hollander E (2016) Excitatory/inhibitory imbalance in autism spectrum disorders: implications for interventions and therapeutics. World J Biol Psychiatry 17:174–186. https://doi. org/10.3109/15622975.2015.1085597
- Vizeli P, Liechti ME (2018) Oxytocin receptor gene variations and socioemotional effects of MDMA: A pooled analysis of controlled studies in healthy subjects. PLoS One 13:e0199384. https://doi.org/10. 1371/journal.pone.0199384
- Vollenweider FX, Gamma A, Liechti M, Huber T. Psychological and cardiovascular effects and short-term sequelae of MDMA ("Ecstasy") in MDMA-naïve healthy volunteers. Neuropsychopharmacology 1998;19(4):241–51. http://dx.doi.org/10.1016/s0893- 133x(98)00013-x.
- von Sydow K, Lieb R, Pfister H, Höfler M, Wittchen HU. Use, abuse and dependence of Ecstasy and related drugs in adolescents and young adults—a transient phenomenon? Results from a longitudinal community study. Drug Alcohol Depend 2002;66(2): 147–59. http://dx.doi.org/10.1016/S0376-8716(01)00195-8
- Walpola IC, Nest T, Roseman L, et al. Altered insula connectivity under MDMA. Neuropsychopharmacology 2017; 42: 2152–62.
- Weathers FW, Keane TM and Davidson JR (2001) Clinician-administered PTSD scale: A review of the first ten years of research. Depress Anxiety 13: 132–156
- Wolff K, Tsapakis EM, Winstock AR, Hartley D, Holt D, Forsling ML, et al. Vasopressin and oxytocin secretion in response to the consumption of Ecstasy in a clubbing population. J Psychopharmacol 2006;20(3):400–10. http://dx.doi.org/10.1177/ 0269881106074514.

Ketamine

- Abdallah CG, Adams TG, Kelmendi B, Esterlis I, Sanacora G, Krystal JH. Ketamine's mechanism of action: a path to rapid acting antidepressants. Depress Anxiety 2016; 33: 689e97
- Amr YM. Multi-day low dose ketamine infusion as adjuvant to oral gabapentin in spinal cord injury related chronic pain: a prospective, randomized, double blind trial. Pain Physician 2010; 13: 245e9
- Andrade C. Ketamine for depression: 3. Does chirality matter? J Clin Psychiatry 2017; 78: e674e7
- Atigari OV, Healy D. Sustained antidepressant response to ketamine. BMJ Case Rep. 2013, http://dx.doi.org/10.1136/ bcr-2013-200370.
- Avidan MS, Maybrier HR, Abdallah AB, et al., PODCAST Research Group. Intraoperative ketamine for prevention of postoperative delirium or pain after major surgery in older adults: an international, multicentre, double-blind, randomised

clinical trial. Lancet 2017; 390: 267e75

- Bakunina N, Pariante CM, Zunszain PA. Immune mechanisms linked to depression via oxidative stress and neuroprogression. Immunology 2015; 144: 365e73

- Berman, R.M., Cappiello, A., Anand, A., Oren, D.A., Heninger, G.R., Charney, D.S., Krystal, J.H., 2000. Antidepressant effects of ketamine in depressed patients. Biol. Psychiatry 47, 351–354.

- Best SR. Combined ketamine/transcranial magnetic stimulation treatment of severe depression in bipolar I disorder. J ECT. 2014;30:e50—1.

- Caddy, C., Giaroli, G., White, T.P., Shergill, S.S., Tracy, D.K., 2014. Ketamine as the prototype glutamatergic antidepressant: pharmacodynamic actions, and a systematic review and meta-analysis of efficacy. Ther. Adv. Psychopharmacol. 4, 75–99.

- Chandley, M.J., Szebeni, A., Szebeni, K., Crawford, J.D., Stockmeier, C.A., Turecki, G., Kostrzewa, R.M., Ordway, G.A., 2014. Elevated gene expression of glutamate receptors in noradrenergic neurons from the locus coeruleus on major depression. Int. J. Neuropsychopharmacol. 17, 1569–1578.

- Cheng PS, Fu CY, Lee CH, Liu C, Chien CS. GC-MS quantification of ketamine, norketamine, and dehydronorketamine in urine specimens and comparative study using ELISA as the preliminary test methodology. J Chromatogr B Analyt Technol Biomed Life Sci. 2007;852(1-2):443-9. DOI: 10.1016/j.jchromb.2007.02.005. PubMed PMID: 17339137.

- Chilukuri, H., Reddy, N.P., Pathapati, R.M., Manu, A.N., Jollu, S., Shaik, A.B., 2014. Acute antidepressant effects of intramuscular versus intravenous ketamine. Indian J. Psychol. Med. 36, 71–76.

- Craven, R. (2007) Ketamine. Anaesthesia 62: S48–53.

- Cusin C, Hilton GQ, Nierenberg AA, Fava M. Long-term maintenance with intramuscular ketamine for treatmentresistant bipolar II depression. Am J Psychiatry. 2012;169: 868—9.

- Dale O, Somogyi AA, Li Y, Sullivan T, Shavit Y. Does intraoperative ketamine attenuate inflammatory reactivity following surgery? A systematic review and metaanalysis. Anesth Analg 2012; 115: 934e43

- Diazgranados, N., Ibrahim, L., Brutsche, N.E., Newberg, A., Kronstein, P., Khalife, S., Kammerer, W.A., Quezado, Z., Luckenbaugh, D.A., Salvadore, G., MachadoVieira, R., Manji, H.K., Zarate Jr., C.A., 2010. A randomized add-on trial of an N-methyl-D-aspartate antagonist in treatment-resistant bipolar depression. Arch. Gen. Psychiatry 67, 793–802.

- Duman, R.S., 2014. Neurobiology of stress, depression, and rapid acting antidepressants: remodeling synaptic connections. Depression Anxiety 31, 291–296.

- Dutta, A., McKie, S., Deakin, J.F., 2015. Ketamine and other potential glutamate antidepressants. Psychiatry Res. 225, 1–13.

- Fond, G., Loundou, A., Rabu, C., Macgregor, A., Lançon, C., Brittner, M., MicoulaudFranchi, J.A., Richieri, R., Courtet, P., Abbar, M., Roger, M., Leboyer, M., Boyer, L., 2014. Ketamine administration in depressive disorders: a systematic review and meta-analysis. psychopharmacol. (Berl) 231, 3663–3676.

- Ghasemi M, Kazemi MH, Yoosefi A, et al. Rapid antidepressant effects of repeated doses of ketamine compared with electroconvulsive therapy in hospitalized patients with major depressive disorder. Psychiatry Res. 2014;215(2):355–361.

- Ghasemi, M., Phillips, C., Trillo, L., De Miquel, Z., Das, D., Salehi, A., 2014. The role of NMDA receptors in the pathophysiology and treatment of mood disorders. Neurosci. Biobehav. Rev. 47, 336–347.

- Han, Chen, Zou, Zheng, Li, Wang, Li, Zhou, Zhang, Liu and Xie. Efficacy of ketamine in the rapid treatment of major depressive disorder: a meta-analysis of randomized, double-blind, placebo-controlled studies. Neuropsychiatric Disease and Treatment 2016:12 2859–2867

- Hijazi Y, Boulieu R. Contribution of CYP3A4, CYP2B6, and CYP2C9 isoforms to N-demethylation of ketamine in human liver microsomes. Drug Metab Dispos. 2002;30(7):853-8. PubMed PMID: 12065445.

- Hirota and Lambert. Ketamine and depression. British Journal of Anaesthesia, 121 (6): 1198e1202 (2018).

- Hirota K, Lambert DG. Ketamine: new uses for an old drug? Br J Anaesth 2011; 107: 123e6

- Hirota K, Okawa H, Appadu BL, Grandy DK, Devi LA, Lambert DG. Stereoselective interaction of ketamine with recombinant mu, kappa, and delta opioid receptors expressed in Chinese hamster ovary cells. Anesthesiology 1999; 90: 174e82

- Hu C, Liu F, Wang X, Chen Y, Zhang T. The effects of ketamine on patients receiving general antidepression therapy. J Clin Anesthesiol. 2014;30(9):848–850.

- Hu YD, Xiang YT, Fang JX, et al. Single iv ketamine augmentation of newly initiated escitalopram for major depression: results from a randomized, placebo-controlled 4-week study. Psychol Med. 2016; 46(03):623–635

- Irwin, S.A., Iglewicz, A., Nelesen, R.A., Lo, J.Y., Carr, C.H., Romero, S.D., Lloyd, L.S., 2013. Daily oral ketamine for the treatment of depression and anxiety in patients receiving hospice care: a 28-day open label proof-of-concept trial. J. Palliat. Med. 16, 958–965.

- Jonkman K, Dahan A, van de Donk T, Aarts L, Niesters M, van Velzen M. Ketamine for pain. F1000Res 2017; 6: 1711

- Kantrowitz JT, Halberstam B, Gangwisch J. Single-dose ketamine followed by daily d-Cycloserine in treatment-resistant bipolar depression. J Clin Psychiatry. 2015;76:737—8.

- Kohler O, Krogh J, Mors O, Benros ME. Inflammation in depression and the potential for anti-inflammatory treatment. Curr Neuropharmacol 2016; 14: 732e42

- Kondo, Koyama Y, Nakamura Y, Shimada S. A novel 5HT3 receptor-IGF1 mechanism distinct from SSRI-induced antidepressant effects. Mol Psychiatry 2018; 23: 833e42

- Krystal, J., Karper, L., Seibyl, J., Freeman, G., Delaney, R., Bremmer, D. et al. (1994) Subanesthetic effects of the noncompetitive NMDA antagonist, ketamine, in humans. Arch Gen Psychiatry 51: 199–214.

- Krystal, J.H., Sanacora, G., Duman, R.S., 2013. Rapid-acting glutamatergic antidepressants: the path to ketamine and beyond. Biol. Psychiatry 73, 1133–1141.

- Lapidus, K.A.B., Levitch, C.F., Perez, A.M., Brallier, J.W., Parides, M.K., Soleimani, L., Feder, A., Iosifescu, D.V., Charney, D.S., Murrough, J.W., 2014. A randomized controlled trial of intranasal ketamine in major depressive disorder. Biol. Psychiatry 76, 970–976.

- Lapidus, K.A.B., Levitch, C.F., Perez, A.M., Brallier, J.W., Parides, M.K., Soleimani, L., Feder, A., Iosifescu, D.V., Charney, D.S., Murrough, J.W., 2014. A randomized controlled trial of intranasal ketamine in major depressive disorder. Biol. Psychiatry 76, 970–976.

- Lara DR, Bisol LW, Munari LR. Antidepressant, mood stabilizing and precognitive effects of very lose dose sublingual ketamine in refractory unipolar and bipolar depression. Int J Neuropsychopharmacol. 2013;16:2111---7.

- Lara, D.R., Bisol, L.W., Munari, L.R., 2014. Antidepressant, mood stabilizing and procognitive effects of very low dose sublingual ketamine in refractory unipolar and bipolar depression. Int. J. Neuropsychopharmacol. 16, 2111–2117.

- Luckenbaugh DA, Ibrahim L, Brutsche N, Franco-Chaves J, Mathews D, Marquardt CA, et al. Family history of alcohol dependence and antidepressant response to an N-methyl-daspartate antagonist in bipolar depression. Bipolar Disord. 2012;14:880---7.

- Malki K, Pain O, Tosto MG, Du Rietz E, Carboni L, Schalkwyk LC. Identification of genes and gene pathways associated with major depressive disorder by integrative brain analysis of rat and human prefrontal cortex transcriptomes. Transl Psychiatry 2015; 5: e519

- Manji, H.K., Quiroz, J.A., Sporn, J., Payne, J.L., Denicoff, K., Gray, A., Zarate, N., Charney, D.S. Jr, C.A., 2003. Enhancing neuronal plasticity and cellular resilience to develop novel, improved therapeutics for difficult-to-treat depression. Biol. Psychiatry 53, 707–742.

- McGirr, A., Berlim, M.T., Bond, D.J., Fleck, M.P., Yatham, L.N., Lam, R.W., 2015. A systematic review and meta-analysis of randomized, double-blind, placebocontrolled trials of ketamine in the rapid treatment of major depressive episodes. Psychol. Med. 45, 693–704.

- Muller J, Pentyala S, Dilger J, Pentyala S. Ketamine enantiomers in the rapid and sustained antidepressant effects. Ther Adv Psychopharmacol 2016; 6: 185e92

- Murrough JW, Iosifescu DV, Chang LC, et al. Antidepressant efficacy of ketamine in treatment-resistant major depression: a twosite randomized controlled trial. Am J Psychiatry. 2013;170(10): 1134–1142.

- Niesters M, Martini C, Dahan A. Ketamine for chronic pain: risks and benefits. Br J Clin Pharmacol 2014; 77: 357e67

- Niwa H, Furukawa KI, Seya K, Hirota K. Ketamine suppresses the proliferation of rat C6 glioma cells. Oncol Lett 2017; 14: 4911e7

- Papolos DF, Teicher MH, Faedda GL, Murphy P, Mattis S. Clinical experience using intranasal ketamine in the treatment of pediatric bipolar disorder/fear of harm phenotype. J Affect Disord. 2013;147:431---6.

- Permoda-Osip A, Dorszewska J, Bartkowska-Sniatkowska A, Chłopocka-Wozniak M, Rybakowski JK. Vitamin B12 level may be related to the efficacy of single ketamine infusion in bipolar depression. Pharmacopsychiatry. 2013;46:227---8.

- Romeo B, Choucha W, Fossati P, Rotge JY. Meta-analysis of short and mid-term efficacy of ketamine in unipolar and bipolar depression. Psychiatry Res. 2015;230(2):682–688

- Rybakowski JK, Permoda-Osip A, Skibinska M, Adamski R, Bartkowska-Sniatkowska A. Single ketamine infusion in bipolar depression resistant to antidepressants: are neurotrophins involved? Hum Psychopharmacol. 2013;28:87---90.

- Sanacora, G., Zarate, C.A., Krystal, J.H., Manji, H.K., 2008. Targeting the glutamatergic system to develop novel, improved therapeutics for mood disorders. Nat. Rev. Drug Discov. 7, 426–437.

- Sheehy KA, Lippold C, Rice AL, Nobrega R, Finkel JC, Quezado ZM. Subanesthetic ketamine for pain management in hospitalized children, adolescents, and young adults: a single-center cohort study. J Pain Res 2017; 10: 787e95

- Short B, Fong J, Galvez V, Shelker W, Loo CK. Side-effects associated with ketamine use in depression: a systematic review. Lancet Psychiatry 2018; 5: 65e78

- Singh JB, Fedgchin M, Daly EJ, et al. A double-blind, randomized, placebo-controlled, dose frequency study of intravenous ketamine in patients with treatment-resistant depression. Am J Psychiatry. 2016; 173(8):816–826.d

- Skolnick, P., Popik, P., Trullas, R., 2009. Glutamate-based antidepressants: 20 years on. Trends Pharmacol. Sci. 30, 563–569.

- Sos P, Klirova M, Novak T, Kohutova B, Horacek J, Palenicek T. Relationship of ketamine's antidepressant and psychotomimetic effects in unipolar depression. Neuro Endocrinol Lett. 2013;34(4):287–293

- Stahl, S.M., 2013. Mechanism of action of ketamine. CNS Spectr. 18, 171–174.

- Taylor, M.J., 2014. Could glutamate spectroscopy differentiate bipolar depression from unipolar? J. Affect. Disord. 167, 80–84.

- Tso MM, Blatchford KL, Callado LF, McLaughlin DP, Stamford JA. Stereoselective effects of ketamine on dopamine, serotonin and noradrenaline release and uptake in rat brain slices. Neurochem Int 2004; 44: 1e7

- Vollenweider FX, Leenders KL, Oye I, Hell D, Angst J. Differential psychopathology and patterns of cerebral glucose utilisation produced by (S)- and (R)-ketamine in healthy volunteers using positron emission tomography (PET). Eur Neuropsychopharmacol 1997; 7: 25e38

- White PF, Way WL, Trevor AJ. Ketamine—its pharmacology and therapeutic uses. Anesthesiology. 1982;56(2):119-36. PubMed PMID: 6892475.

- Williams NR, Heifets BD, Blasey C, et al. Attenuation of antidepressant effects of ketamine by opioid receptor antagonism. Am J Psychiatry 2018. https://doi.org/10.1176/ appi.ajp.2018.18020138. Advance Access published on August 29

- YaDeau JT, Morelli CM, Billingsley JK. Ketamine stimulates secretion of b-endorphin from a mouse pituitary cell line. Reg Anesth Pain Med 2003; 28: 12e6

- Yang C, Shirayama Y, Zhang JC, et al. R-ketamine: a rapidonset and sustained antidepressant without psychotomimetic side effects. Transl Psychiatry 2015; 5: e632

- Yang Y, Cui Y, Sang K, et al. Ketamine blocks bursting in the lateral habenula to rapidly relieve depression. Nature 2018; 554: 317e22

- Zarate CA Jr, Singh JB, Carlson PJ, Brutsche NE, Ameli R, Luckenbaugh DA, et al. A randomized trial of an N-methyl-daspartate antagonist in treatment-resistant major depression. Arch Gen Psychiatry. 2006;63:856—64.

- Zarate, Brutsche, Ibrahim, Franco-Chaves, Diazgranados, Cravchik, Selter, Marquardt, Liberty, and Luckenbaugh. Replication of Ketamine's Antidepressant Efficacy in Bipolar Depression: A Randomized Controlled Add-on Trial. Biol Psychiatry. 2012 June 1; 71(11): 939–946. doi:10.1016/j.biopsych.2011.12.010.

- Zhang K, Xu T, Yuan Z, et al. Essential roles of AMPA receptor GluA1 phosphorylation and presynaptic HCN channels in fast-acting antidepressant responses of ketamine. Sci Signal 2016; 9: ra123

ABOUT THE AUTHOR

Oliver Rumle Hovmand (born 1990) is a psychiatry resident in Denmark. He has been interested in the clinical use of psychedelics for several years. His other interests include CrossFit, Lego and riding motorcycles.

Made in the USA
Monee, IL
14 February 2020